ABSOLUTE BEGINNER'S GUIDE

TO

VBA

Paul McFedries

800 East 96th Street,
Indianapolis, Indiana 46240

Absolute Beginner's Guide to VBA
Copyright © 2004 by Que Publishing

International Standard Book Number: 0-7897-3076-6

Library of Congress Catalog Card Number: 2003116158

Printed in the United States of America

First Printing: March 2004

12 11 10 09   15 14 13 12 11

Trademarks

Warning and Disclaimer

Bulk Sales

Que Publishing offers excellent discounts on this book when ordered in quantity for bulk purchases or special sales. For more information, please contact

U.S. Corporate and Government Sales
1-800-382-3419
corpsales@pearsontechgroup.com

For sales outside of the U.S., please contact

International Sales
international@pearsoned.com

Publisher
Paul Boger

Associate Publisher
Michael Stephens

Acquisitions Editor
Loretta Yates

Development Editor
Sean Dixon

Managing Editor
Charlotte Clapp

Project Editor
Tricia Liebig

Production Editor
Benjamin Berg

Indexer
Mandie Frank

Proofreader
Tonya Fenimore

Technical Editor
Bob Villareal

Publishing Coordinator
Cindy Teeters

Interior Designer
Anne Jones

Cover Designer
Anne Jones

Page Layout
Susan Geiselman

Contents at a Glance

Table of Contents

About the Author

Paul McFedries is the president of Logophilia Limited, a technical writing company. While now primarily a writer, Paul has worked as a programmer, consultant, database developer, and Web site developer. He started programming when he was a teenager in the mid-1970s and has worked with everything from mainframes to desktops to bar code scanners. He has programmed in many different languages, including Fortran, assembly language, C++, Java, JavaScript, Visual Basic, VBScript, and, of course, Visual Basic for Applications. Paul has written more than forty books that have sold nearly three million copies worldwide. These books include *Special Edition Using JavaScript*, *Excel 2003 Formulas and Functions*, and *The Complete Idiot's Guide to Windows XP*.

Dedication

To Karen and Gypsy.

Acknowledgments

Robert Pirsig, in *Zen and the Art of Motorcycle Maintenance*, wrote that "a person who sees Quality and feels it as he works, is a person who cares." If this book is a quality product (and I immodestly think that it is), it's because the people at Que editorial cared enough to make it so.

So a round of hearty thanks is in order for all the good people who worked on this project. You'll find them all listed near the front of the book, but I'd like to extend special kudos to the folks I worked with directly: Acquisitions Editor Loretta Yates, Development Editor Sean Dixon, Production Editor Tricia Liebig, Copy Editor Ben Berg, and Tech Editor Bob Villareal.

We Want to Hear from You!

As the reader of this book, *you* are our most important critic and commentator. We value your opinion and want to know what we're doing right, what we could do better, what areas you'd like to see us publish in, and any other words of wisdom you're willing to pass our way.

As an associate publisher for Que Publishing, I welcome your comments. You can email or write me directly to let me know what you did or didn't like about this book—as well as what we can do to make our books better.

Please note that I cannot help you with technical problems related to the topic of this book. We do have a User Services group, however, where I will forward specific technical questions related to the book.

When you write, please be sure to include this book's title and author as well as your name, email address, and phone number. I will carefully review your comments and share them with the author and editors who worked on the book.

Email: feedback@quepublishing.com

Mail: Paul Boger
           Publisher
           Que Publishing
           800 East 96th Street
           Indianapolis, IN 46240 USA

For more information about this book or another Que Publishing title, visit our Web site at www.quepublishing.com. Type the ISBN (excluding hyphens) or the title of a book in the Search field to find the page you're looking for.

Introduction

Visual Basic for Applications is a mouthful to say (which is why I'll use the standard short form—VBA—from now on), but it also seems like it would be a real handful to learn. After all, this is a *programming language* we're talking about, right?

True, but VBA was designed to be easy to learn and straightforward to apply. I've learned a couple of dozen programming languages over the past 30 years or so, and I can tell you that VBA is, hands down, the easiest language I've ever worked with.

Okay, but isn't this stuff just for power users and the staff of the Information Technology department?

Yes, VBA is a useful tool for hardcore users and those who need to design major projects. But VBA can be immensely useful for *every* user. As a writer, I use Word constantly, and over the years I've developed dozens of small macros, functions, and forms that streamline or automate repetitive chores. Most of these routines consist of only a few lines of code, and each one saves me only about 30 seconds to a minute, depending on the task. But I use these routines 50 or 100 times a day, so I end up saving myself anywhere from 30 to 90 minutes a day! That's pretty remarkable, but the proof is in the pudding: I can now write far more pages in a day than I used to. (Don't tell my editor!)

Whether your concern is ease-of-use or personal productivity, there's little doubt VBA can make working with the Office applications a better experience. So now all you have to do is learn how to use it, and that's where this book comes in. My goal in writing this book was to give you an introduction to the VBA language, and to give you plenty of examples for putting the language to good use. Even if you've never even programmed your VCR, this book will teach you VBA programming from the ground up. The first six chapters, in particular, give you all the know-how you'll need to be a competent and productive programmer.

What You Should Know Before Reading This Book

First and foremost, this book does *not* assume that you've programmed before. Absolute VBA beginners are welcome here and will find the text to their liking.

I've tried to keep the chapters focused on the topic at hand and unburdened with long-winded theoretical discussions. For the most part, each chapter gets right down to brass tacks without much fuss and bother. To keep the chapters uncluttered, I've made a few assumptions about what you know and don't know:

- I assume you have knowledge of rudimentary computer concepts such as files and folders.
- I assume you're familiar with Windows and that you know how to launch applications and work with tools such as menus, dialog boxes, and the Help system.
- I assume you can operate peripherals attached to your computer, such as the keyboard, mouse, printer, and modem.
- This book's examples use the Office 2003 applications, although they also work with Office 2000 and Office XP. Therefore, I assume you've used these Office programs for a while and are comfortable working with these programs.

This Book's Special Features

The Absolute Beginner's Guide to VBA is designed to give you the information you need without making you wade through ponderous explanations and interminable technical background. To make your life easier, this book includes various features and conventions that help you get the most out of the book and VBA itself.

Steps: Throughout this book, each VBA task is summarized in step-by-step procedures.

Things you type: Whenever I suggest that you type something, what you type appears in a **bold** font.

Visual Basic keywords: Keywords reserved in the Visual Basic for Applications language appear in monospace type.

Commands: I use the following style for application menu commands: **File, Open**. This means that you pull down the File menu and select the Open command.

The code continuation character (➥): When a line of code is too long to fit on one line of this book, it is broken at a convenient place, and the code continuation character appears at the beginning of the next line.

This book also uses the following boxes to draw your attention to important (or merely interesting) information.

note

The Note box presents asides that give you more information about the topic under discussion. These tidbits provide extra insights that give you a better understanding of the task at hand. In many cases, they refer you to other sections of the book for more information.

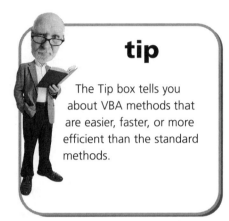

tip

The Tip box tells you about VBA methods that are easier, faster, or more efficient than the standard methods.

caution

The Caution box tells you about potential accidents waiting to happen. There are always ways to mess things up when you're working with computers. These boxes help you avoid at least some of the pitfalls.

PART

i

GETTING STARTED WITH VBA

1

RECORDING YOUR FIRST MACRO

This chapter gets your VBA education off to a rousing start by introducing you to some macro basics. You'll begin, appropriately enough, at the beginning by learning just what macros are, what you can do with them, and why you should learn any of this stuff. You'll then get a brief introduction to VBA procedures, but that will be the end of the theoretical portion of the show. You'll also get down to brass tacks by learning to compose macros the easy way: by recording them automatically. From there, you'll learn how to view the resulting macro and how to edit it using the Visual Basic Editor. This will set the stage for the next few chapters where you take a closer look at the specifics of the VBA language.

What Is a Macro?

It doesn't matter which Office program you're working in—it could be Word, it could be Excel, it could be PowerPoint—a few times a day, you probably find yourself performing some chore that either you've done dozens of times in the past or that you have to repeat a bunch of times in a row. It could be typing and formatting a section of text, running a series of menu commands, or editing a document in a particular way. If you're like me, when faced with these repetitive chores, you probably find yourself wishing there was some way to ease the drudgery and reduce the time taken by this mindless but necessary work.

Sure, most of the Office applications have a Repeat command on the Edit menu that lets you repeat your most recent action. That's handy, but it only repeats a single action. If you need to repeat two or more actions, this solution won't work.

What's a person to do about this? Well, what if I told you that it was possible to *automate* just about any routine and repetitive task? What if I told you that it was possible to take this automated task and run it immediately simply by selecting a command or even by just pressing a key or clicking a toolbar button?

It sounds too good to be true, I know, but that's just what Visual Basic for Applications (VBA) can do for you. You use VBA to create something called a *macro*, which is really just a list of tasks that you want a program to perform. Therfore, a macro is not unlike a recipe, which is a set of instructions that tells you what tasks to perform to cook or bake something. A macro is a set of instructions that tells a program (such Word or Excel) what tasks to perform to accomplish some goal.

The big difference, however, is that a macro combines all these instructions into a single script that you can invoke using a menu command, a toolbar button, or a keystroke. In this sense, then, a macro isn't so much like a recipe for, say, how to bake bread, but is more akin to a bread machine which, once it has been loaded with ingredients, bakes a loaf with the push of a button.

This list of instructions is composed mostly of *macro statements*. Some of these statements perform specific macro-related tasks, but most correspond to the underlying application's menu commands and dialog box options. For example, in any application, you can close the current (active) window by selecting the File menu's Close command. In a VBA macro, the following statement does the same thing:

```
ActiveWindow.Close
```

What Does VBA Have to Do with Macros?

VBA is a programming environment designed specifically for application macros. That sounds intimidating, I'm sure, but VBA's biggest advantage is that it's just plain easier to use than most programming languages. If you don't want to do any programming, VBA enables you to record macros and attach them to buttons, either inside a document or on a menu or toolbar. You can also create dialog boxes by simply drawing the appropriate controls onto a document. Other visual tools enable you to customize menus and toolbars as well, so you have everything you need to create simple scripts without writing a line of code.

Of course, if you want to truly unleash VBA's capabilities, you'll need to augment your interface with programming code. That sounds pretty fancy, but the VBA language is constructed in such a way that it's fairly easy to get started and to figure things out as you go along. More than any other programming language, VBA enables you to do productive things without a huge learning curve.

Understanding VBA Procedures

Before you get to the nitty-gritty of recording your first macro, let's take a second to understand what exactly you'll be recording. In a nutshell, when you record a macro (or, as you'll see in Chapter 2, "Writing Your Own Macros," when you create VBA code by hand), what you're creating is something called a *procedure*. In VBA, a procedure is, broadly speaking, a collection of related statements that forms a unit and performs some kind of task. For our purposes in this book, VBA procedures come in two flavors: command macros and user-defined functions. Here's a summary of the differences:

- *Command macros* (which are also known as *Sub procedures*, for reasons that will become clear in Chapter 2) are the most common types of procedures; they usually contain statements that are the equivalent of menu options and other program commands. The distinguishing feature of command macros is that, like regular application commands, they have an effect on their surroundings. (In Word, for example, this means the macro affects the current document, a section of text, and so on.) Whether it's formatting some text, printing a document, or creating custom menus, command macros *change* things. I show you how to create command macros in the section of Chapter 2 entitled "Writing Your Own Command Macro."

- *User-defined functions* (also called *Function procedures*) work just like a program's built-in functions. Their distinguishing characteristic is that they accept input values—called *arguments*—and then manipulate those values and return a result. A properly designed function has no effect on the current environment. I show you how to create these functions in the section of Chapter 2 entitled "Creating User-Defined Functions with VBA."

Recording a VBA Macro

By far, the easiest way to create a command macro is to use the Macro Recorder. With this method, you just start the recorder and then run through the operations you want to automate (which can include selecting text, running menu commands, and choosing dialog box options), and the Recorder translates everything into the appropriate VBA statements. These are copied to a separate area called a *module*, where you can then replay the entire procedure any time you like. This section shows you how to record a command macro in Word, Excel, or PowerPoint. (The other programs in the Office suite don't have macro recording capabilities.)

Here are the steps to follow:

1. Set up the application so that it's ready to record. In Word, for example, if you want to record a series of formatting options, select the text you want to work with.

2. Select Tools, Macro, Record New Macro. You'll see the Record Macro dialog box appear. Figure 1.1 shows the Excel version.

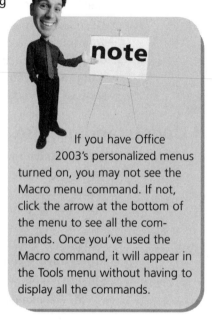

note

If you have Office 2003's personalized menus turned on, you may not see the Macro menu command. If not, click the arrow at the bottom of the menu to see all the commands. Once you've used the Macro command, it will appear in the Tools menu without having to display all the commands.

FIGURE 1.1

Use the Record Macro dialog box to name and describe your macro.

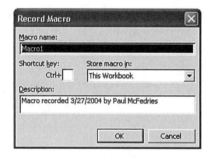

3. The application proposes a name for the macro (such as Macro1), but you can use the Macro name text box to change the name to anything you like. However, you must follow a few naming conventions:

   ■ There can be no more than 255 characters. (That sounds like a lot, and it is. Since you'll often have to type macro names, I recommend keeping the names relatively short to save wear and tear on your typing fingers.)

- ◼ The first character must be a letter or an underscore (_).
- ◼ No spaces or periods are allowed.

4. In Word and Excel, assign an optional shortcut to the macro:

- ◼ In Word, click Toolbars to assign a toolbar button to the macro; you can also click Keyboard to assign a shortcut key to the macro.
- ◼ In Excel, enter a letter in the text box labeled Shortcut key: Ctrl+.

5. In Word, Excel, and PowerPoint, use the Store macro in the drop-down list to specify where the macro will reside:

- ◼ In Word, you can store the macro in any open template (which makes the macro available to any document that uses the template), or in any open document (which makes the macro available only to that document).
- ◼ In Excel, you can store the macro in the current workbook, a new workbook, or in the Personal Macro Workbook. If you use the Personal Macro Workbook, your macros will be available to all your workbooks.
- ◼ In PowerPoint, you can store the macro in any open presentation.

Excel's Personal Macro Workbook is a hidden workbook (it's filename is `Personal.xls`) that opens automatically when you start Excel. This is useful because any macros contained in this file will be available to all your workbooks, which makes them easy to reuse. If you want to use this workbook, however, you first have to unhide it. To do this, select the Window, Unhide command, make sure that `PERSONAL.XLS` is highlighted in the Unhide dialog box, and then click OK.

6. Enter an optional description of the macro in the Description text box.

7. Click OK. The application returns you to the document, displays Recording or REC in the status bar, and displays the Stop Recording Macro toolbar, as shown in Figure 1.2. (This is the tiny toolbar shown more or less in the middle of the window, which shows only "St" in the title bar.)

8. Perform the tasks you want to include in the macro. Because the macro recorder takes note of *everything* you do (except clicking the buttons in the Stop Recording Macro toolbar), be careful not to perform any extraneous actions or commands during the recording.

9. When you finish the tasks, select Tools, Macro, Stop Recording or click the Stop Macro button in the Stop Recording Macro toolbar.

FIGURE 1.2

While you're
recording, you
see Recording or
REC in the sta-
tus bar as well
as the Stop
Recording
Macro toolbar.

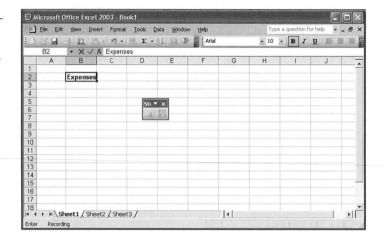

Viewing the Resulting Module

When you record a macro, the application creates a "VBA project." This is a container that includes both the document you used for the macro and a special object called a *module* that contains the macro statements.

To see your macro, follow these steps:

1. Select Tools, Macro, Macros (or press Alt+F8) to display the Macro dialog box.

2. In the Macro name list, highlight the name of the macro you just recorded.

3. Click the Edit button. The application opens the Visual Basic Editor window and then opens the module and displays the macro. As you can see in Figure 1.3, the application (Excel, in this case) translates your actions into VBA statements and combines everything into a single macro.

FIGURE 1.3

A sample
recorded macro.

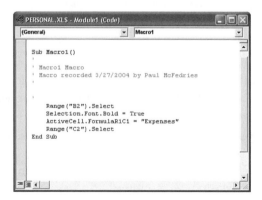

A typical macro has the following features:

Sub—This keyword marks the beginning of a macro. The Sub keyword (it's short for *subroutine*) is the reason why command macros also are called *Sub procedures*.

Macro Name—After the Sub keyword, Excel enters the name of the macro followed by left and right parentheses (the parentheses are used for input values—the arguments—as you'll see in Chapter 2).

Comments—The first few lines begin with an apostrophe ('), which tells VBA that these lines are *comments*. As the name implies, comments are for show only; they aren't processed when you run the macro. In each recorded macro, the comments display the name of the macro and the description you entered in the Record Macro dialog box. (In Excel, the comments also display the keyboard shortcut, if you entered one.)

Macro statements—The main body of the macro (in other words, the lines between Sub and End Sub, not including the initial comments) consists of a series of statements. These are the application's interpretations of the actions you performed during the recording. In the example, four actions were performed in Excel:

1. Cell B2 was selected:
   ```
   Range("B2").Select
   ```

2. The cell was formatted as boldface:
   ```
   Selection.Font.Bold = True
   ```

3. The word "Expenses" was typed into the cell:
   ```
   ActiveCell.FormulaR1C1 = "Expenses"
   ```

4. The right arrow key was pressed (which moved the selection over to cell C2):
   ```
   Range("C2").Select
   ```

End Sub—These keywords mark the end of the macro.

Editing a Recorded Macro

As you're learning VBA, you'll often end up with recorded macros that don't turn out quite right the first time. Whether the macro runs a command it shouldn't or is missing a command altogether, you'll often have to patch things up after the fact.

The lines within a VBA module are just text, so you make changes the same way you would in a word processor or text editor. If your macro contains statements that you want to remove, just delete the offending lines from the module.

If you want to add new recorded actions to the macro, VBA doesn't give you any way to record new statements into an existing macro. Instead, you should first record a new macro that includes the actions you want and then display the macro. From there, you can use the standard Windows cut-and-paste techniques (including drag-and-drop) to move the statements from the new macro into the other macro.

THE ABSOLUTE MINIMUM

This chapter introduced you to VBA macros. You learned what macros are and why they're useful. You also learned how to record a macro, see the result in the Visual Basic Editor, and edit a recorded macro.

The few VBA statements that you've seen so far probably look more than a little strange to you. Yes, recorded statements correspond to specific actions you took while the Macro Recorder was running, but the resulting code contains weird constructions, such as Selection.Font.Bold and ActiveCell.FormulaR1C1. It's perfectly normal to feel a bit intimidated by these barely decipherable statements. My job, over the next five chapters, in particular, will be to dispel the inherent strangeness of VBA and show you that the language is actually quite comprehensible once you learn what it's all about. To that end, you'll find related information in the following chapters:

- You'll learn more about the Visual Basic Editor as well as how to create you own procedures and enter your own VBA statements in Chapter 2, "Writing Your Own Macros."

- You won't get too far writing VBA code without learning about variables, and you'll do that in Chapter 3, "Understanding Program Variables."

- Your procedures will also rely heavily on operators and expressions. Turn to Chapter 4, "Building VBA Expressions," to learn more.

- Objects are one of the most important concepts in VBA. You'll find out how they work in Chapter 5, "Working with Objects." Also, see Part II, "Putting VBA to Work," to get the specifics on the objects used in Word, Excel, and other Office applications.

- VBA, like any programming language worth its salt, contains a number of statements that control program flow. I discuss these statements in Chapter 6, "Controlling Your VBA Code."

IN THIS CHAPTER

- Understanding the advantages of writing your own macros
- Getting to know the Visual Basic Editor
- The basic steps required to write a macro
- Learning how to craft your very own user-defined functions
- Creating and using procedures
- Understanding and working with VBA modules

2

WRITING YOUR OWN MACROS

Letting VBA do all the work by recording your macros is an easy way to automate tasks, and it's a technique you'll use often. However, to get the most out of VBA, you need to do some full-fledged programming, which means writing your own macros, either from scratch or by using a recorded macro as a starting point. Here are just a few of the advantages you gain by doing this:

- If you make a mistake while recording a macro, particularly one that requires a large number of steps, you can *edit* the macro to fix the mistake rather than re-recording the whole thing from scratch.

- You get full control over each macro, which means you ensure that your macros do exactly what you need them to do.

- You can take advantage of the hidden power of VBA to manipulate the Office programs and to perform some impressive programming feats that are simply not available via the recording process.

To help you realize these advantages and many more, this chapter introduces you to the basics of writing simple procedures and functions, as well as how to get around in the Visual Basic Editor, which is the tool that VBA provides for writing macros by hand. This will set the stage for the next few chapters when I take a closer look at the specifics of the VBA language.

Displaying the Visual Basic Editor

To get the Visual Basic Editor onscreen in any Office program, select Tools, Macro, Visual Basic Editor. (Note, however, that for simplicity's sake, I use a single Office application—Excel—for the examples throughout this chapter.) Figure 2.1 shows the new window that appears.

> **tip**
>
> You can also get to the Visual Basic Editor by pressing Alt+F11. In fact, this key combination is a toggle that switches you between the Visual Basic Editor and the underlying application.

FIGURE 2.1

You use the Visual Basic Editor to craft and edit your macros.

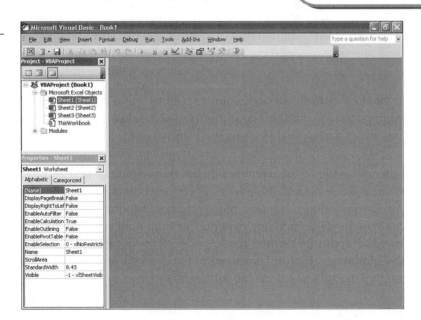

Touring the Visual Basic Editor

The idea behind the Visual Basic Editor is simple: It's a separate program that's designed to do nothing else but help you create and edit VBA macros. (In professional programming circles, the Visual Basic Editor is called an *integrated development environment* or *IDE*.)

When you open the Visual Basic Editor for the first time, you don't see much. The left side of the editor has two windows labeled Project and Properties. The latter you don't need to worry about right now. (I'll talk about it in Chapter 5, "Working with Objects.") The Project window (technically, it's called the Project Explorer) shows you the contents of the current VBA project. In simplest terms, a *project* is an Office file and all of its associated VBA items, including its macros and its user forms. (You learn about user forms in Chapter 13, "Creating Custom VBA Dialog Boxes.")

Opening an Existing Module

To do some work in the Visual Basic Editor, you usually start by opening a *module*, which is a VBA item that contains one or more macros. Here's how you do that:

1. In the Project window, open the Modules branch by clicking the plus sign (+) to its left.
2. Double-click the name of the module you want to open.

If you recorded a macro in Chapter 1, you should see a module named Module1. Go ahead and double-click that module to open it, as shown in Figure 2.2.

FIGURE 2.2

To write or edit a macro, first open the module you want to work with.

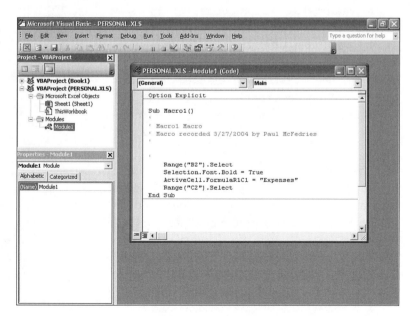

As you can see in Figure 2.2, the open module contains the macro code from my example in Chapter 1. I should also point out that each module window has two drop-down lists beneath the title bar:

Object list—This is the list on the left and it contains a list of the available objects for whatever project item you're working with. (I explain objects in detail in Chapter 5.) Modules don't contain objects, so this list contains only (General) for a module window.

Procedure list—This is the list on the right and it contains all the procedures and functions in the module. When you select an item from this list, the editor displays that item in the module window.

Creating a New Module

If you don't have an existing module, you can create one any time you like by selecting the Insert, Module command. The Visual Basic Editor assigns the module a generic name, such as Module1 or Module2, but you're free to rename the module. See "Renaming a Module," later in this chapter.

Writing Your Own Command Macro

As I mentioned at the start of this chapter, recording macros is limiting because there are plenty of macro features that you can't access with mouse or keyboard actions or by selecting menu options. In Excel, for example, VBA has a couple dozen information macro functions that return data about cells, worksheets, workspaces, and more. Also, the VBA control functions enable you to add true programming structures, such as looping, branching, and decision-making (see Chapter 6, "Controlling Your VBA Code").

To access these macro elements, you need to write your own VBA routines from scratch. This is easier than it sounds because all you really need to do is enter a series of statements in a module.

note

Although this section tells you how to create VBA macros, I realize there's an inherent paradox here: How can you write your own macros when you haven't learned anything about them yet? Making you familiar with VBA's statements and functions is the job of the next four chapters of the book. This section will get you started, and you can use this knowledge as a base on which to build your VBA skills in the chapters that follow.

With a module window open and active, follow these steps to write your own command macro:

1. Place the insertion point where you want to start the macro. (Make sure the insertion point isn't inside an existing macro.)

2. If you want to begin your macro with a few notes—called *comments* in programming parlance—that describe what the macro does, type an apostrophe (') at the beginning of each comment line.

3. To start the macro, type **Sub**, followed by a space and the name of the macro. The name should consist of only letters, numbers, or the underscore character (_). Don't use spaces or any other characters in the name.

4. Press Enter. VBA automatically adds a pair of parentheses at the end of the macro name. It also tacks on an End Sub line to mark the end of the procedure.

5. Between the Sub and End Sub lines, type the VBA statements you want to include in the macro.

> **tip**
>
> To make your code easier to read, you should indent each statement by pressing the Tab key at the beginning of the line. (Don't do this for the Sub and End Sub lines, just the statements that go between them.) Conveniently, VBA preserves the indentation on subsequent lines, so you only have to indent the first line.

Each time you press Enter to start a new line, VBA analyzes the line you just entered and performs three chores:

- It formats the color of each word in the line: by default, VBA keywords are blue, comments are green, errors are red, and all other text is black.

- VBA keywords are converted to their proper case. For example, if you type **end sub**, VBA converts this to End Sub when you press Enter.

- It checks for *syntax errors*, which are errors that occur when a word is misspelled, a function is entered incorrectly, and so on. VBA signifies a syntax error either by displaying a dialog box to let you know what the problem is or by not converting a word to its proper case or color.

> **tip**
>
> By always entering VBA keywords in lowercase letters, you'll be able to catch typing errors by looking for those keywords that VBA doesn't recognize (in other words, the ones that remain in lowercase).

Let's run through a simple example:

1. Type `sub Hello_World` and press Enter.
2. Press Tab, type `msgbox "Hello VBA World!"`, and press Enter.

The macro should appear as shown in Figure 2.3. The code you entered in Step 2 is an example of a VBA *statement*: an instruction that gives VBA a specific task. In this case, the statement contains VBA's MsgBox function, which is used to display a simple dialog box to the user. (See Chapter 12, "Interacting with the User," for details.)

FIGURE 2.3

The example macro, ready for execution.

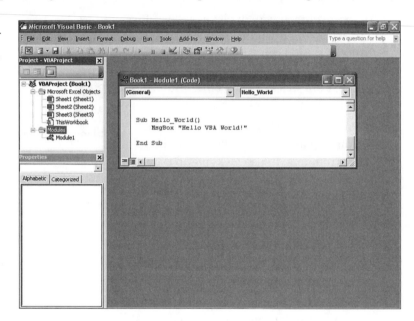

Running a VBA Macro

The Office applications offer several methods for running your VBA macros, but there are two that you'll use most often:

- In a module, place the insertion point anywhere inside the macro and then either select Run, Run Sub/UserForm or press the F5 key.
- In the Office application, select Tools, Macro, Macros (or press Alt+F8) to display the Macro dialog box. If necessary, use the Macros In box to choose the document that contains the macro you want to work with. Now use the Macro Name list to highlight the macro; then click the Run button.

If you try this on the sample macro that you created in the previous section, you should see dialog box appear with the text `Hello VBA World!`. Click OK to close the dialog box.

Creating User-Defined Functions with VBA

The Office applications come with a large number of built-in functions. Excel, for example, has hundreds of functions—one of the largest function libraries of any spreadsheet package. However, even with this vast collection, you'll still find that plenty of applications are not covered. For example, you might need to calculate the area of a circle of a given radius or the gravitational force between two objects. You could, of course, easily calculate these things on a worksheet, but if you need them frequently, it makes sense to define your own functions that you can use any time. The next three sections show you how it's done.

Understanding User-Defined Functions

As I mentioned Chapter 1, the defining characteristic of user-defined functions is that they return a result. They can perform any number of calculations on numbers, text, logical values, or whatever, but they're not allowed to affect their surroundings. In a worksheet, for example, they can't move the active cell, format a range, or change the workspace settings. In fact, anything you can access using the application menus is off-limits in a user-defined function.

So, what *can* you put in a user-defined function? All the application's built-in functions are fair game, and you can use any VBA function that isn't the equivalent of a menu command or desktop action.

All user-defined functions have the same basic structure, as shown in Listing 2.1.

LISTING 2.1 An Example of a User-defined Function

```
Function HypotenuseLength(x, y)
    HypotenuseLength = Sqr(x ^ 2 + y ^ 2)
End Function
```

This is a function named HypotenuseLength that calculates the length of a right triangle's hypotenuse given the other two sides (x and y). Using this example, here's a summary of the various parts of a user-defined function:

The Function statement—This keyword identifies the procedure as a user-defined function. The Function keyword is the reason that user-defined functions are also known as Function procedures.

The function name—This is a unique name for the function. Names must begin with an alphabetic character, they can't include a space or a period, and they can't be any longer than 255 characters.

The function arguments—Just as many application functions accept arguments, so do user-defined functions. Arguments (or parameters, as they're sometimes called) are typically one or more values that the function uses as the raw materials for its calculations. You always enter arguments between parentheses after the function name, and you separate multiple arguments with commas.

The VBA statements—This is the code that actually performs the calculations. Each statement is a combination of values, operators, variables, and VBA or application functions that, together, produce a result.

The return value—User-defined functions usually return a value. To do this, include a statement where you set the name of the function equal to an expression. For example, in the HypotenuseLength function, the following statement defines the return value:

HypotenuseLength = Sqr(x ^ 2 + y ^ 2)

The End Function keywords—These keywords indicate the end of the Function procedure.

All your user-defined functions will have this basic structure, so you need to keep three things in mind when designing these kinds of macros:

- What arguments will the function take?
- What formulas will you use within the function?
- What value or values will be returned?

Writing User-Defined Functions

User-defined functions can't contain menu commands or mouse and keyboard actions. This means, of course, that there is no way to record user-defined functions. You have to write them out by hand, and the process is very similar to creating a command macro from scratch. Here are the general steps to follow to write a user-defined function:

1. Open the module you want to use for the function.

2. Place the insertion point where you want to start the function.

3. If you like, enter one or more comments that describe what the function does. Be sure to type an apostrophe (') at the beginning of each comment line.

4. Start the procedure by typing Function followed by a space and then the name of the macro. If your function uses arguments, enclose them in parentheses after the function name (be sure to separate each argument with a comma). When you press Enter, VBA inserts the End Function statement.

5. Between the `Function` and `End Function` lines, enter the VBA statements that you want to include in the function. As with Sub procedures, you should indent each line for clarity by pressing the Tab key at the beginning of the line.

6. Be sure to include a line that defines the return value.

Employing User-Defined Functions

You'll probably find that user-defined functions are most useful in Excel. In this case, you can employ these functions only within worksheet formulas or in other VBA statements. You have two choices:

- In the cell, enter the function the same way you would any of Excel's built-in functions. In other words, enter the name of the function and then the necessary arguments enclosed in parentheses. Here's a sample formula that uses the `HypotenuseLength` function:

  `=HypotenuseLength(3,4)`

- Select Insert, Function to display the Insert Function dialog box. Highlight All in the Or Select a Category list and then highlight the macro in the Select a Function list. Click OK and enter the arguments. When you're done, click OK.

Working with Procedures

The basic unit of VBA programming is the *procedure*, which is a block of code in a module that you reference as a unit. So far, you've seen that there are two types of procedures: command macros (also known as Sub procedures) and user-defined functions (or Function procedures).

The Structure of a Procedure

To recap what you learned earlier, a Sub procedure is allowed to modify its environment, but it can't return a value. Here is the basic structure of a Sub procedure:

```
Sub ProcedureName (argument1, argument2, ...)
    [VBA statements]
End Sub
```

For example, Listing 2.2 presents a Sub procedure that enters some values for a loan in various worksheet ranges and then adds a formula to calculate the loan payment. (I'll show you how to work with ranges and other Excel objects in Chapter 8, "Programming Excel.")

LISTING 2.2 A Sample Sub Procedure

```
Sub EnterLoanData()
    Range("IntRate").Value = .08
    Range("Term").Value = 10
    Range("Principal").Value = 10000
    Range("Payment").Formula = "=PMT(IntRate/12, Term*12, Principal)"
End Sub
```

A Function procedure, on the other hand, can't modify its environment, but it does return a value. Here is its structure:

```
Function ProcedureName (argument1, argument2, ...)
    [VBA statements]
    ProcedureName = returnValue
End Function
```

For example, Listing 2.3 is a Function procedure that sums two ranges, stores the results in variables named totalSales and totalExpenses (see Chapter 3, "Understanding Program Variables," to learn more about variables), and then uses these values and the fixedCosts argument to calculate the net margin.

LISTING 2.3 A Sample Function Procedure

```
Function CalcNetMargin(fixedCosts)
    totalSales = Application.Sum(Range("Sales"))
    totalExpenses = Application.Sum(Range("Expenses"))
    CalcNetMargin = (totalSales-totalExpenses-fixedCosts)/totalSales
End Function
```

Calling a Procedure

After you've written a procedure, you can use it either in a worksheet formula or in another procedure. This is known as *calling* the procedure.

Calling a Procedure Name in the Same Project

If a procedure exists in the current module or in a different module that's part of the current VBA project, you call it just by entering the procedure name and then including any necessary arguments. For example, as you learned earlier, you can call the HypotenuseLength procedure from a worksheet cell by entering a formula such as the following:

```
=HypotenuseLength(3,4)
```

If you like, you also can call a procedure from another procedure. For example, the following VBA statement sets a variable named TotalPerimeter equal to the total perimeter of a right triangle that has two sides of length x and y:

```
TotalPerimeter = X + Y + HypotenuseLength(X,Y)
```

If the procedure exists in a different module, but it has the same name as a procedure in the current module, you need to preface the call with the name of the module that contains the procedure:

```
ModuleName.ProcedureName
```

For example, the following statement calls the CalcNetMargin function from another module:

```
Module2.CalcNetMargin(100000)
```

Calling a Procedure in Another Project

If you have a VBA statement that needs to call a procedure in another project, you first need to set up a *reference* to the project. Doing this gives you access to all the project's procedures. The following steps show you what to do:

1. In the Visual Basic Editor, select Tools, References to display the References dialog box.

2. You have two ways to proceed from here:

   ■ If the project is from the same application and is open, the name of the project will appear in the Available References list (probably using the default project name: VBAProject). Select the check box beside the project name. If there are multiple projects in the list, you can be certain you've got the right one by highlighting each one and looking at the Location info near the bottom of the dialog box, which tells you the name of the project file.

   ■ If the project isn't open, click the Browse button and then highlight the document you want from the Add Reference dialog box that appears. (To ensure that you find the file, select the All Files (*.*) item in the Files of Type list box. Click Open to return to the References dialog box. You'll see the project in the Available References list, and its check box will be activated for you automatically.

3. Click OK to return to the Visual Basic Editor. In the Project Explorer, you'll see that your project sprouts a new References folder and that the referenced project appears within that folder.

After you have the reference established, you call the procedure the same way you call the procedures in the current project. If the two projects have procedures with the same names, you need to add the project's name, surrounded by square brackets ([]), to the call:

[ProjectName].ProcedureName

For example, the following statement calls the HypotenuseLength function in the VBAProject01 project:

[VBAProject01].HypotenuseLength(3,4)

Taking Advantage of IntelliSense

VBA's IntelliSense feature is like a mini version of the VBA Help system. It offers you assistance with VBA syntax, either on-the-fly or on-demand. You should find this an incredibly useful tool because, as you'll see as you work through this book, VBA contains dozens of statements and functions, and VBA-enabled programs offer hundreds of objects to work with. Few people are capable of committing all this to memory, and it's a pain to be constantly looking up the correct syntax. IntelliSense helps by giving you hints and alternatives as you type. To see what I mean, let's look at the four most useful types of IntelliSense help available.

List Properties/Methods

In Chapter 4, you'll learn how to work with the objects that each VBA-enabled application makes available. In particular, you'll learn about *properties* and *methods* which, put simply, define the characteristics of each object. (In broad terms, properties describe an object's appearance, and methods describe what you can do with an object.)

As you'll see, however, each object can have dozens of properties and methods. To help you code your procedures correctly, IntelliSense can display a list of the available properties and methods as you type your VBA statements. To try this out,

caution

If the project you select in the References dialog box has the same name as the project in the current document, VBA will display an error message because no two open projects can have the same name. To avoid this, make sure you give each of your VBA projects a unique name. To rename a project, click the project name in the Project Explorer and then use the Name property in the Properties window to change the name. Save the project by pulling down the File menu and selecting the Save *File* command, where *File* is the name of the current document.

activate a module in the Visual Basic Editor and type `application` followed by a period (.). As shown in Figure 2.4, VBA will display a pop-up menu. The items on this menu are the properties and methods that are available for the Application object. Use the following methods to work with this menu:

- Keep typing to display different items in the list. In Excel, for example, if you type `cap`, VBA highlights Caption in the list.
- Double-click an item to insert it in your code.
- Highlight an item (by clicking it or by using the up and down arrow keys) and then press Tab to insert the item and continue working on the same statement.
- Highlight an item and then press Enter to insert the item and start a new line.
- Press Esc to remove the menu without inserting an item.

FIGURE 2.4

IntelliSense displays the available properties and methods as you type.

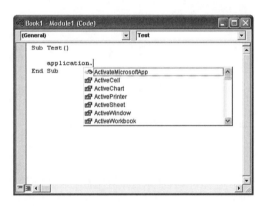

Note that if you press Esc to remove the pop-up menu, VBA won't display it again for the same object. If you would like to display the menu again, use any of the following techniques:

- Select Edit, List Properties/Methods.
- Press Ctrl+J.
- Right-click the module and click List Properties/Methods.

List Constants

IntelliSense has a List Constants feature that's similar to List Properties/Methods. In this case, you get a pop-up menu that displays a list of the available constants for a property or method. (A *constant* is a fixed value that corresponds to a specific state or result.) For example, type the following in a module:

```
Application.ActiveWindow.WindowState=
```

Figure 2.5 shows the pop-up menu that appears in Excel. This is a list of constants that correspond to the various settings for a window's WindowState property. For example, you would use the xlMaximized constant to maximize a window. You work with this list using the same techniques that I outlined for List Properties/Methods.

If you need to display this list by hand, use any of the following methods:

■ Select Edit, List Constants.

■ Press Ctrl+Shift+J.

■ Right-click the module and click List Constants.

FIGURE 2.5

The List Constants feature in action.

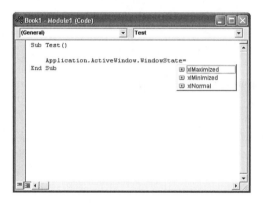

Parameter Info

You learned earlier that a user-defined function typically takes one or more arguments (or parameters) to use in its internal calculations. Many of the functions and statements built into VBA also use parameters, and some have as many as a dozen separate arguments! The syntax of such statements is obviously very complex, so it's easy to make mistakes. To help you out when entering a user-defined function or one of VBA's built-in functions or statements, IntelliSense provides the Parameter Info feature. As its name implies, this feature displays information on the parameters you can utilize in a function. To see an example, enter the following text in any Excel module:

```
activecell.formula=pmt(
```

As soon as you type the left parenthesis, a banner pops up that tells you the available arguments for (in this case) VBA's Pmt function (see Figure 2.6). Here are the features of this banner:

■ The current argument is displayed in boldface. When you enter an argument and then type a comma, VBA displays the next argument in boldface.

■ Arguments that are optional are surrounded by square brackets ([]).

- The various As statements (for example, As Double) tell you the *data type* of each argument. I'll explain data types in the next chapter but, for now, think of them as defining what kind of data is associated with each argument (text, numeric, and so on).

- To remove the banner, press Esc.

As usual, IntelliSense also enables you to display this information by hand. Here are the techniques to use:

- Select Edit, Parameter Info.

- Press Ctrl+Shift+I.

- Right-click the module and click Parameter Info.

FIGURE 2.6

The Parameter Info feature shows you the defined arguments for the current function or statement.

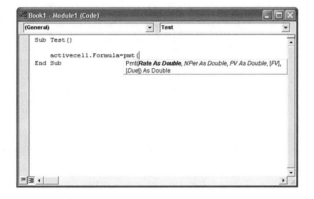

Complete Word

The last of the IntelliSense features that I'll discuss is Complete Word. You use this feature to get VBA to complete a keyword that you've started typing and thus save some wear and tear on your typing fingers. To use Complete Word, type in the first few letters of a keyword and do one of the following:

- Select Edit, Complete Word.

- Press Ctrl+Alt+A.

- Right-click the module and click Complete Word.

If the letters you typed are enough to define a unique keyword, IntelliSense fills in the rest of the word. For example, if you type **appl** and run Complete Word, IntelliSense changes your typing to Application. However, if there are multiple keywords that begin with the letters you typed, IntelliSense displays a pop-up menu that you can use to select the word you want.

Working with Comment Blocks

Although comments aren't executed when you run a procedure, they still have an important role to play in VBA programming. In particular, you can use comments to document a procedure:

- Provide an overall explanation of what the procedure does.
- Discuss assumptions you've made about how the procedure runs, as well as any background information necessary to operate the procedure.
- Explain the arguments the procedure uses, if any.
- Create a "running commentary" throughout the procedure that explains what the procedure is doing and why.

Why go to all this trouble? Well, the VBA language uses a fairly straightforward syntax, but it is still (like most programming languages) inherently somewhat cryptic. So, although *you* might know exactly what your program is trying to accomplish, other people will have a harder time deciphering your code. A copiously commented procedure removes some of this burden and makes it easier for other people to work with your procedures. Not only that, but you'll find comments are an invaluable tool for getting up to speed when you haven't looked at a procedure for a few months.

However, there is yet another way that comments are useful: to prevent VBA from executing troublesome statements. If you're pulling your hair out trying to figure out why a particular statement won't run properly, it's often best to just skip the statement altogether and come back to it later. Or, you might want to try an alternative statement. Either way, tacking an apostrophe onto the beginning of the statement is all you need to do to "comment out" the pesky line and move on to more productive matters.

Suppose, however, that instead of a single line of troublesome code you have 10 lines, or even 20 or 30. Again, you can bypass these lines by commenting them out, but it's pain to have to insert apostrophes at the beginning of every line. To relieve you of this hassle, VBA has a Comment Block feature that can toggle any number of statements between "commented" and "uncommented." To use this feature, highlight the statements you want to work with and then do one of the following:

- To comment the statements, click the Comment Block button in the Edit toolbar.
- To uncomment the statements, click the Uncomment Block button in the Edit toolbar.

Working with Modules

So far, you've seen that modules are where most of the VBA action takes place. True, as you'll see in subsequent chapters, you'll also be working in user form windows and the Properties window, but modules are really the heart of VBA. Given that, it will help to have a few module manipulation techniques under your belt. To that end, the next four sections show you how to rename, export, import, and remove modules.

Renaming a Module

When you insert a new module, VBA gives it an uninspiring name such as Module1. That's fine if you'll just be using the one module in your project, but if you'll be working with multiple modules, you should consider giving meaningful names to each module to help differentiate them.

To rename a module, follow these steps:

1. Select the module in the Project Explorer.
2. In the Properties window, use the (Name) property to rename the module. Make sure the name you use begins with a letter, contains no spaces or punctuation marks (underscores are acceptable, however), and is no longer than 31 characters.

Exporting a Module

The procedures and functions in a module will usually be specific to the application in which the project was created. For example, procedures in a Word-based module will usually reference Word-specific objects such as bookmarks and paragraphs. However, you might have generic procedures and functions that can be used in different contexts. How, then, can you share code between applications?

One way to do it is to use the Clipboard to copy data from one module and paste it into a module in a different application. Another way is to *export* the module to a .BAS file. In the next section, I'll show you how to import .BAS files into your VBA projects.

The .BAS (Basic) file format is the one used by Visual Basic modules (which means you could use your VBA code in a Visual Basic project), but it's really just a simple text file. Here are the steps to follow to export a module:

1. In the Project Explorer, highlight the module you want to export.
2. Select File, Export File or press Ctrl+E. VBA displays the Export File dialog box.
3. Select a location and name for the .BAS file.
4. Click Save. VBA creates the new .BAS file.

Importing a Module

If you exported a module to a .BAS file, you can import that file as a module in another application's VBA project. Also, if you've used Visual Basic before, you can leverage your existing code by importing Visual Basic modules into your project. Here are the steps to follow:

1. If you have multiple projects open, use the Project Explorer to highlight any object in the project you want to use to store the imported file.

2. Select File, Import File or press Ctrl+M, to display the Import File dialog box.

3. Highlight the .BAS file that you want to import.

4. Click Open. VBA adds a new module for the .BAS file.

Removing a Module

If you no longer need a module, you should remove it from your project to reduce the clutter in the Project Explorer. Use the following technique:

1. Highlight the module in the Project Explorer.

2. Select File, Remove *Module,* where *Module* is the name of the module.

3. The Visual Basic Editor asks if you want to export the module before removing it:

   ■ If you want to export the module first, click Yes and use the Export File dialog box to export the module to a .BAS file.

   ■ Otherwise, click No to remove the module.

Shutting Down the Visual Basic Editor

When you've completed your VBA chores, you can shut down the Visual Basic Editor by using either of the following techniques:

■ Pull down the File menu and select the Close and Return to *Application* command, where *Application* is the name of the program you're running (such as Microsoft Excel).

■ Press Alt+Q.

THE ABSOLUTE MINIMUM

This chapter got you started down the road to writing your own macros by showing a few necessary techniques. If you feel a little uncertain about anything you read here, that's perfectly natural because I've been telling you the *how* of creating macros without also telling you the *what*. As I've said, the specifics of the VBA language will be covered in detail throughout the rest of the book, particularly the next four chapters.

Everything you learned in this chapter will become second nature to you before your VBA education is complete. However, there are a few things you should be sure you know cold before moving on.

First, you need to know the basic structure of a Sub procedure, which is allowed to modify its environment, but can't return a value:

```
Sub ProcedureName (argument1, argument2, ...)
    [VBA statements]
End Sub
```

Similarly, you need to know the basic structure of a Function procedure, which can't modify its environment, but can return a value:

```
Function ProcedureName (argument1, argument2, ...)
    [VBA statements]
    ProcedureName = returnValue
End Function
```

Secondly, I'd like to impress upon you the advantages to taking a neat, orderly approach to your programming. Humans can and do thrive in messy environments, but we're many times smarter and infinitely more intuitive than any macro. Procedures live in a world of strict and unyielding logic, and programming is always many times easier if you supplement that logic with a sense of order. Fortunately, there are only two things you need to do to achieve most of the order you need to be a successful programmer:

- Don't skimp on the comments. Any procedure will be much easier to read if it is sprinkled liberally with comments throughout the code. Also, adding comments as you go is a great way of getting a grip on your own thoughts and logical leaps as you go.

- Indent your code. Again, this is mostly a readability exercise, but as you'll see later in the book—especially when you learn fun stuff such as programming loops in Chapter 6—properly indenting your code can prevent many errors.

3

UNDERSTANDING PROGRAM VARIABLES

Your VBA procedures often will need to store temporary values for use in statements and calculations that come later in the code. For example, you might want to store values for total sales and total expenses to use later in a gross margin calculation. Although you probably could get away with using the underlying application to store these values (in, say, a cell in an Excel worksheet), this almost always isn't very practical. Instead, VBA (like all programming languages) lets you store temporary values in *variables*. This chapter explains this important topic and shows you how to use variables in your VBA procedures.

Declaring Variables

Declaring a variable tells VBA the name of the variable you're going to use. (It also serves to specify the *data type* of the variable, which I'll explain later in this chapter.) You declare variables by including Dim statements (Dim is short for *dimension*) at the beginning of each Sub or Function procedure.

In its simplest form, a Dim statement has the following syntax:

```
Dim variableName
```

Here, variableName is the name of the variable. You make up these names yourself, but there are a few restrictions you need to bear in mind:

- The name must begin with a letter
- The name can't be longer than 255 characters
- The name can't be a VBA keyword (such as Dim or Sub or End)
- The name can't contain a space or any of the following characters: . ! # $ % & @

For example, the following statement declares a variable named totalSales:

```
Dim totalSales
```

Most programmers set up a declaration section at the beginning of each procedure and use it to hold all their Dim statements. Then, after the variables have been declared, you can use them throughout the procedure. Listing 3.1 shows a Function procedure that declares two variables—totalSales and totalExpenses—and then uses Excel's Sum function to store a range sum in each variable. Finally, the GrossMargin calculation uses each variable to return the function result.

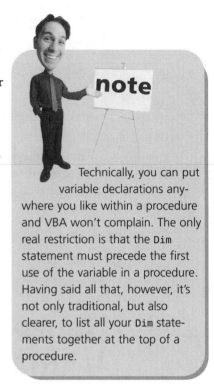

note

Technically, you can put variable declarations anywhere you like within a procedure and VBA won't complain. The only real restriction is that the Dim statement must precede the first use of the variable in a procedure. Having said all that, however, it's not only traditional, but also clearer, to list all your Dim statements together at the top of a procedure.

tip

To conserve space, you can declare multiple variables on a single line. In the GrossMargin function, for example, you could declare totalSales and totalExpenses using the following statement:

```
Dim totalSales, totalExpenses
```

LISTING 3.1   A Function that Uses Variables to Store the Intermediate Values of a Calculation

```
Function GrossMargin()
    '
    ' Declarations
    '
    Dim totalSales
    Dim totalExpenses
    '
    ' Code
    '
    totalSales = Application.Sum(Range("Sales"))
    totalExpenses = Application.Sum(Range("Expenses"))
    GrossMargin = (totalSales - totalExpenses) /
totalSales
End Function
```

In the `GrossMargin` function, notice that you store a value in a variable with a simple assignment statement of the following form:

variableName = value

Avoiding Variable Errors

One of the most common errors in VBA procedures is to declare a variable and then later misspell the name. For example, suppose I had entered the following statement in the `GrossMargin` procedure from Listing 3.1:

```
totlExpenses =
Application.Sum(Range("Expenses"))
```

Here, `totlExpenses` is a misspelling of the variable named `totalExpenses`. VBA supports *implicit declarations*, which means that if it sees a name it doesn't recognize, it assumes that the name belongs to a new variable. In this case, VBA would assume that `totlExpenses` is a new variable, proceed normally, and calculate the wrong answer for the function.

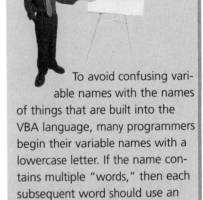

note

To avoid confusing variable names with the names of things that are built into the VBA language, many programmers begin their variable names with a lowercase letter. If the name contains multiple "words," then each subsequent word should use an uppercase first letter (for example, `totalSales` or `newFileName`). This is the style I use in this book.

Also, note that VBA preserves the case of your variable names throughout a procedure. For example, if you declare a variable named `totalSales` and you later enter this variable name as, say, `totalsales`, VBA will convert the name to `totalSales` automatically as part of its syntax checking. This means two things:

- If you want to change the case used in a variable, change the *first* instance of the variable (usually the `Dim` statement).

- After you've declared a variable, you should enter all subsequent references to the variable entirely in lowercase.

To avoid this problem, you can tell VBA to generate an error whenever it comes across a name that hasn't been declared explicitly with a Dim statement. There are two ways to do this:

- For an individual module, enter the following statement at the top of the module:
  Option Explicit

- To force VBA to add this statement automatically to all your modules, in the Visual Basic Editor, select Tools, Options, display the Editor tab in the Options dialog box that appears, and activate the Require Variable Declaration check box.

note

Activating the Require Variable Declaration check box forces VBA to add the Option Explicit statement at the beginning of each new module. However, it *doesn't* add this statement to any existing modules; you need to do that by hand.

Variable Data Types

The *data type* of a variable determines the kind of data the variable can hold. You specify a data type by including the As keyword in a Dim statement. Here is the general syntax:

```
Dim variableName As DataType
```

variableName is the name of the variable and DataType is one of the data types. Here's a rundown of the most useful VBA data types:

String—This type holds *strings*, which are simple text values. Here's a sample declaration and an assignment statement (note the use of quotation marks in the assignment statement value; this tells VBA that the value is a string):

```
Dim newFileName As String
newFileName = "Budget Notes.doc"
```

Date—This type holds *date* values, which refer to dates and/or times. Here are a few examples (note the use of the # character around the values; this tells VBA that the values are dates and/or times):

```
Dim myBirthDate As Date
Dim myBirthTime As Date
Dim anotherDate As Date
myBirthDate = #8/23/59#
myBirthTime = #3:02 AM#
anotherDate = #4/27/04 16:05#
```

Integer—This type holds *integer* values, which VBA defines as whole numbers between –32,768 and 32,767. Here's an example:

```
Dim paragraphNumber As Integer
paragraphNumber = 1
```

Long—This type holds *long integer* values, which VBA defines as whole numbers between –2,147,483,648 to 2,147,483,647. Here's an example (note that you don't include commas in numbers that would normally use one or more thousands separators):

```
Dim wordCount As Long
wordCount = 100000
```

Boolean—This type holds *Boolean* values, which take one of two values: True or False. Here's an example:

```
Dim documentSaved As Boolean
documentSaved = False
```

Currency—This type holds monetary values. The value range is from –922,337,203,685,477.5808 to 922,337,203,685,477.5807.

Single—This type holds *single-precision floating point* values, which are numbers that have a decimal component. Here's an example:

```
Dim averageUnitSales As Single
averageUnitSales = 50.3
```

Double—This type holds *double-precision floating point*, which can accommodate much larger or smaller numbers than the Single type. Note, however, that the range available with the Single type should be more than enough for your VBA macros, so you'll probably never use the Double type. Here's an example:

```
Dim atomsInTheUniverse As Double
atomsInTheUniverse = 2.0E+79
```

> **note**
>
> Double values often use *exponential notation*, such as the value 2.0E+79 used in the Double example. A positive number, say *X*, after the E symbol means that you move the decimal point *X* positions to the right to get the actual number. So, for example, 2.0E+3 is the same thing as 2000. A negative number, say –*X*, after the E means that you move the decimal point *X* positions to the left. So 3.14E-4 is the equivalent of 0.000314.

Here are a few notes to keep in mind when using data types:

- If you don't include a data type when declaring a variable, VBA assigns the Variant data type. This enables you to store any kind of data in the variable. However, this isn't a good idea because Variant variables use more memory and are much slower than the other data types. Therefore, always give your variables a specific data type.

- If you declare a variable to be one data type and then try to store a value of a different data type in the variable, VBA will often display an error. For example, if you declare a variable using the Single type and you try to assign a value that's outside the Single type's allowable range, VBA will display an "Overflow" error message when you attempt to run the procedure.

- To specify the data type of a procedure argument, use the As keyword in the argument list. For example, the following Function statement declares variables x and y to be Single:

```
Function HypotenuseLength(x As Single, y As Single)
```

- To specify the data type of the return value for a Function procedure, use the As keyword at the end of the Function statement:

```
Function HypotenuseLength(x, y) As Single
```

Using Array Variables

In VBA, an *array* is a group of variables of the same data type. Why would you need to use an array? Well, suppose you wanted to store 20 employee names in variables to use in a procedure. One way to do this would be to create 20 variables named, say, employee1, employee2, and so on. However, it's much more efficient to create a single employee array variable that can hold up to 20 names. Here's how you would do that:

```
Dim employee(19) As String
```

As you can see, this declaration is very similar to one you would use for a regular variable. The difference is the 19 enclosed in parentheses. The parentheses tell VBA that you're declaring an array, and the number tells VBA how many elements you'll need in the array. Why 19 instead of 20? Well, each element in the array is assigned a *subscript*, where the first element's subscript is 0, the second is 1, and so on up to, in this case, 19. Therefore, the total number of elements in this array is 20.

You use the subscript to refer to any element simply by enclosing its index number in the parentheses, like so:

```
employee(0) = "Ponsonby"
```

By default, the subscripts of VBA arrays start at 0 (this is called the *lower bound* of the array) and run up to the number you specify in the Dim statement (this is called the *upper bound* of the array). If you would prefer your array index numbers to start at 1, include the following statement at the top of the module (in other words, before declaring your first array and before your first procedure):

```
Option Base 1
```

Working with Constants

Constants are values that don't change. They can be numbers, strings, or other values, but, unlike variables, they keep their values throughout your code. VBA recognizes two types of constants: built-in and user-defined.

Using Built-In Constants

Many properties and methods have their own predefined constants. For Excel objects, these constants begin with the letters xl. For Word objects, the constants begin with wd. For VBA objects, the constants begin with vb.

For example, Excel's Window object has a WindowState property that recognizes three built-in constants: xlNormal (to set a window in its normal state), xlMaximized (to maximize a window), and xlMinimized (to minimize a window). To maximize the active window, for example, you would use the following statement:

```
ActiveWindow.WindowState = xlMaximized
```

Creating User-Defined Constants

To create your own constants, use the Const statement:

```
Const CONSTANTNAME [As type] = expression
```

CONSTANTNAME	The name of the constant. Most programmers use all-uppercase names for constants.
As type	Use this optional expression to assign a data type to the constant.
expression	The value (or a formula that returns a value) that you want to use for the constant.

For example, the following statement creates a constant named DISCOUNT and assigns it the value 0.4:

```
Const DISCOUNT = 0. 4
```

The Absolute Minimum

This chapter gave you the nitty-gritty on VBA's variables. You learned what variables are and how to declare them, and you learned the various data types supported by VBA. I finished by showing you how to work with arrays and constants.

You also learned a few things that will help you avoid the most common variable-related errors made by beginning programmers:

- Declare all your variables.

- To ensure you declare all your variables, add the Option Explicit statement to the top of all your modules (or get VBA to do it for you automatically).

- Assign a specific data type to each variable.

- Put all your variable declarations at the top of each procedure (that is, immediately after the Sub or Function statement).

- To avoid confusing a variable with a built-in VBA name, use a lowercase first letter in each of your variable names.

- After a variable has been declared, enter all subsequent instances of the variable entirely in lowercase. After you move the cursor away from the variable name, the Visual Basic Editor should change the case to match what you have in the original declaration. If it doesn't do this, it likely means you spelled the variable name wrong.

Here's a list of chapters where you'll find related information:

- You often use operators and expressions to assign values to variables. I discuss this in detail in Chapter 4, "Building VBA Expressions."

- Objects have a separate variable type. I talk about it, as well as about assigning objects to variables, in Chapter 5, "Working with Objects."

- See Chapter 12, "Interacting with the User," to learn more about the details of the MsgBox statement.

4

BUILDING VBA EXPRESSIONS

The VBA variables you learned about in the Chapter 3, "Understanding Program Variables," don't amount to a hill of beans unless you do something with them. In other words, a procedure is merely a lifeless collection of Dim statements until you define some kind of relationship among the variables and your program objects. (I'll talk about the latter in Chapter 5, "Working with Objects.")

To establish these relationships, you need to create *expressions* that perform calculations and produce results. This chapter takes you through some expression basics and shows you a number of techniques for building powerful expressions using not only variables, but also VBA's built-in functions.

You can think of an expression as being like a compact version of a user-defined function. In other words, in the same way that a function takes one or more arguments, combines them in various ways, and returns a value, so too does an expression take one or more inputs (called operands), combine them with special symbols (called operators), and produce a result. The main difference, though, is that an expression must do all its dirty work in a single VBA statement.

For example, consider the following statement:

```
might = "right"
```

Here, the left side of the equation is a variable named `might`. The right side of the equation is the simplest of all expressions: a text string. So, in other words, a string value is being stored in a variable.

Here's a slightly more complex example:

```
energy = mass * (speedOfLight ^ 2)
```

Again, the left side of the equation is a variable (named `energy`), and the right side of the equation is an expression. For the latter, a variable named `speedOfLight` is squared, and then this result is multiplied by another variable named `mass`. In this example, you see the two main components of any expression:

Operands—These are the "input values" used by the expression. They can be variables, object properties, function results, or literals. (A *literal* is a specific value, such as a number or a text string. In the first expression example, "right" is a string literal.)

Operators—These are symbols that combine the operands to produce a result. Common operators are the familiar + (addition) and - (subtraction). In the example just shown, the * symbol represents multiplication and the ^ symbol represents exponentiation.

This combination of operands and operators produces a result that conforms to one of the variable data types outlined in the last chapter: String, Date, Boolean, or one of the numeric data types (Integer, Long, Currency, Single, or Double). When building your expressions, the main point to keep in mind is that you must maintain *data type consistency* throughout the expression. This means you must watch for three things:

- The operands must use compatible data types. Although it's okay to combine, say, an `Integer` operand with a `Long` operand (because they're both numeric data types), it wouldn't make sense to use, say, a `Double` operand and a `String` operand.

- The operators you use must match the data types of the operands. For example, you wouldn't want to multiply two strings together.

- If you're storing the expression result in a variable, make sure the variable's data type is consistent with the type of result produced by the expression. For example, don't use a `Boolean` variable to store the result of a string expression.

VBA divides expressions into four groups: numeric, string, date, and logical. I discuss each type of expression later in this chapter, but let's first run through all the available VBA operators.

Working with VBA Operators

You've already seen the first of VBA's operators: the *assignment operator*, which is just the humble equals sign (=). You use the assignment operator to assign the result of an expression to a variable (or, as you'll see in Chapter 5, to an object property).

Bear in mind that VBA always derives the result of the right side of the equation (that is, the expression) before it modifies the value of the left side of the equation. This seems like obvious behavior, but it's the source of a handy trick that you'll use quite often. In other words, you can use the current value of whatever is on the left side of the equation *as part of the expression* on the right side. For example, consider the following code fragment:

```
currentYear = 2004
currentYear = currentYear + 1
```

The first statement assigns the value 2004 to the currentYear variable. The second statement also changes the value stored in the currentYear, but it uses the expression currentYear + 1 to do it. This looks weird until you remember that VBA always evaluates the expression first. In other words, it takes the current value of currentYear, which is 2004, and adds 1 to it. The result is 2005 and *that* is what's stored in currentYear when all is said and done.

Consider, again, the generic assignment statement:

```
variable = expression
```

Because of VBA's evaluate-the-expression-and-*then*-store-the-result behavior, this assignment statement should *not* be read like this:

```
variable is the same as expression.
```

Instead, it makes more sense to think of it in either of the following terms:

```
variable is set to expression
variable assumes the value given by expression.
```

This helps to reinforce the important concept that the expression result is being stored in the variable.

VBA has a number of different operators that you use to combine functions, variables, and values in a VBA expression. These operators work much like the operators—such as addition (+) and multiplication (*)—that you use to build formulas in Excel worksheets and Word tables. VBA operators fall into five general categories: arithmetic, concatenation, comparison, logical, and miscellaneous.

Arithmetic Operators

VBA's arithmetic operators are similar to those you use to build Excel formulas. Table 4.1 lists each of the arithmetic operators you can use in your VBA statements.

TABLE 4.1   The VBA Arithmetic Operators

Operator	Name	Example	Result
+	Addition	10+5	15
-	Subtraction	10-5	5
-	Negation	-10	-10
*	Multiplication	10*5	50
/	Division	10/5	2
\	Integer division	11\5	2
^	Exponentiation	10^5	100000
Mod	Modulus	10 Mod 5	0

The Mod operator works like Excel's MOD() worksheet function. In other words, it divides one number by another and returns the remainder. Here's the general form to use:

```
result = dividend Mod divisor
```

Here, *dividend* is the number being divided; *divisor* is the number being divided into *dividend*; and *result* is the remainder of the division. For example, 16 Mod 5 returns 1 because 5 goes into 16 three times with a remainder of 1.

The Concatenation Operator

You use the concatenation operator (&) to combine text strings within an expression. One way to use the concatenation operator is to combine string literals. For example, consider the following expression:

```
"soft" & "ware"
```

The result of this expression is the following string:

```
software
```

You can also use & to combine not just `String` operands, but numeric and `Date` operands, too. Just remember that the result will always be of the `String` data type. For more information on the concatenation operator, check out the section "Working with String Expressions" later in this chapter.

Comparison Operators

You use the comparison operators in an expression that compares two or more numbers, text strings, variables, or function results. If the statement is true, the result of the formula is given the logical value True (which is equivalent to any nonzero value). If the statement is false, the formula returns the logical value False (which is equivalent to 0). Table 4.2 summarizes VBA's comparison operators.

TABLE 4.2   The VBA Comparison Operators

Operator	Name	Example	Result
=	Equal to	10=5	False
>	Greater than	10>5	True
<	Less than	10<5	False
>=	Greater than or equal to	"a">="b"	False
<=	Less than or equal to	"a"<="b"	True
<>	Not equal to	"a"<>"b"	True

Logical Operators

You use the logical operators to combine or modify True/False expressions. Table 4.3 summarizes VBA's logical operators. I provide more detail about each operator later in this chapter (see "Working with Logical Expressions").

TABLE 4.3   The VBA Logical Operators

Operator	General Form	What It Returns
And	*Expr1* And *Expr2*	True if both *Expr1* and *Expr2* are True; False otherwise.
Or	*Expr1* Or *Expr2*	True if at least one of *Expr1* and *Expr2* are True; False otherwise.
Xor	*Expr1* Xor *Expr2*	False if both *Expr1* and *Expr2* are True or if both *Expr1* and *Expr2* are False; True otherwise.
Not	Not *Expr*	True if *Expr* is False; False if *Expr* is True.

Understanding Operator Precedence

You'll often use simple expressions that contain just two values and a single operator. In practice, however, many expressions you use will have a number of values and operators. In these more complex expressions, the order in which the calculations are performed becomes crucial. For example, consider the expression 3+5^2. If you calculate from left to right, the answer you get is 64 (3+5 equals 8 and 8^2 equals 64). However, if you perform the exponentiation first and then the addition, the result is 28 (5^2 equals 25 and 3+25 equals 28). As this example shows, a single expression can produce multiple answers depending on the order in which you perform the calculations.

To control this problem, VBA evaluates an expression according to a predefined *order of precedence*. This order of precedence lets VBA calculate an expression unambiguously by determining which part of the expression it calculates first, which part second, and so on.

The Order of Precedence

The order of precedence that VBA uses is determined by the various expression operators I outlined in the preceding section. Table 4.4 summarizes the complete order of precedence used by VBA.

TABLE 4.4   The VBA Order of Precedence

Operator	Operation	Order of Precedence
^	Exponentiation	First
--	Negation	Second
* and /	Multiplication and division	Third
\	Integer division	Fourth
Mod	Modulus	Fifth
+ and --	Addition and subtraction	Sixth
&	Concatenation	Seventh
= < > <= >= <>	Comparison	Eighth
And Eqv Imp Or Xor Not	Logical	Ninth

From this table, you can see that VBA performs exponentiation before addition. Therefore, the correct answer for the expression 3+5^2 (just discussed) is 28.

Notice, as well, that some operators in Table 4.4 have the same order of precedence (for example, multiplication and division). This means that it doesn't matter in which order these operators are evaluated. For example, consider the expression 5*10/2. If you perform the multiplication first, the answer you get is 25 (5*10 equals 50, and 50/2 equals 25). If you perform the division first, you also get an answer of 25 (10/2 equals 5, and 5*5 equals 25). By convention, VBA evaluates operators with the same order of precedence from left to right.

Controlling the Order of Precedence

Sometimes you want to override the order of precedence. For example, suppose you want to create an expression that calculates the pre-tax cost of an item. If you bought something for $10.65, including 7 percent sales tax, and you wanted to find the cost of the item less the tax, you'd use the expression 10.65/1.07, which gives you the correct answer of $9.95. In general, the expression to use is given by the following formula:

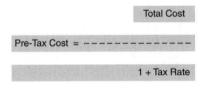

Listing 4.1 shows a function that attempts to implement this formula.

LISTING 4.1   A First Attempt at Calculating the Pre-Tax Cost

```
Function PreTaxCost(totalCost As Currency, taxRate As Single) As Currency
    PreTaxCost = totalCost / 1 + taxRate
End Function
```

Figure 4.1 shows an Excel worksheet that uses this function. The value in cell B4 is passed to the totalCost argument and the value in cell B1 is passed to the taxRate argument.

FIGURE 4.1

A function that attempts to calculate the pre-tax cost of an item.

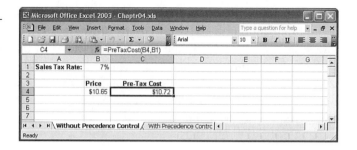

As you can see, the result is incorrect. What happened? Well, according to the rules of precedence, VBA performs division before addition, so the totalCost value first is divided by 1 and then is added to the taxRate value, which isn't the correct order.

To get the correct answer, you have to override the order of precedence so the addition 1 + taxRate is performed first. You do this by surrounding that part of the expression with parentheses, as in Listing 4.2. Using this revised function, you get the correct answer, as shown in Figure 4.2.

LISTING 4.2 The Correct Way to Calculate the Pre-Tax Cost

```
Function PreTaxCost2(totalCost As Currency, taxRate As Single) As Currency
    PreTaxCost2 = totalCost / (1 + taxRate)
End Function
```

FIGURE 4.2

The revised function calculates the pre-tax cost correctly.

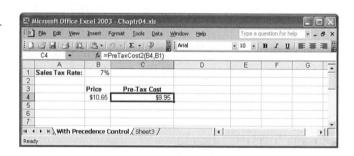

In general, you can use parentheses to control the order that VBA uses to calculate expressions. Terms inside parentheses are always calculated first; terms outside parentheses are calculated sequentially (according to the order of precedence). To

gain even more control over your expressions, you can place parentheses inside one another; this is called *nesting* parentheses, and VBA always evaluates the innermost set of parentheses first. Here are a few sample expressions:

Expression	First Step	Second Step	Third Step	Result
3^(15/5)*2–5	3^3*2–5	27*2–5	54–5	49
3^((15/5)*2–5)	3^(3*2–5)	3^(6–5)	3^1	3
3^(15/(5*2–5))	3^(15/(10–5))	3^(15/5)	3^3	27

Notice that the order of precedence rules also hold within parentheses. For example, in the expression (5*2–5), the term 5*2 is calculated before 5 is subtracted.

Using parentheses to determine the order of calculations allows you to gain full control over VBA expressions. This way, you can make sure that the answer given by an expression is the one *you* want.

Working with Numeric Expressions

Numeric expressions are what I normally think of when I use the generic term "expression." Whether it's calculating gross margin, figuring out commissions, or determining the monthly payment on a loan, many expressions perform some kind of number crunching. You saw VBA's arithmetic operators earlier in this chapter. This section adds to that by giving you a quick look at VBA's built-in math and financial functions.

> **caution**
>
> One of the most common mistakes when using parentheses in expressions is to forget to close a parenthetic term with a right parenthesis. If you do this, VBA displays an `Expected:` `)` message. To make sure you've closed each parenthetic term, count all the left parentheses and count all the right parentheses. If these totals don't match, you know you've left out a parenthesis.

VBA's Math Functions

The operands you use in your numeric expressions will usually be numeric literals or variables declared as one of VBA's numeric data types. However, VBA also boasts quite a few built-in math functions that your expressions can use as operands. These functions are outlined in Table 4.5.

TABLE 4.5 VBA's Math Functions

Function	What It Returns
Abs(*number*)	The absolute value of *number*.
Atn(*number*)	The arctangent of *number*.
Cos(*number*)	The cosine of *number*.
Exp(*number*)	*e* (the base of the natural logarithm) raised to the power of *number*.
Fix(*number*)	The integer portion of *number*. If *number* is negative, Fix returns the first negative integer greater than or equal to *number*.
Hex(*number*)	The hexadecimal value, as a Variant, of *number*.
Hex$(*number*)	The hexadecimal value, as a String, of *number*.
Int(*number*)	The integer portion of *number*. If *number* is negative, Int returns the first negative integer less than or equal to *number*.
Log(*number*)	The natural logarithm of *number*.
Oct(*number*)	The octal value, as a Variant, of *number*.
Oct$(*number*)	The octal value, as a String, of *number*.
Rnd(*number*)	A random number between 0 and 1, as a Single. You use the optional *number* as a "seed" value, as follows:

	number	*What It Generates*
	Less than 0	The same number every time (varies with *number*).
	Equal to 0	The most recently generated number.
	Greater than 0	The next random number in the sequence.

Function	What It Returns
Sgn(*number*)	The sign of *number*.
Sin(*number*)	The sine of *number*.
Sqr(*number*)	The square root of *number*.
Tan(*number*)	The tangent of *number*.

The need for random numbers comes up quite a bit in programming. However, instead of random numbers between 0 and 1, you might need to generate numbers within a larger range. Here's the general formula to use to get Rnd to generate a random number between a lower bound and an upper bound:

```
Int((upper - lower) * Rnd + lower)
```

For example, here's some code that generates a random 8-digit integer:

```
Randomize
fileName = Int((99999999 - 10000000) * Rnd +
10000000)
```

VBA's Financial Functions

VBA has quite a few financial functions that offer you powerful tools for building applications that manage both business and personal finances. You can use these functions to calculate such things as the monthly payment for a loan, the future value of an annuity, or the yearly depreciation of an asset.

Although VBA has a baker's dozen financial functions that use many different arguments, the following list covers the arguments you'll use most frequently:

The random numbers generated by Rnd are only pseudo-random. In other words, if you use the same seed value, you get the same sequence of numbers. If you need truly random numbers, run the Randomize statement just before using Rnd. This initializes the random number generator with the current system time. Here's an example:

```
Randomize
myRandomNumber = Rnd()
```

rate	The fixed rate of interest over the term of the loan or investment.
nper	The number of payments or deposit periods over the term of the loan or investment.
pmt	The periodic payment or deposit.
pv	The present value of the loan (the principal) or the initial deposit in an investment.
fv	The future value of the loan or investment.
type	The type of payment or deposit. Use 0 (the default) for end-of-period payments or deposits and 1 for beginning-of-period payments or deposits.

For most financial functions, the following rules apply:

■ The underlying unit of both the interest rate and the period must be the same. For example, if the *rate* is the annual interest rate, you must express *nper* in years. Similarly, if you have a monthly interest rate, you must express *nper* in months.

- You enter money you receive as a positive quantity, and you enter money you pay as a negative quantity. For example, you always enter the loan principal as a positive number because it's money you receive from the bank.

- The *nper* argument should always be a positive integer quantity.

Table 4.6 lists all of VBA's financial functions.

TABLE 4.6 The Built-In Financial Functions in VBA

Function	What It Returns
DDB(*cost,salvage,life,period,factor*)	The depreciation of an asset over a specified period using the double-declining balance method.
FV(*rate,nper,pmt,pv,type*)	The future value of an investment or loan.
IPmt(*rate,per,nper,pv,fv,type*)	The interest payment for a specified period of a loan.
IRR(*values,guess*)	The internal rate of return for a series of cash flows.
MIRR(*values,finance_rate,reinvest_rate*)	The modified internal rate of return for a series of periodic cash flows.
NPer(*rate,pmt,pv,fv,type*)	The number of periods for an investment or loan.
NPV(*rate,value1,value2...*)	The net present value of an investment based on a series of cash flows and a discount rate.
Pmt(*rate,nper,pv,fv,type*)	The periodic payment for a loan or investment.
PPmt(*rate,per,nper,pv,fv,type*)	The principal payment for a specified period of a loan.
PV(*rate,nper,pmt,fv,type*)	The present value of an investment.
Rate(*nper,pmt,pv,fv,type,guess*)	The periodic interest rate for a loan or investment.
SLN(*cost,salvage,life*)	The straight-line depreciation of an asset over one period.
SYD(*cost,salvage,life,period*)	Sum-of-years' digits depreciation of an asset over a specified period.

Working with String Expressions

A *string expression* is an expression that returns a value that has a String data type. String expressions can use as operands string literals (one or more characters enclosed in double quotation marks), variables declared as String, or any of VBA's built-in functions that return a String value. Table 4.7 summarizes all of the VBA functions that deal with strings.

TABLE 4.7   VBA's String Functions

Function	What It Returns
Asc(*string*)	The ANSI character code of the first letter in *string*.
Chr(*charcode*)	The character, as a Variant, that corresponds to the ANSI code given by *charcode*.
Chr$(*charcode*)	The character, as a String, that corresponds to the ANSI code given by *charcode*.
CStr(*expression*)	Converts *expression* to a String value.
InStr(*start,string1,string2*)	The character position of the first occurrence of *string2* in *string1*, starting at *start*.
InStrB(*start,string1,string2*)	The byte position of the first occurrence of *string2* in *string1*, starting at *start*.
InStrRev(*string1,string2, start*)	The character position of the final occurrence of *string2* in *string1*, starting at *start*.
LCase(*string*)	*string* converted to lowercase, as a Variant.
LCase$(*string*)	*string* converted to lowercase, as a String.
Left(*string,length*)	The leftmost *length* characters from *string*, as a Variant.
Left$(*string,length*)	The leftmost *length* characters from *string*, as a String.
LeftB(*string*)	The leftmost *length* bytes from *string*, as a Variant.
LeftB$(*string*)	The leftmost *length* bytes from *string*, as a String.
Len(*string*)	The number of characters in *string*.
LenB(*string*)	The number of bytes in *string*.
LTrim(*string*)	A string, as a Variant, without the leading spaces in *string*.
LTrim$(*string*)	A string, as a String, without the leading spaces in *string*.
Mid(*string,start,length*)	*length* characters, as a Variant, from *string* beginning at *start*.
Mid$(*string,start,length*)	*length* characters, as a String, from *string* beginning at *start*.
MidB(*string,start,length*)	*length* bytes, as a Variant, from *string* beginning at *start*.
MidB$(*string,start,length*)	*length* bytes, as a String, from *string* beginning at *start*.
Right(*string*)	The rightmost *length* characters from *string*, as a Variant.
Right$(*string*)	The rightmost *length* characters from *string*, as a String.
RightB(*string*)	The rightmost *length* bytes from *string*, as a Variant.
RightB$(*string*)	The rightmost *length* bytes from *string*, as a String.
RTrim(*string*)	A string, as a Variant, without the trailing spaces in *string*.
RTrim$(*string*)	A string, as a String, without the trailing spaces in *string*.

TABLE 4.7 (continued)

Function	What It Returns
Trim(*string*)	A string, as a Variant, without the leading and trailing spaces in *string*.
Trim$(*string*)	A string, as a String, without the leading and trailing spaces in *string*.
Space(*number*)	A string, as a Variant, with *number* spaces.
Space$(*number*)	A string, as a String, with *number* spaces.
Str(*number*)	The string representation, as a Variant, of *number*.
Str$(*number*)	The string representation, as a String, of *number*.
StrComp(*string2*,*string2*,*compare*)	A value indicating the result of comparing *string1* and *string2*.
StrConv(*string*, *conversion*)	The *string* converted into another format, as specified by *conversion* (such as vbUpperCase, vbLowerCase, and vbProperCase).
String(*number*,*character*)	*character*, as a Variant, repeated *number* times.
String$(*number*,*character*)	*character*, as a String, repeated *number* times.
UCase(*string*)	*string* converted to uppercase, as a Variant.
UCase$(*string*)	*string* converted to uppercase, as a String.
Val(*string*)	All the numbers contained in *string*, up to the first non-numeric character.

Listing 4.3 shows a procedure that uses some of these string functions.

LISTING 4.3 A Procedure that Uses a Few String Functions

```
Function ExtractLastName(fullName As String) As String
    Dim spacePos As Integer
    spacePos = InStr(fullName, " ")
    ExtractLastName = Mid$(fullName, _
                          spacePos + 1, _
                          Len(fullName) - spacePos)
End Function

Sub TestIt()
    MsgBox ExtractLastName("Millicent Peeved")
End Sub
```

note

Note the use of the underscore (_) in Listing 4.3. This is VBA's *code continuation character*—it's useful for breaking up long statements into multiple lines for easier reading. One caveat, though: Make sure you add a space before the underscore, or VBA will generate an error.

The purpose of this procedure is to take a name (first and last, separated by a space, as shown in the `TestIt` procedure) and extract the last name. The full name is brought into the function as the `fullName` argument. After declaring an `Integer` variable named `spacePos`, the procedure uses the `InStr` function to check `fullName` and find out the position of the space that separates the first and last names. The result is stored in `spacePos`:

```
spacePos = InStr(fullName, " ")
```

The real meat of the function is provided by the `Mid$` string function, which uses the following syntax to extract a substring from a larger string:

```
Mid$(string,start,length)
```

> *string*   The string from which you want to extract the characters. In the `ExtractLastName` function, this parameter is the `fullName` variable.
>
> *start*   The starting point of the string you want to extract. In `ExtractLastName`, this parameter is the position of the space, plus 1 (in other words, `spacePos + 1`).
>
> *length*   The length of the string you want to extract. In the `ExtractLastName` function, this is the length of the full string—`Len(fullName)`—minus the position of the space.

Working with Logical Expressions

A logical expression is an expression that returns a Boolean result. A Boolean value is almost always either True or False, but VBA also recognizes some Boolean equivalents:

- A False result can be used in an expression as though it was 0. Similarly, you can use 0 in a logical expression as though it was False.

- A True result can be used in an expression as though it was –1. However, *any* nonzero value can be used in a logical expression as though it was True.

In Chapter 6, "Controlling Your VBA Code," I'll show you various VBA statements that let your procedures make decisions and loop through sections of code. In most cases, the mechanism that controls these statements will be a logical expression. For example, if *x* is a logical expression, you can tell VBA to run one set of statements if *x* returns True and a different set of statements if *x* returns False.

You'll see that these are powerful constructs, and they'll prove invaluable in all of your VBA projects. To help you prepare, let's take a closer look at VBA's logical operators.

The And Operator

You use the And operator when you want to test two Boolean operands to see if they're both True. For example, consider the following generic expression (where *Expr1* and *Expr2* are Boolean values):

```
Expr1 And Expr2
```

- If both *Expr1* and *Expr2* are True, this expression returns True.
- If either or both *Expr1* and *Expr2* are False, the expression returns False.

The Or Operator

You use the Or operator when you want to test two Boolean operands to see if one of them is True:

```
Expr1 Or Expr2
```

- If either or both *Expr1* and *Expr2* are True, this expression returns True.
- If both *Expr1* and *Expr2* are False, the expression returns False.

The Xor Operator

Xor is the exclusive Or operator. It's useful when you need to know if two operands have the opposite value:

```
Expr1 Xor Expr2
```

- If one of the values is True and the other is False, the expression returns True.
- If *Expr1* and *Expr2* are both True or are both False, the expression returns False.

The Not Operator

The Not operator is the logical equivalent of the negation operator. In this case, Not returns the opposite value of an operand. For example, if *Expr* is True, Not *Expr* returns False.

Working with Date Expressions

A *date expression* is an expression that returns a Date value. For operands in date expressions, you can use either a variable declared as Date or a date literal. For the latter, you enclose the date in pound signs, like so:

```
dateVar = #8/23/04#
```

When working with dates, it helps to remember that VBA works with dates internally as *serial numbers*. Specifically, VBA uses December 31, 1899 as an arbitrary starting point and then represents subsequent dates as the number of days that have passed since then. So, for example, the date serial number for January 1, 1900 is 1, January 2, 1900 is 2, and so on. Table 4.8 displays some sample date serial numbers.

TABLE 4.8   Examples of Date Serial Numbers

Serial Number	Date
366	December 31, 1900
16229	June 6, 1944
38222	August 23, 2004

Similarly, VBA also uses serial numbers to represent times internally. In this case, though, VBA expresses time as a fraction of the 24-hour day to get a number between 0 and 1. The starting point, midnight, is given the value 0, noon is 0.5, and so on. Table 4.9 displays some sample time serial numbers.

TABLE 4.9   Examples of Time Serial Numbers

Serial Number	Time
0.25	6:00:00 AM
0.375	9:00:00 AM
0.70833	5:00:00 PM
.99999	11:59:59 PM

You can combine the two types of serial numbers. For example, 38222.5 represents 12 noon on August 23, 2004.

The advantage of using serial numbers in this way is that it makes calculations involving dates and times very easy. Because a date or time is really just a number, any mathematical operation you can perform on a number can also be performed on a date. This is invaluable for procedures that track delivery times, monitor accounts receivable or accounts payable aging, calculate invoice discount dates, and so on.

VBA also comes equipped with quite a few date and time functions. Table 4.10 summarizes them all.

TABLE 4.10   VBA's Date and Time Functions

Function	Returns
CDate(*expression*)	Converts *expression* into a Date value.
Date	The current system date, as a Variant.
Date$()	The current system date, as a String.
DateSerial(*year*,*month*,*day*)	A Date value for the specified *year*, *month*, and *day*.
DateValue(*date*)	A Date value for the *date* string.
Day(*date*)	The day of the month given by *date*.
Hour(*time*)	The hour component of *time*.
Minute(*time*)	The minute component of *time*.
Month(*date*)	The month component of *date*.
Now	The current system date and time.
Second(*time*)	The second component of *time*.
Time	The current system time, as a Variant.
Time$	The current system time, as a String.
Timer	The number of seconds since midnight.
TimeSerial(*hour*,*minute*,*second*)	A Date value for the specified *hour*, *minute*, and *second*.
TimeValue(*time*)	A Date value for the *time* string.
Weekday(*date*)	The day of the week, as a number, given by *date*.
Year(*date*)	The year component of *date*.

Listing 4.4 shows a couple of procedures that take advantage of a few of these date functions.

LISTING 4.4   A Function Procedure that Uses Various Date Functions to Calculate a Person's Age

```
Function CalculateAge(birthDate As Date) As Byte
    Dim birthdayNotPassed As Boolean
    birthdayNotPassed = CDate(Month(birthDate) & "/" & _
                             Day(birthDate) & "/" & _
                             Year(Now)) > Now
    CalculateAge = Year(Now) - Year(birthDate) + birthdayNotPassed
End Function
```

LISTING 4.4   (continued)

```
'
' Use this procedure to test CalculateAge.
'
Sub TestIt2()
    MsgBox CalculateAge(#8/23/59#)
End Sub
```

The purpose of the CalculateAge function is to figure out a person's age given the date of birth (as passed to CalculateAge through the Date variable named birthDate). You might think the following formula would do the job:

Year(Now) - Year(birthDate)

This works, but only if the person's birthday has already passed this year. If the person hasn't had his or her birthday yet, this formula reports the person's age as being one year greater than it really is.

To solve this problem, you need to take into account whether or not the person's birthday has occurred. To do this, CalculateAge first declares a Boolean variable birthdayNotPassed and then uses the following expression to test whether or not the person has celebrated his or her birthday this year:

CDate(Month(birthDate) & "/" & Day(birthDate) & "/" & Year(Now)) > Now

This expression uses the Month, Day, and Year functions to construct the date of the person's birthday this year and uses the CDate function to convert this string into a date. The expression then checks to see if this date is greater than today's date (as given by the Now function). If it is, the person hasn't celebrated his or her birthday, so birthdayNotPassed is set to True; otherwise, birthdayNotPassed is set to False.

The key is that, to VBA, a True value is equivalent to -1, and a False value is equivalent to 0. Therefore, to calculate the person's correct age, you need only add the value of birthdayNotPassed to the expression Year(Now) - Year(birthDate).

THE ABSOLUTE MINIMUM

This chapter showed you how to build expressions in VBA. This is a crucial topic because much of your VBA coding will involve creating expressions of one kind or another. With that in mind, I designed this chapter to give you a solid grounding in expression fundamentals. After first learning about basic expression structure, you were given a quick tour of the various VBA operators and the all-important topic of operator precedence. From there, you went through more detailed lessons on the four main expression types: numeric, string, logical, and date. For related information, see the following chapters:

■ Objects will play a big part in your expressions. For example, you'll use expressions to set the values of object properties. I explain all this and more in Chapter 5, "Working with Objects."

■ You can put your newfound knowledge of logical expressions to good use in Chapter 6, "Controlling Your VBA Code."

■ VBA boasts an impressive function collection, and you'll be learning about many more of these functions as you progress through this book. However, you also have access to the huge collection of built-in functions exposed by the underlying application (for example, Excel's worksheet functions). The chapters in Part 2, "Putting VBA to Work," will show you how to access application functions from your VBA procedures.

■ You'll find a complete list of VBA functions in Appendix B, "VBA Functions."

5

Working with Objects

Many of your VBA procedures will perform calculations using simple combinations of numbers, operators, and the host application's built-in functions. You'll probably find, however, that most of your code manipulates the application environment in some way, whether it's formatting document text, entering data in a worksheet range, or setting application options. Each of these items—the document, the range, and the application—is called an *object* in VBA. Objects are perhaps the most crucial concept in VBA programming, and I'll explain them in detail in this chapter.

The dictionary definition of an object is "anything perceptible by one or more of the senses, especially something that can be seen and felt." Now, of course, you can't *feel* anything in an Office application, but you can *see* all kinds of things. To VBA, an object is anything in an application that you can see *and* manipulate in some way.

For example, a paragraph in a Word document is something you can see, and you can manipulate it by inserting text, changing the style, setting the font, and so on. A paragraph, therefore, is an object.

What isn't an object? The Office programs are so customizable that most things you can see qualify as objects, but not everything does. For example, the Maximize and Minimize buttons in document windows aren't objects. Yes, you can operate them, but you can't change them. Instead, the window itself is the object, and you manipulate it so that it's maximized or minimized.

You can manipulate objects in VBA in any of the following three ways:

- You can make changes to the object's *properties*.
- You can make the object perform a task by activating a *method* associated with the object.
- You can define a procedure that runs whenever a particular *event* happens to the object.

To help you understand properties, methods, events, and objects, I'll put things in real-world terms. First, let's consider a simple analogy using a car. A car is an object, to be sure, but what does it mean to say that it has its own "properties, methods, and events"? Let's see:

- The car's "properties" would be its physical characteristics: its model, color, engine size, and so on.
- The car's "methods" define what you can do with the car: accelerate, brake, turn, and so on.
- The car's "events" are the actions that happen to the car that generate an automatic response from the car. For example, on most modern cars, if you exit the vehicle with the key still in the ignition (the event), a warning bell will sound (the response).

Let's run through a more detailed example. Specifically, let's look at your computer as though it were an object. For starters, you can think of your computer in one of two ways: as a single object or as a *collection* of objects (such as the monitor, the keyboard, the system unit, and so on).

If you wanted to describe your computer as a whole, you would mention things like the name of the manufacturer, the price, the color, and so on. Each of these items is a *property* of the computer. You also can use your computer to perform tasks, such as writing letters, crunching numbers, and playing games. These are the *methods* associated with your computer. There are also a number of things that happen to the computer that cause it to respond in predefined ways. For example, when the On button is pressed, the computer runs through its Power On Self-Test, initializes its components, and so on. The actions to which the computer responds automatically are its *events*.

The sum total of all these properties, methods, and events gives you an overall description of your computer.

But your computer is also a collection of objects, each with its own properties, methods, and events. The CD-ROM drive, for example, has various properties, including its speed and data rate. Its methods would be actions such as ejecting a disk and adjusting the sound level. A CD-ROM event might be the insertion of a disc that contains a file that causes the disc's program to run automatically.

In the end, you have a complete description of the computer: what its distinguishing features are (its properties), how you interact with it (its methods), and to what actions it responds (its events).

The Object Hierarchy

As you've seen, your computer's objects are arranged in a hierarchy with the most general object (the computer as a whole) at the top. Lower levels progress through more specific objects (such as the system unit, the motherboard, and the processor).

Each Office application's objects are arranged in a hierarchy also. The most general object—the `Application` object—refers to the program itself. In Word, for example, the `Application` object contains more than 30 objects, including the `Documents` object (the collection of all open documents, each one being a Document object), the `Options` object (the settings available in the Options dialog box), and the `RecentFiles` object (the names of the files that have been used most recently).

Many of these objects have objects beneath them in the hierarchy. A Document object, for example, contains objects that represent the document's characters, words, sentences, paragraphs, bookmarks, and much more. Similarly, a Paragraph object contains objects for the paragraph format and the tab stops.

To specify an object in the hierarchy, you usually start with the uppermost object and add the lower objects, separated by periods. For example, here's one way you could specify the first word in the second paragraph in a document named `Memo.doc`:

`Application.Documents("Memo.doc").Paragraphs(2).Range.Words(1)`

As you'll see, there are ways to shorten such long-winded "hierarchical paths."

Working with Object Properties

Every object has a defining set of characteristics. These characteristics are called the object's *properties*, and they control the appearance and position of the object. For example, each Window object has a `WindowState` property you can use to display a window as maximized, minimized, or normal. Similarly, a Word Document object has a `Name` property to hold the filename, a `Saved` property that tells you whether or not the document has changed since the last save, a `Type` property to hold the document type (regular or template), and many more.

When you refer to a property, you use the following syntax:

`Object.Property`

For example, the following expression refers to the `ActiveWindow` property of the `Application` object:

`Application.ActiveWindow`

One of the most confusing aspects of objects and properties is that some properties do double-duty as objects. Figure 5.1 uses an Excel example to illustrate this. The `Application` object has an `ActiveWindow` property that tells you the name of the active window. However, `ActiveWindow` is also a `Window` object. Similarly, the `Window` object has an `ActiveCell` property that specifies the active cell, but `ActiveCell` is also a `Range` object. Finally, a `Range` object has a `Font` property, but a font is also an object with its own properties (`Italic`, `Name`, `Size`, and so on).

note

You'll come across the word "active" quite often in your VBA travels, so let's make sure you know what it means. In the VBA world, *active* describes the item you're currently working with. In Word, for example, the document that you're currently working with is the active document. Similarly, in Excel the worksheet cell that you're editing or formatting is the active cell. In programming lingo, the active item is said to have the *focus*.

FIGURE 5.1

Some Excel properties also can be objects.

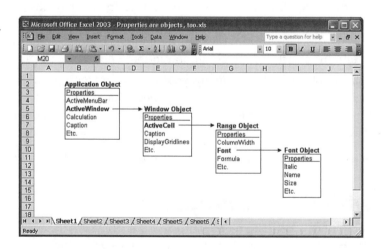

In other words, lower-level objects in the object hierarchy are really just properties of their parent objects. This idea will often help you to reduce the length of a hierarchical path (and thus reduce the abuse your typing fingers must bear). For example, consider the following object path:

```
Application.ActiveWindow.ActiveCell.Font.Italic
```

Here, an object such as ActiveCell implicitly refers to the ActiveWindow and Application objects, so you can knock the path down to size, as follows:

```
ActiveCell.Font.Italic
```

Setting the Value of a Property

To set a property to a certain value, you use the following syntax:

```
Object.Property=value
```

Here, value is an expression that returns the value to which you want to set the property. As such, it can be any of VBA's recognized data types, including the following:

- A numeric value. For example, the following statement sets the size of the font in the active cell to 14:

```
ActiveCell.Font.Size = 14
```

- A string value. The following example sets the font name in the active cell to Times New Roman:

```
ActiveCell.Font.Name = "Times New Roman"
```

- A logical value (in other words, True or False). The following statement turns on the Italic property in the active cell:

```
ActiveCell.Font.Italic = True
```

Returning the Value of a Property

Sometimes you need to know the current setting of a property before changing the property or performing some other action. You can find out the current value of a property by using the following syntax:

```
variable=Object.Property
```

Here, *variable* is a variable or another property. For example, the following statement stores the contents of the active cell in a variable named `cellContents`:

```
cellContents = ActiveCell.Value
```

Working with Object Methods

An object's properties describe what the object is, whereas its *methods* describe what you can do with the object. For example, in Word you can spell check a Document object using the `CheckSpelling` method. Similarly, you can sort a Table object by using the `Sort` method.

How you refer to a method depends on whether or not the method uses any arguments. If it doesn't, the syntax is similar to that of properties:

```
Object.Method
```

For example, the following statement saves the active document:

```
ActiveDocument.Save
```

If the method requires arguments, you use the following syntax:

```
Object.Method (argument1, argument2, ...)
```

Technically, the parentheses around the argument list are necessary only if you'll be storing the result of the method in a variable or object property:

```
variable = Object.Method
➥(argument1, argument2, ...)
```

For example, Word's Document object has a `Close` method that you can use to close a document programmatically. Here's the syntax:

```
Object.Close(SaveChanges, OriginalFormat, RouteDocument)
```

Object	The Document object you want to work with.
SaveChanges	A constant that specifies whether or not the file is saved before closing.

OriginalFormat   A constant that specifies whether or not the file is saved in its original format.

RouteDocument   A True or False value that specifies whether or not the document is routed to the next recipient.

For example, the following statement prompts the user to save changes, saves the changes (if applicable) in the original file format, and routes the document to the next recipient:

```
ActiveDocument.Close wdPromptToSaveChanges,
wdOriginalFormat, True
```

To make your methods clearer to read, you can use VBA's predefined *named arguments*. For example, the syntax of the Close method has three named arguments: SaveChanges, OriginalFormat, and RouteDocument. Here's how you would use them in the preceding example:

```
ActiveDocument.Close
SaveChanges:=wdPromptToSaveChanges, _
   OrignalFormat:=wdOriginalFormat, _
   RouteDocument:=True
```

Notice how the named arguments are assigned values by using the := operator.

Named arguments make your code easier read, but they also bring two other advantages to the table:

note

For many VBA methods, not all the arguments are required. For the Close method, for example, only the SaveChanges argument is required. Throughout this book, I differentiate between required and optional arguments by displaying the required arguments in bold type.

To skip a non-required argument (and thus use its default value), leave it blank, although you still need to enter all the commas that separate the arguments. For example, to exclude the OriginalFormat argument in the Close method, you use a statement like this:

```
ActiveDocument.Close
wdPromptToSaveChanges, , True
```

- You can enter the arguments in any order you like.

- You can ignore any arguments you don't need (except necessary arguments, of course).

Handling Object Events

In simplest terms, an *event* is something that happens to an object. For example, the opening of an Excel workbook would be an event for that workbook. Don't confuse a method with an event, however. Yes, Word has an Open method that you can use to open a document, but this method only *initiates* the procedure; the actual process of the file being opened is the event. Note, too, that events can happen either programmatically (by including the appropriate method in your code, such as `File.Open`) or by user intervention (by selecting a command, such as File, Open).

In VBA, the event itself isn't as important as how your procedures *respond* to the event. In other words, you can write special procedures called *event handlers* that will run every time a particular event occurs. In a Word document, for example, you can specify event handlers for both opening the file and closing the file. (Excel's Workbook object has an even larger list of events, including not just opening the file, but also activating the workbook window, saving the file, inserting a new worksheet, closing the file, and much more.)

For example, Figure 5.2 shows a module window for a document. (Specifically, it's the module window for the project's `ThisDocument` object.) Notice that the module window has two drop-down lists just below the title bar:

Object list—This is the list on the left and it tells you what kind of object you're working with. If you select (General) in this list, you can use the module window to enter standard VBA procedures and functions. If you select an object from this list, however, you can enter event handlers for the object.

Procedure list—This is the list on the right and it tells you which procedure is active in the module. If you select (General) in the Object list, the Procedure list contains all the standard VBA procedures and functions in the module. If you select an object in the Object list, however, the Procedure list changes to show all the events recognized by the object.

FIGURE 5.2

An example of an event procedure. Here, this procedure runs each time the document is opened.

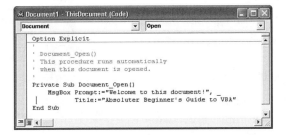

```
Document1 - ThisDocument (Code)
Document                          Open
    Option Explicit
'
' Document_Open()
' This procedure runs automatically
' when this document is opened.
'
Private Sub Document_Open()
    MsgBox Prompt:="Welcome to this document!", _
            Title:="Absoluter Beginner's Guide to VBA"
End Sub
```

In Figure 5.2, I've selected Document in the Object list, so the Procedure list contains all the events recognized by the Document object. For the Open event, I've inserted a MsgBox statement into the Document_Open event handler. This statement will display a message each time the document is opened. (I show you how to use MsgBox in Chapter 12, "Interacting with the User.")

Working with Object Collections

A *collection* is a set of similar objects. For example, Word's Documents collection is the set of all the open Document objects. Similarly, the Paragraphs collection is the set of all Paragraph objects in a document. Collections are objects, too, so they have their own properties and methods, and you can use these properties and methods to manipulate one or more objects in the collection.

The members of a collection are called the *elements* of the collection. You can refer to individual elements using either the object's name or an *index*. For example, the following statement closes a document named Budget.doc:

`Documents("Budget.doc").Close`

On the other hand, the following statement uses an index to select the first Bookmark object in the active document:

`ActiveDocument.Bookmarks(1).Select`

note

It's important to understand that you often can't refer to objects by themselves. Instead, you must refer to the object as an element in a collection. For example, when referring to the Budget.doc document, you can't just use Budget.doc. You have to use Documents("Budget.doc") so that VBA knows you're talking about a currently open document.

If you don't specify an element, VBA assumes you want to work with the entire collection.

Assigning an Object to a Variable

As I mentioned at the end of Chapter 3, "Understanding Program Variables," objects have their own data types. You can declare a variable as an object by using the following form of the Dim statement:

```
Dim variableName As ObjectType
```

Here, `ObjectType` is the data type of the object you want to work with. For example, if you want to work with a Document object, you'd use a Dim statement similar to this:

```
Dim currentDocument As Document
```

It's a good idea to use object variables whenever you can because it enables you to use the Visual Basic Editor's handy IntelliSense features that I described in detail in Chapter 1 (see "Taking Advantage of IntelliSense").

<aside>
note

Object variables take up memory. For optimum code performance, you can reclaim the memory used by unneeded object variables by setting the variable equal to Nothing, like so:

```
Set budgetSheet = Nothing
```
</aside>

After you've set up your object variable, you can assign an object to it by using the Set statement. Set has the following syntax:

```
Set variableName = ObjectName
```

variableName	The name of the variable.
ObjectName	The object you want to assign to the variable.

For example, the following statements declare a variable named budgetSheet to be a Worksheet object and then assign it to the 2004 Budget worksheet in the Budget.xls workbook:

```
Dim budgetSheet As Worksheet
Set budgetSheet = Workbooks("Budget.xls").Worksheets("2004 Budget")
```

The Is Operator

When you looked at comparison operators in the last chapter, the operands you used were simple numbers and strings. Indeed, most of the comparison operators don't make sense in the context of objects (for example, it's absurd to think of one object being "greater than" another). However, VBA does have a comparison operator specifically for objects—the Is operator:

```
result = Object1 Is Object2
```

Here, *Object1* and *Object2* are objects or Object variables. If they're the same, *result* takes the value True; otherwise, *result* is False.

Working with Multiple Properties or Methods

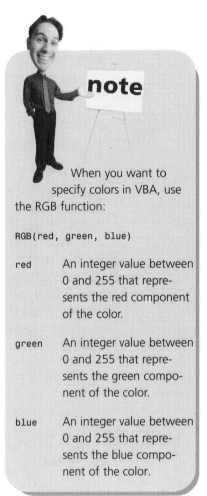

Because most objects have many different properties and methods, you'll often need to perform multiple actions on a single object. This is accomplished easily with multiple statements that set the appropriate properties or run the necessary methods. However, this can be a pain if you have a long object name.

For example, take a look at the FormatParagraph procedure shown in Listing 5.1. This procedure formats a paragraph with six statements. Note that the Paragraph object name—
ThisDocument.Paragraphs(1)—is quite long and is repeated in all six statements.

note

When you want to specify colors in VBA, use the RGB function:

```
RGB(red, green, blue)
```

red	An integer value between 0 and 255 that represents the red component of the color.
green	An integer value between 0 and 255 that represents the green component of the color.
blue	An integer value between 0 and 255 that represents the blue component of the color.

LISTING 5.1   A Procedure That Formats a Range

```
Sub FormatParagraph()
    ThisDocument.Paragraphs(1).Style = "Heading 1"
    ThisDocument.Paragraphs(1).Alignment = wdAlignParagraphCenter
    ThisDocument.Paragraphs(1).Range.Font.Size = 16
    ThisDocument.Paragraphs(1).Range.Font.Bold = True
    ThisDocument.Paragraphs(1).Range.Font.Color = RGB(255, 0, 0) ' Red
    ThisDocument.Paragraphs(1).Range.Font.Name = "Times New Roman"
End Sub
```

To shorten this procedure, VBA provides the With statement. Here's the syntax:

```
With object
    [statements]
End With
```

object	The name of the object.
statements	The statements you want to execute on object.

The idea is that you strip out the common object and place it on the With line. Then, all the statements between With and End With need only reference a specific method or property of that object. In the FormatParagraph procedure, the common object in all six statements is ThisDocument.Paragraphs(1). Listing 5.2 shows the FormatParagraph2 procedure, which uses the With statement to strip out this common object and make the previous macro more efficient.

> **note**
>
> You can make the FormatParagraph2 procedure even more efficient when you realize that the Font object also is repeated several times. In this case, you can *nest* another With statement inside the original one. The new With statement would look like this:
>
> ```
> With .Range.Font
>     .Size = 16
>     .Bold = True
>     .Color = RGB(255, 0, 0)
>     .Name = "Times New Roman"
> End With
> ```

LISTING 5.2   A More Efficient Version of FormatParagraph()

```
Sub FormatParagraph2()
    With ThisDocument.Paragraphs(1)
        .Style = "Heading 1"
        .Alignment = wdAlignParagraphCenter
        .Range.Font.Size = 16
        .Range.Font.Bold = True
        .Range.Font.Color = RGB(255, 0, 0) ' Red
        .Range.Font.Name = "Times New Roman"
    End With
End Sub
```

Example: The `Application` Object

You'll be seeing plenty of objects when you turn your attention to the Microsoft Office programs in Part 2, "Putting VBA to Work." For now, though, let's take a look at an object that is common to all programs: the `Application` object. The `Application` object refers to the application as a whole; therefore, it acts as a container for all of the program's objects. However, the `Application` object does have a few useful properties and methods of its own, and many of these members are applicable to all the Office applications.

Properties of the `Application` Object

The `Application` object has dozens of properties that affect a number of aspects of the program's environment. For starters, any control in the application's Options dialog box (select Tools, Options) has an equivalent `Application` object property. For example, the `StatusBar` property in Word and Excel takes a True or False value that toggles the status bar on or off.

Here's a rundown of a few other `Application` object properties you'll use most often in your VBA code:

`Application.ActivePrinter`—Returns or sets the name of the application's current printer driver.

`ActiveWindow`—Returns a `Window` object that represents the window that currently has the focus.

`Application.Caption`—Returns or sets the name that appears in the title bar of the main application window. In Excel, for example, to change the title bar caption from "Microsoft Excel" to "ACME Coyote Supplies," you would use the following statement:

`Application.Caption = "ACME Coyote Supplies"`

`Application.Dialogs`—Returns the collection of all the application's built-in dialog boxes. See Chapter 12 to learn how to display these dialog boxes from your VBA procedures.

`Application.DisplayAlerts`—Determines whether or not the application displays alert dialog boxes. For example, if your code deletes an Excel worksheet, Excel normally displays an alert box asking you to confirm the deletion. To suppress this alert box and force Excel to accept the default action (which is, in this case, deleting the sheet), set the `DisplayAlerts` property to False.

note

The application restores the `DisplayAlerts` property to its default state (True) when your procedure finishes. If you would prefer to turn the alerts back on before then, set the `DisplayAlerts` property to True.

`Application.Height`—Returns or sets the height, in points, of the application window.

`Application.Left`—Returns or sets the distance, in points, of the left edge of the application window from the left edge of the screen.

`Application.Path`—Returns the path of the `Application` object. In other words, it tells you the drive and folder where the application's executable file resides (such as C:\Program Files\Microsoft Office\Office). Note that the returned path does not include a trailing back slash (\).

`Application.ScreenUpdating`—Returns or sets the application's screen updating. When ScreenUpdating is set to True (the default), the user sees the results of all your code actions: cut-and-paste operations, drawing objects added or deleted, formatting, and so on. Applications look more professional (and are noticeably faster) if the user just sees the end result of all these actions. To do this, turn off screen updating (by setting the `ScreenUpdating` property to False), perform the actions, and turn screen updating back on.

`Application.Top`—Returns or sets the distance, in points, of the top of the application window from the top of the screen.

`Application.UsableHeight`—The maximum height, in points, that a window can occupy within the application's window. In other words, this is the height of the application window less the vertical space taken up by the title bar, menu bar, toolbars, status bar, and so on.

`Application.UsableWidth`—The maximum width, in points, that a window can occupy within the application's window. This is the width of the application window less the horizontal space taken up by items such as the vertical scroll bar.

`Application.Version`—Returns the version number of the application.

`Application.Visible`—A Boolean value that either hides the application (False) or displays the application (True).

`Application.Width`—Returns or sets the width, in points, of the application window.

`Application.Windows`—The collection of all the application's open `Window` objects.

`Application.WindowState`—Returns or sets the state of the main application window. This property is controlled via three built-in constants that vary between applications:

Window State	Excel	Word	PowerPoint
Maximized	xlMaximized	wdWindowStateMaximize	ppWindowMaximized
Minimized	xlMinimized	wdWindowStateMinimize	ppWindowMinimized
Normal	xlNormal	wdWindowStateNormal	ppWindowNormal

Methods of the `Application` Object

The `Application` object features a few dozen methods that perform actions on the program's environment. Here's a summary of the most common methods:

`Application.CheckSpelling`—When used with the Word or Excel `Application` object, the `CheckSpelling` method checks the spelling of a single word using the following syntax (note that Word's method has a few extra arguments):

`Application.CheckSpelling(word,customDictionary,ignoreUppercase)`

word	The word you want to check.
customDictionary	The filename of a custom dictionary that the application can search if *word* wasn't found in the main dictionary.
ignoreUppercase	Set to True to tell the application to ignore words entirely in uppercase.

For example, the code shown in Listing 5.3 gets a word from the user, checks the spelling, and tells the user whether or not the word is spelled correctly. (You also can use this property with a `Document`, `Worksheet`, or `Range` object, as described in Chapter 7, "Programming Word," and 8, "Programming Excel." Also, see Chapter 12 to learn more about the `InputBox` function.)

LISTING 5.3 A Procedure that Checks the Spelling of an Entered Word

```
Sub SpellCheckTest()
    '
    ' Get the word from the user
    '
    word2Check = InputBox("Enter a word:")
    '
    ' Spell-check it
    '
    result = Application.CheckSpelling(word2Check)
    '
    ' Display the result to the user
    '
    If result = True Then
        MsgBox "'" & word2Check & "' is spelled correctly!"
    Else
        MsgBox "Oops! '" & word2Check & "' is spelled incorrectly."
    End If
End Sub
```

`Application.EnableCancelKey`—This property controls what the application does when the user presses Esc (or Ctrl+Break), which, under normal circumstances, interrupts the running procedure. If you don't want the user to interrupt a critical section of code, you can disable the Esc key (and Ctrl+Break) by disabling the `EnableCancelKey` property. (In Word, for example, you do this by setting the property to `wdCancelDisabled`.) To restore interrupts to their default state, enable the `EnableCancelKey` property.

> **caution**
>
> Wield the `EnableCancelKey` property with care. If you disable the Esc key and your code ends up in an infinite loop (see Chapter 6, "Controlling Your VBA Code"), there's no way to shut down the procedure short of shutting down the application itself. Therefore, while you're testing and building your application, you should always make sure the `EnableCancelKey` property is set to True.

`Application.Help`—Displays the application's Help system.

`Application.Quit`—Quits the application. If there are any open documents with unsaved changes, the application will ask if you want to save the changes. To prevent this, either save the documents before running the `Quit` method (I tell you how to do this in the appropriate chapters in Part 2), or set the `DisplayAlerts` property to False. (In the latter case, note that the application will *not* save changes to the documents. Also, Word's version of Quit accepts an argument that specifies whether or not to save changes.)

`Application.Repeat`—Repeats the user's last action. This is equivalent to selecting the Edit, Repeat command.

Example: The `Window` Object

Another object that's common to almost all applications is the `Window` object, which represents an open window in an application. Note that this isn't the same as an open document. Rather, the `Window` object is just a container for a document, so the associated properties and methods have no effect on the document data. You can use VBA to change the window state (maximized or minimized), size and move windows, navigate open windows, and much more. In the next section, I'll show you how to specify a `Window` object in your code; you'll also look at some `Window` object properties and methods.

Specifying a `Window` Object

If you need to perform some action on a window or change a window's properties, you need to tell the application which window you want to use. VBA gives you two ways to do this:

Use the `Windows` object—The `Windows` object is the collection of all the open windows in the application. To specify a window, either use its index number (as given by the numbers beside the windows on the application's Windows menu) or enclose the window caption (in other words, the text that appears in the window's title bar) in quotation marks. For example, if the `Budget.doc` window is listed first in the Window menu, the following two statements would be equivalent:

```
Windows(1)
Windows("Budget.doc")
```

Use the ActiveWindow object—The `ActiveWindow` object represents the window that currently has the focus.

Opening a New Window

If you need to create a new window, use the Window object's `NewWindow` method:

Window.NewWindow

> *Window*   The Window object from which you want to create the new window.

Note that this argument is optional in some applications. In Word, for example, if you omit *Window,* the active window is used.

Window Object Properties

Here's a rundown of some common properties associated with `Window` objects:

Window.Caption—Returns or sets the text that appears in the title bar of the specified *Window.*

Window.Height—Returns or sets the height, in points, of the specified *Window.*

Window.Left—Returns or sets the distance, in points, of the left edge of the specified *Window* from the left edge of the application window.

Window.Top—Returns or sets the distance, in points, of the top of the specified *Window* from the top of the application window.

Window.UsableHeight—The maximum height, in points, that data can occupy within the specified *Window.*

Window.UsableWidth—The maximum width, in points, that data can occupy within the specified *Window*.

Window.Visible—A Boolean value that either hides the specified *Window* (False) or displays the *Window* (True).

Window.Width—Returns or sets the width, in points, of the specified *Window*.

Window.WindowNumber—Returns the window number of the specified *Window*. For example, a window named Chaptr05.doc:2 has window number 2.

Window.WindowState—Returns or sets the state of the specified *Window*. See the Application.WindowState property, discussed earlier, for a list of the constants that control this property.

Window Object Methods

Window objects have a few methods that you can use to control your windows programmatically. Here are a few methods that you'll use most often:

Window.Activate—Activates the specified open *Window*. For example, the following statement activates the Finances.xls window:

Windows("Finances.xls").Activate

Window.Close—Closes the specified Window.

Window.LargeScroll—Scrolls through the specified Window by screens, using the following syntax:

Window.LargeScroll(Down, Up, ToRight, ToLeft)

Window	The Window object you want to scroll through.
Down	The number of screens to scroll down.
Up	The number of screens to scroll up.
ToRight	The number of screens to scroll to the right.
ToLeft	The number of screens to scroll to the left.

Window.SmallScroll—Scrolls through the specified *Window* by lines, using the following syntax:

Window.SmallScroll(Down, Up, ToRight, ToLeft)

The arguments are the same as those in the LargeScroll method.

THE ABSOLUTE MINIMUM

This chapter discussed the all-important topics of objects and how to work with them in your VBA procedures. After some introductory information on objects and the object hierarchy, you learned about the three types of members of any object class: properties, methods, and events. I also showed you how to assign objects to variables, how to wield the Is operator, and how to work with multiple properties or methods. I closed this chapter with a look at the properties and methods of the Application and Window objects.

One thing I didn't mention but that you may want to check out is the Object Browser. This is a handy tool that shows you the objects available for your procedures, as well as the properties, methods, and events for each object. To display the Object Browser in the Visual Basic Editor, select View, Object Browser (you can also press F2). In the Object Browser dialog box that appears, use the Classes list to select the object you want to see and its properties, methods, and events will appear in the Members list on the right.

Here's a list of chapters where you'll find related information:

- The With...End With statement is an example of a VBA control structure. I'll discuss a few more of these control structures in Chapter 6, "Controlling Your VBA Code."

- Part 2, "Putting VBA to Work," is a veritable "object fest" as I examine the object hierarchies in the main Office applications.

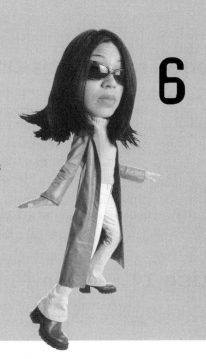

6

- Creating "smart" procedures that make decisions
- Handling everything from simple True/False decisions to complex multiple-decision logic
- Learning about the handy VBA functions that make decisions
- Eliminating repetitive coding by making good use of programming loops

CONTROLLING YOUR VBA CODE

One of the advantages of writing your own VBA procedures instead of simply recording them is that you end up with much more control over what your code does and how it performs its tasks. In particular, you can create procedures that make *decisions* based on certain conditions and that can perform *loops*—the running of several statements repeatedly. The statements that handle this kind of processing—*control structures*—are the subject of this chapter.

Code That Makes Decisions

A smart procedure performs tests on its environment and then decides what to do next based on the results of each test. For example, suppose you've written a Function procedure that uses one of its arguments as a divisor in a formula. You should test the argument before using it in the formula to make sure that it isn't 0 (to avoid producing a "division by zero" error). If it is, you could then display a message that alerts the user of the illegal argument.

Similarly, a well-designed application will interact with the user and ask for feedback in the form of extra information or a confirmation of a requested action. The program can then take this feedback and redirect itself accordingly.

Using If...Then to Make True/False Decisions

The most basic form of decision is the simple true/false decision (which could also be seen as a yes/no or an on/off decision). In this case, your program looks at a certain condition, determines whether it is currently true or false, and acts accordingly. As you might expect from the discussion of expressions in Chapter 4, "Building VBA Expressions," logical expressions (which, you'll recall, always return a True or False result) play a big part here.

In VBA, simple true/false decisions are handled by the If...Then statement. You can use either the *single-line* syntax:

```
If condition Then statement
```

or the *block* syntax:

```
If condition Then
    [statements]
End If
```

condition — You can use either a logical expression that returns True or False, or you can use any expression that returns a numeric value. In the latter case, a return value of zero is functionally equivalent to False, and any nonzero value is equivalent to True.

note

The code for this chapter is available on my Web site at the following address:

http://www.mcfedries.com/ABGVBA/Chapter06.xls

statement(s)   The VBA statement or statements to run if *condition* returns True. If *condition* returns False, VBA skips over the statements.

Whether you use the single-line or block syntax depends on the statements you want to run if the *condition* returns a True result. If you have only one statement, you can use either syntax. If you have multiple statements, you must use the block syntax.

Listing 6.1 shows a revised version of the GrossMargin procedure from Chapter 3, "Understanding Program Variables" (see Listing 3.1). This version—called GrossMargin2—uses If...Then to check the totalSales variable. The procedure calculates the gross margin only if totalSales isn't zero.

tip

You can make the If...Then statement in the GrossMargin2 procedure slightly more efficient by taking advantage of the fact that in the condition, zero is equivalent to False and any other number is equivalent to True. This means you don't have to explicitly test the totalSales variable to see whether it's zero. Instead, you can use the following statements:

```
If totalSales Then
        GrossMargin = (totalSales-totalExpenses)/totalSales
End If
```

On the other hand, many programmers feel that including the explicit test for a nonzero value (totalSales <> 0) makes the procedure easier to read and more intuitive. Since, in this case, the efficiency gained is only minor, you're probably better off leaving in the full expression.

LISTING 6.1   An If...Then Example

```
Function GrossMargin2()
    Dim totalSales
    Dim totalExpenses
    totalSales = Application.Sum(Range("Sales"))
    totalExpenses = Application.Sum(Range("Expenses"))
    If totalSales <> 0 Then
        GrossMargin2 = (totalSales - totalExpenses) / totalSales
    End If
End Function
```

Using If...Then...Else to Handle a False Result

Using the If...Then statement to make decisions adds a powerful new weapon to your VBA arsenal. However, this technique suffers from an important drawback: A False result only bypasses one or more statements; it doesn't execute any of its own. This is fine in many cases, but there will be times when you need to run one group of statements if the condition returns True and a different group if the result is False. To handle this, you need to use an If...Then...Else statement:

```
If condition Then
    [TrueStatements]
Else
    [FalseStatements]
End If
```

condition	The logical expression that returns True or False.
TrueStatements	The statements to run if condition returns True.
FalseStatements	The statements to run if condition returns False.

If the condition returns True, VBA runs the group of statements between If...Then and Else. If it returns False, VBA runs the group of statements between Else and End If.

Let's look at an example. Suppose you want to calculate the future value of a series of regular deposits, but you want to differentiate between monthly deposits and quarterly deposits. Listing 6.2 shows a Function procedure called FutureValue that does the job.

LISTING 6.2 A Procedure that Uses If...Then...Else

```
Function FutureValue(Rate, Nper, Pmt, Frequency)
    If Frequency = "Monthly" Then
        FutureValue = FV(Rate / 12, Nper * 12, Pmt / 12)
    Else
        FutureValue = FV(Rate / 4, Nper * 4, Pmt / 4)
    End If
End Function
```

The first three arguments—Rate, Nper, and Pmt—are, respectively, the annual interest rate, the number of years in the term of the investment, and the total deposit available annually. The fourth argument—Frequency—is either "Monthly" or "Quarterly". The idea is to adjust the first three arguments based on the Frequency. To do that, the If...Then...Else statement runs a test on the Frequency argument:

```
If Frequency = "Monthly" Then
```

If the logical expression `Frequency = "Monthly"` returns True, the procedure runs the following statement:

```
FutureValue = FV(Rate / 12, Nper * 12, Pmt / 12)
```

This statement divides the interest rate by 12, multiplies the term by 12, and divides the annual deposit by 12. Otherwise, if the logical expression returns False, a quarterly calculation is assumed and the procedure executes the following statement:

```
FutureValue = FV(Rate / 4, Nper * 4, Pmt / 4)
```

This statement divides the interest rate by 4, multiplies the term by 4, and divides the annual deposit by 4. In both cases, VBA's `FV` function (see Chapter 4) is used to return the future value.

> **tip**
>
> `If...Then...Else` statements are much easier to read when you indent the expressions between `If...Then`, `Else`, and `End If`, as I've done in Listing 6.2. This lets you easily identify which group of statements will be run if there is a True result and which group will be run if the result is False. Pressing the Tab key once at the beginning of the first line in the block does the job.

Making Multiple Decisions

The problem with `If...Then...Else` is that normally you can make only a single decision. The statement calculates a single logical result and performs one of two actions. However, plenty of situations require multiple decisions before you can decide which action to take.

For example, the `FutureValue` procedure discussed in the preceding section probably should test the `Frequency` argument to make sure it's either `Monthly` or `Quarterly` and not something else. The next few sections show you three solutions to this problem.

Using the `And` and `Or` Operators

One solution to our multiple-decision problem is to combine multiple logical expressions in a single `If...Then` statement. From Chapter 4, you'll recall that you can combine logical expressions by using VBA's `And` and `Or` operators. In our example, we want to calculate the future value only if the `Frequency` argument is either `Monthly` *or* `Quarterly`. The following `If...Then` statement uses the `And` operator to test this:

```
If Frequency = "Monthly" Or Frequency = "Quarterly" Then
```

As shown in Listing 6.3, if `Frequency` equals either of these values, the entire condition returns True, and the procedure runs the calculation in the usual way. Otherwise, if `Frequency` doesn't equal either value, then the procedure returns a message to the user.

LISTING 6.3 A Procedure that Uses the Or Operator to Perform Multiple Logical Tests

```
Function FutureValue2(Rate, Nper, Pmt, Frequency)
    If Frequency = "Monthly" Or Frequency = "Quarterly" Then
        If Frequency = "Monthly" Then
            FutureValue2 = FV(Rate / 12, Nper * 12, Pmt / 12)
        Else
            FutureValue2 = FV(Rate / 4, Nper * 4, Pmt / 4)
        End If
    Else
        MsgBox "The Frequency argument must be either " & _
               """"Monthly"" or ""Quarterly""!"
    End If
End Function
```

Note that this procedure isn't particularly efficient because you end up testing the Frequency argument in two places. However, that just means that this example isn't the best use of the And and Or operators. The overall principle of using these operators to perform multiple logical tests is a useful one, however, and you should keep it in mind when constructing your decision-making code.

Using Multiple If...Then...Else Statements

There is a third syntax for the If...Then...Else statement that lets you string together as many logical tests as you need:

```
If condition1 Then
    [condition1 TrueStatements]
ElseIf condition2 Then
    [condition2 TrueStatements]
<etc.>
Else
    [FalseStatements]
End If
```

tip

In Listing 6.3, if Frequency equals either Monthly or Quarterly, the result of the first If...Then...Else is true, and the procedure then executes a *second* If...Then...Else structure. This is called *nesting* one control structure within another. This is very common in VBA procedures, but it can also get very confusing very quickly. To help you keep things straight, not only indent the statements within the first If...Then...Else, but *double-indent* the statements within the second If...Then...Else (refer to Listing 6.3 for an example).

condition1	A logical expression.
condition1 TrueStatements	The statements to run if *condition1* returns True.
condition2	A different logical expression.
Condition2 TrueStatements	The statements to run if *condition2* returns True.
FalseStatements	The statements to run if both *condition1* and *condition2* return False.

VBA first tests *condition1*. If this returns True, VBA runs the group of statements between If...Then and ElseIf...Then. If it returns False, VBA then tests *condition2*. If this test is True, VBA runs the group of statements between ElseIf...Then and Else. Otherwise, VBA runs the statements between Else and End If. Here are two things you should note about this structure:

- You can have as many ElseIf conditions as you need.
- You don't have to use the Else part if you don't need it.

Listing 6.4 shows FutureValue3, a revised version of FutureValue that makes allowances for an improper Frequency argument.

LISTING 6.4   A Procedure that Uses Multiple If...Then...Else Statements

```
Function FutureValue3(Rate, Nper, Pmt, Frequency)
    If Frequency = "Monthly" Then
        FutureValue3 = FV(Rate / 12, Nper * 12, Pmt / 12)
    ElseIf Frequency = "Quarterly" Then
        FutureValue3 = FV(Rate / 4, Nper * 4, Pmt / 4)
    Else
        MsgBox "The Frequency argument must be either " & _
            """Monthly"" or ""Quarterly""!"
    End If
End Function
```

As before, the If...Then statement checks to see if Frequency equals Monthly and, if it does, calculates the future value accordingly. If it's doesn't, the ElseIf...Then statement checks to see if Frequency equals Quarterly and calculates the future value if the expression returns True. If it returns False, the user entered the Frequency argument incorrectly, so a warning message is displayed.

Using the Select Case Statement

Performing multiple tests with If...ElseIf is a handy technique—it's a VBA tool you'll reach for quite often. However, it quickly becomes unwieldy as the number of tests you need to make gets larger. It's okay for two or three tests, but any more than that makes the logic harder to follow.

For these situations, VBA's Select Case statement is a better choice. The idea is that you provide a logical expression at the beginning and then list a series of possible results. For each possible result—called a *case*—you provide one or more VBA statements to execute should the case prove to be true. Here's the syntax:

```
Select Case TestExpression
    Case FirstCaseList
        [FirstStatements]
    Case SecondCaseList
        [SecondStatements]
    <etc.>
    Case Else
        [ElseStatements]
End Select
```

> **note**
>
> If more than one *CaseList* contains an element that matches the *TestExpression*, VBA runs only the statements associated with the *CaseList* that appears *first* in the Select Case structure.

TestExpression	This expression is evaluated at the beginning of the structure. It must return a value (logical, numeric, string, and so on).
CaseList	A list of one or more possible results for *TestExpression*. These results are values or expressions separated by commas. VBA examines each element in the list to see whether one matches the *TestExpression*. The expressions can take any one of the following forms:

Expression

Expression To *Expression*

Is *LogicalOperator Expression*

The To keyword defines a range of values (for example, 1 To 10). The Is keyword defines an open-ended range of values (for example, Is >= 100).

Statements	These are the statements VBA runs if any part of the associated *CaseList* matches the *TestExpression*. VBA runs the optional *ElseStatements* if no *CaseList* contains a match for the *TestExpression*.

Listing 6.5 shows how you would use Select Case to handle the Frequency argument problem.

LISTING 6.5 A Procedure that Uses Select Case to Test Multiple Values

```
Function FutureValue4(Rate, Nper, Pmt, Frequency)
    Select Case Frequency
        Case "Monthly"
            FutureValue4 = FV(Rate / 12, Nper * 12, Pmt / 12)
        Case "Quarterly"
            FutureValue4 = FV(Rate / 4, Nper * 4, Pmt / 4)
        Case Else
            MsgBox "The Frequency argument must be either " & _
                    """Monthly"" or ""Quarterly""!"
    End Select
End Function
```

A Select Case Example: Converting Test Scores to Letter Grades

To help you get a better feel for the Select Case statement, let's take a look at another example that better showcases the unique talents of this powerful structure. Suppose you want to write a procedure that converts a raw test score into a letter grade according to the following table:

Raw Score	Letter Grade
80 and over	A
Between 70 and 79	B
Between 60 and 69	C
Between 50 and 59	D
Less than 50	F

Listing 6.6 shows the LetterGrade procedure, which uses a Select Case statement to make the conversion.

LISTING 6.6   A Procedure that Uses `Select Case` to Convert a Raw Test Score into a Letter Grade

```
Function LetterGrade(rawScore As Integer) As String
    Select Case rawScore
        Case Is < 0
            LetterGrade = "ERROR! Score less than 0!"
        Case Is < 50
            LetterGrade = "F"
        Case Is < 60
            LetterGrade = "D"
        Case Is < 70
            LetterGrade = "C"
        Case Is < 80
            LetterGrade = "B"
        Case Is <= 100
            LetterGrade = "A"
        Case Else
            LetterGrade = "ERROR! Score greater than 100!"
    End Select
End Function
```

The `rawScore` argument is an integer value between 0 and 100. The `Select Case` structure first checks to see if `rawScore` is negative and, if so, the function returns an error message. The next `Case` statement checks to see if the score is less than 50, and the function returns the letter grade "F" if it is. The next `Case` statement looks for a score that is less than 60. If we get this far, we already know (thanks to the preceding `Case` statement) that the score is at least 50. Therefore, this case is really checking to see if the score is between 50 and 60 (including 50, but not including 60). If so, the letter grade "D" is returned. The rest of the `Case` statements proceed in the same manner. The `Case Else` checks for a score greater than 100 and returns another error message if it is.

Another Example: Taming the RGB Function

In Chapter 5, "Working with Objects," I mentioned briefly that you can use the RGB (*red,green,blue*) VBA function any time you need to specify a color for a property. Each of the three named arguments (*red*, *green*, and *blue*) are integers between 0 and 255 that determine how much of each component color is mixed into the final color. In the *red* component, for example, 0 means no red is present, and 255 means that pure red is present. If all three values are the same, you get a shade of gray.

Here are some sample values for each component that produce common colors:

Red	Green	Blue	Result
0	0	0	Black
0	0	255	Blue
0	255	0	Green
0	255	255	Cyan
255	0	0	Red
255	0	255	Magenta
255	255	0	Yellow
255	255	255	White

However, rather than memorize these combinations, let's put VBA and select Case to work to make choosing colors easier. Listing 6.7 shows the VBAColor function, which lets you set 16 of the most common colors using names (for example, "red" or "blue") rather than cryptic number combinations.

LISTING 6.7   A Function That Accepts a Color Name as a String and Return the Corresponding RGB Value

```
Function VBAColor(colorName As String) As Long

    Select Case LCase(Trim(colorName))
        Case "black"
            VBAColor = RGB(0, 0, 0)
        Case "white"
            VBAColor = RGB(255, 255, 255)
        Case "gray"
            VBAColor = RGB(192, 192, 192)
        Case "dark gray"
            VBAColor = RGB(128, 128, 128)
        Case "red"
            VBAColor = RGB(255, 0, 0)
        Case "dark red"
            VBAColor = RGB(128, 0, 0)
        Case "green"
            VBAColor = RGB(0, 255, 0)
        Case "dark green"
            VBAColor = RGB(0, 128, 0)
        Case "blue"
            VBAColor = RGB(0, 0, 255)
```

LISTING 6.7 (continued)

```
        Case "dark blue"
            VBAColor = RGB(0, 0, 128)
        Case "yellow"
            VBAColor = RGB(255, 255, 0)
        Case "dark yellow"
            VBAColor = RGB(128, 128, 0)
        Case "magenta"
            VBAColor = RGB(255, 0, 255)
        Case "dark magenta"
            VBAColor = RGB(128, 0, 128)
        Case "cyan"
            VBAColor = RGB(0, 255, 255)
        Case "dark cyan"
            VBAColor = RGB(0, 128, 128)
    End Select
End Function


Sub ColorTester()
    ActiveCell.Font.Color = VBAColor("red")
End Sub
```

VBAColor takes a single argument, colorName, which is the name of the color you want to work with. Notice how the Select Case statement massages the argument to prevent errors:

```
Select Case LCase(Trim(colorName))
```

The Trim function removes any extraneous spaces at the beginning and end of the argument, and the LCase function converts colorName to lowercase. This ensures that the function is not case sensitive, which means it doesn't matter whether you send *black*, *BLACK*, or *Black*: the function will still work.

The rest of the function uses Case statements to check for the various color names and return the appropriate RGB values. You can use the ColorTester procedure to give VBAColor a whirl. This procedure just formats the font color of the currently selected worksheet cell.

VBA also defines eight color constants that you can use when you just need the basic colors: vbBlack, vbBlue, vbCyan, vbGreen, vbMagenta, vbRed, vbWhite, and vbYellow.

Functions That Make Decisions

Much of what we're talking about in this chapter involves ways to make your procedures cleaner and more efficient. These are laudable goals for a whole host of reasons, but the following are the main ones:

- Your code will execute faster.
- You'll have less code to type.
- Your code will be easier to read and maintain.

This section looks at three powerful VBA functions that can increase the efficiency of your procedures.

The `IIf` Function

You've seen how the decision-making prowess of the `If...Then...Else` structure lets you create "intelligent" procedures that can respond appropriately to different situations. However, sometimes `If...Then...Else` just isn't efficient. For example, suppose you're writing a document that can't be longer than 1,000 words and you want to devise a test that will alert you when the document's word count exceeds that number. Here's a code fragment that includes an `If...Then...Else` structure that performs this test:

```
Dim DocTooLong As Boolean
If ActiveDocument.Range.Words.Count > 1000 Then
    DocTooLong = True
Else
    DocTooLong = False
End If
```

In Word, the `ActiveDocument.Range.Words.Count` property tells you the total number of words in the active document. As it stands, there's nothing wrong with this code. However, it seems like a lot of work to go through just to assign a value to a variable. For these types of situations, VBA has an `IIf` function that's more efficient. `IIf`, which stands for "inline If," performs a simple If test on a single line:

```
IIf (condition, TrueResult, FalseResult)
```

condition	A logical expression that returns True or False.
TrueResult	The value returned by the function if *condition* is True.
FalseResult	The value returned by the function if *condition* is False.

Listing 6.8 shows a function procedure that checks the word count by using `IIf` to replace the `If...Then...Else` statement shown earlier.

LISTING 6.8   A Function that Uses IIf to Test a Document's Word Count

```
Function DocTooLong() As Boolean
    DocTooLong = IIf(ActiveDocument.Range.Words.Count > 1000, True, False)
End Function
```

If the number of words exceeds 1000, IIf returns True; otherwise, the function returns False.

The Choose Function

In the previous section, I showed you how the IIf function is an efficient replacement for If...Then...Else when all you need to do is assign a value to a variable based on the results of the test. Suppose now that you have a similar situation with the Select Case structure. In other words, you want to test a number of possible values and assign the result to a variable.

For example, you saw in Chapter 4 that VBA's Weekday function returns the current day of the week as a number. Here's a procedure fragment that takes the day number and uses a Select Case structure to assign the name of the deity associated with that day to the dayDeity variable:

```
Dim dayDeity As String
Select Case Weekday(Now)
    Case 1
        dayDeity = "Sun"
    Case 2
        dayDeity = "Moon"
    Case 3
        dayDeity = "Tiw"
    Case 4
        dayDeity = "Woden"
    Case 5
        dayDeity = "Thor"
    Case 6
        dayDeity = "Freya"
    Case 7
        dayDeity = "Saturn"
End Select
```

Again, this seems like *way* too much effort for a simple variable assignment. And, in fact, it *is* too much work, thanks to VBA's Choose function. Choose encapsulates the essence of the preceding Select Case structure—the test value and the various possible results—into a single statement. Here's the syntax:

Choose(*index, value1, value2,...*)

index	A numeric expression that determines which of the values in the list is returned. If *index* is 1, *value1* is returned. If *index* is 2, *value2* is returned, and so on.
value1, value2...	A list of values from which Choose selects the return value. The values can be any valid VBA expression.

Listing 6.9 shows a function called DayDeity that returns the name of a day's deity by using Choose to replace the Select Case structure shown earlier.

LISTING 6.9   A Function that Uses the Choose Function to Select from a List of Values

```
Function DayDeity(weekdayNum As Integer) As String
    DayDeity = Choose(weekdayNum, "Sun", "Moon", _
        "Tiw", "Woden", "Thor", "Freya", "Saturn")
End Function
```

The Switch Function

Choose is a welcome addition to the VBA function library, but its use is limited because of two constraints:

- You can use Choose only when the *index* argument is a number or a numeric expression.
- Choose can't handle logical expressions.

To illustrate why the last point is important, consider the Select Case structure used earlier in this chapter to convert a test score into a letter grade:

```
Select Case rawScore
    Case Is < 0
        LetterGrade = "ERROR! Score less than 0!"
    Case Is < 50
        LetterGrade = "F"
    Case Is < 60
        LetterGrade = "D"
    Case Is < 70
        LetterGrade = "C"
    Case Is < 80
```

```
        LetterGrade = "B"
    Case Is <= 100
        LetterGrade = "A"
    Case Else
        LetterGrade = "ERROR! Score greater than 100!"
End Select
```

At first blush, this structure seems to satisfy the same inefficiency criteria that I mentioned earlier for If...Then...Else and Select Case. In other words, each Case runs only a single statement and that statement serves only to assign a value to a variable. The difference, though, is that the Case statements use logical expressions, so we can't use Choose to make this code more efficient.

However, we *can* use VBA's Switch function to do the job:

Switch(*expr1, value1, expr2, value2,...*)

expr1, expr2...	These are logical expressions that determine which of the values in the list is returned. If *expr1* is True, *value1* is returned. If *expr2* is True, *value2* is returned, and so on.
value1, value2...	A list of values from which Switch selects the return value. The values can be any valid VBA expression.

Switch trudges through the logical expressions from left to right. When it comes across the first True expression, it returns the value that appears immediately after the expression. Listing 6.10 puts Switch to work to create a more efficient version of the LetterGrade function.

LISTING 6.10   A Procedure that Uses the Switch Function to Convert a Test Score into a Letter Grade

```
Function LetterGrade2(rawScore As Integer) As String
    LetterGrade2 = Switch( _
        rawScore < 0, "ERROR! Score less than 0!", _
        rawScore < 50, "F", _
        rawScore < 60, "D", _
        rawScore < 70, "C", _
        rawScore < 80, "B", _
        rawScore <= 100, "A", _
        rawScore > 100, "ERROR! Score greater than 100!")
End Function
```

Code That Loops

You've seen in this chapter and in previous chapters that it makes sense to divide up your VBA chores and place them in separate procedures or functions. That way, you only need to write the code once and then call it any time you need it. This is known in the trade as *modular programming*, and it saves time and effort by helping you avoid reinventing too many wheels.

This code fragment uses the Excel Application object's `Wait` method to produce a delay. The argument `Now + TimeValue("00:00:05")` pauses the procedure for about five seconds before continuing.

There are also wheels to avoid reinventing *within* your procedures and functions. For example, consider the following code fragment:

```
MsgBox "The time is now " & Time
Application.Wait Now + TimeValue("00:00:05")
MsgBox "The time is now " & Time
Application.Wait Now + TimeValue("00:00:05")
MsgBox "The time is now " & Time
Application.Wait Now + TimeValue("00:00:05")
```

This code does nothing more than display the time, delay for five seconds, and repeat this two more times. Besides being decidedly useless, this code just reeks of inefficiency. It's clear that a far better approach would be to take just the first two statements and somehow get VBA to repeat them as many times as necessary.

The good news is that not only is it possible to do this, but VBA also gives you a number of different methods to perform this so-called *looping*. I spend the rest of this chapter investigating each of these methods.

Using Do...Loop Structures

What do you do when you need to loop but you don't know in advance how many times to repeat the loop? This could happen if, for example, you want to loop only until a certain condition is met, such as encountering a blank cell in an Excel worksheet. The solution is to use a Do...Loop.

The Do...Loop has four different syntaxes:

`Do While condition` `[statements] Loop`	Checks *condition* before entering the loop. Executes the *statements* only while *condition* is True.
`Do [statements]` `Loop While condition`	Checks *condition* after running through the loop once. Executes the *statements* only while *condition* is True. Use this form when you want the loop to be processed at least once.

`Do Until` *condition* [*statements*] `Loop`	Checks *condition* before entering the loop. Executes the *statements* only while *condition* is False.
`Do` [*statements*] `Loop Until` *condition*	Checks *condition* after running through the loop once. Executes the *statements* only while *condition* is False. Again, use this form when you want the loop to be processed at least once.

Listing 6.11 shows a procedure called `BigNumbers` that runs down a worksheet column and changes the font color to magenta whenever a cell contains a number greater than or equal to 1,000.

LISTING 6.11   A Procedure That Uses a `Do...Loop` to Process Cells Until It Encounters a Blank Cell

```
Sub BigNumbers()
    Dim rowNum As Integer, colNum As Integer, currCell As Range
    '
    ' Initialize the row and column numbers
    '
    rowNum = ActiveCell.Row
    colNum = ActiveCell.Column
    '
    ' Get the first cell
    '
    Set currCell = ActiveSheet.Cells(rowNum, colNum)
    '
    ' Loop while the current cell isn't empty
    '
    Do While currCell.Value <> ""
        '
        ' Is it a number?
        '
        If IsNumeric(currCell.Value) Then
            '
            ' Is it a big number?
            '
            If currCell.Value >= 1000 Then
                '
                ' If so, color it magenta
                '
                currCell.Font.Color = VBAColor("magenta")
            End If
```

LISTING 6.11   (condition)

```
        End If
        '
        ' Increment the row number and get the next cell
        '
        rowNum = rowNum + 1
        Set currCell = ActiveSheet.Cells(rowNum, colNum)
    Loop
End Sub
```

The idea is to loop until the procedure encounters a blank cell. This is controlled by the following Do While statement:

```
Do While currCell.Value <> ""
```

currCell is an object variable that is set using the Cells method (which I describe in Chapter 8, "Programming Excel"). Next, the first If...Then uses the IsNumeric function to check whether the cell contains a number, and the second If...Then checks whether the number is greater than or equal to 1,000. If both conditions are True, the font color is set to magenta using the VBAColor function described earlier in this chapter.

Using For...Next Loops

The most common type of loop is the For...Next loop. Use this loop when you know exactly how many times you want to repeat a group of statements. The structure of a For...Next loop looks like this:

```
For counter = start To end [Step increment]
    [statements]
Next [counter]
```

counter	A numeric variable used as a *loop counter*. The loop counter is a number that counts how many times the procedure has gone through the loop.
start	The initial value of *counter*. This is usually 1, but you can enter any value.
end	The final value of *counter*.
increment	This optional value defines an increment for the loop counter. If you leave this out, the default value is 1. Use a negative value to decrement *counter*.
statements	The statements to execute each time through the loop.

The basic idea is simple. When VBA encounters the `For...Next` statement, it follows this five-step process:

1. Set `counter` equal to `start`.

2. Test `counter`. If it's greater than `end`, exit the loop (that is, process the first statement after the `Next` statement). Otherwise, continue. If `increment` is negative, VBA checks to see whether `counter` is less than `end`.

3. Execute each statement between the `For` and `Next` statements.

4. Add `increment` to `counter`. Add 1 to `counter` if `increment` isn't specified.

5. Repeat steps 2 through 4 until done.

Listing 6.12 shows a simple `Sub` procedure—`LoopTest`—that uses a `For...Next` statement. Each time through the loop, the procedure uses the `Application` object's `StatusBar` property to display the value of counter (the loop counter) in the status bar. (See Chapter 12, "Interacting with the User," to learn more about the `StatusBar` property.) When you run this procedure, `counter` gets incremented by 1 each time through the loop, and the new value gets displayed in the status bar.

LISTING 6.12   A Simple `For...Next` Loop

```
Sub LoopTest()
    Dim counter
    For counter = 1 To 10
        '
        'Display the message
        '
        Application.StatusBar = "Counter value: " & counter
        '
        ' Wait for 1 second
        '
        Application.Wait Now + TimeValue("00:00:01")
    Next counter
    Application.StatusBar = False
End Sub
```

Here are some notes on `For...Next` loops:

■ If you use a positive number for `increment` (or if you omit `increment`), `end` must be greater than or equal to `start`. If you use a negative number for `increment`, `end` must be less than or equal to `start`.

■ If `start` equals `end`, the loop will execute once.

■ As with `If...Then...Else` structures, indent the statements inside a `For...Next` loop for increased readability.

■ To keep the number of variables defined in a procedure to a minimum, always try to use the same name for all your `For...Next` loop counters. The letters *i* through *n* traditionally are used for counters in programming. For greater clarity, you might want to use names such as "counter."

■ For the fastest loops, don't use the counter name after the `Next` statement. If you'd like to keep the counter name for clarity (which I recommend), precede the name with an apostrophe (') to comment out the name, like this:

```
For counter = 1 To 10
    [statements]
Next 'counter
```

■ If you need to break out of a `For...Next` loop before the defined number of repetitions is completed, use the `Exit For` statement, described in the section "Using `Exit For` or `Exit Do` to Exit a Loop."

note

The `LoopTest` procedure works fine in Excel, but it will fail in the other Office applications because they don't implement the `Wait` method. If you need to get your code to delay for a short while, here's a simple procedure that does the trick:

```
Sub VBAWait(delay As Integer)
    Dim startTime As Long
    startTime = Timer
    Do While Timer - startTime < delay
        DoEvents
    Loop
End Sub
```

Note the use of the `DoEvents` function inside the `Do While...Loop` structure. This function yields execution to the operating system so that events such as keystrokes and application messages are processed while the procedure delays.

Using For Each...Next Loops

A useful variation of the `For...Next` loop is the `For Each...Next` loop, which operates on a collection of objects. You don't need a loop counter because VBA just loops through the individual elements in the collection and performs on each element whatever operations are inside the loop. Here's the structure of the basic For Each...Next loop:

```
For Each element In collection
    [statements]
Next [element]
```

     element   A variable used to hold the name of each element in the collection.

     collection   The name of the collection.

     statements   The statements to be executed for each element in the collection.

As an example, let's create a command procedure that converts a range of text into proper case (that is, the first letter of each word is capitalized). This function can come in handy if you import mainframe text into your worksheets because mainframe reports usually appear entirely in uppercase. This process involves three steps:

1. Loop through the selected range with For Each...Next.

2. Convert each cell's text to proper case. Use Excel's Proper() worksheet function to handle this:

   ```
   WorksheetFunction(Proper(text))
   ```

        text   The text to convert to proper case.

3. Enter the converted text into the selected cell. This is the job of the Range object's Formula method:

   ```
   object.Formula = expression
   ```

        object   The Range object in which you want to enter *expression*.

        expression   The data you want to enter into *object*.

Listing 6.13 shows the resulting procedure, ConvertToProper. Note that this procedure uses the Selection object to represent the currently selected range.

LISTING 6.13 A Sub Procedure that Uses For Each...Next to Loop through a Selection and Convert Each Cell to Proper Text

```
Sub ConvertToProper()
    Dim cellObject As Range
    For Each cellObject In Selection
        cellObject.Formula = WorksheetFunction.Proper(cellObject.Formula)
    Next
End Sub
```

How would you use this procedure in practice? You'd highlight the cells you want to convert and then use the Tools, Macro, Macros command to find and run the ConvertToProper procedure.

Using Exit For or Exit Do to Exit a Loop

Most loops run their natural course and then the procedure moves on. There might be times, however, when you want to exit a loop prematurely. For example, you might come across a certain type of cell, an error might occur, or the user might enter an unexpected value. To exit a For...Next loop or a For Each...Next loop, use the Exit For statement. To exit a Do...Loop, use the Exit Do statement.

Listing 6.14 shows a revised version of the BigNumbers procedure, which exits the Do...Loop if it comes across a cell that isn't a number.

LISTING 6.14 Version of the BigNumbers Procedure That Terminates with the Exit Do Statement if the Current Cell Isn't a Number

```
Sub BigNumbers2()
    Dim rowNum As Integer, colNum As Integer, currCell As Range
    '
    ' Initialize the row and column numbers
    '
    rowNum = ActiveCell.Row
    colNum = ActiveCell.Column
    '
    ' Get the first cell
    '
    Set currCell = ActiveSheet.Cells(rowNum, colNum)
    '
    ' Loop while the current cell isn't empty
    '
    Do While currCell.Value <> ""
        '
        ' Is it a number?
        '
        If IsNumeric(currCell.Value) Then
            '
            ' Is it a big number?
            '
            If currCell.Value >= 1000 Then
                '
```

LISTING 6.14 (continued)

```
                ' If so, color it magenta
                '
                currCell.Font.Color = VBAColor("magenta")
            End If
        '
        ' Otherwise, exit the loop
        '
        Else
            Exit Do
        End If
        '
        ' Increment the row number and get the next cell
        '
        rowNum = rowNum + 1
        Set currCell = ActiveSheet.Cells(rowNum, colNum)
    Loop
End Sub
```

THE ABSOLUTE MINIMUM

This chapter showed you a number of methods for gaining maximum control over your VBA code. We began with a look at various VBA structures that allow your procedures to make decisions and act accordingly. In particular, I showed you how to work with If...Then...Else for true/false decisions; for multiple decisions I told you about the And and Or operators, the If...ElseIf...Else structure, and Select Case. I also included material on three decision-making functions: IIf, Choose, and Switch. You then learned about looping, including the structures Do...Loop, For...Next, and For Each...Next.

For beginning programmers, one of the most common causes of confusion when using these control structures is keeping track of which statements belong to which If...Then test or Do...While loop. This is particularly true if you end up with control structures nested within other control structure (see, for example, Listings 6.3, 6.11, and 6.14). I've stressed indenting your code throughout this book, and I want to underline this programming principle once again here:

■ In the main test or loop, indent the statements once (press Tab at the beginning of the first statement).

■ In a secondary (that is, nested) test or loop, double indent the statements (press Tab again at the beginning of the first statement).

■ In a tertiary (that is, nested within a nested structure) test or loop, triple indent the statements (press Tab again at the beginning of the first statement).

Here's a general example of how this indenting looks:

```
If MainExpression Then
    If SecondaryExpression Then
        If TertiaryExpression Then
            [TertiaryTrueStatements]
        Else
            [TeriaryFalseStatements]
        End If
    Else
        [SecondayFalseStatements]
    EndIf
Else
    [MainFalseStatements]
End If
```

Here's a list of chapters where you'll find related information:

■ This chapter used a few Word and Excel objects as examples. To get the full scoop on other objects available for these programs, see Chapter 7, "Programming Word" and Chapter 8, "Programming Excel."

■ Controlling code often depends on interaction with the user. For example, you might use If...Then...Else to test the value of a check box or Select Case to process a group of option buttons. See Chapter 12, "Interacting with the User," and Chapter 13, "Creating Custom VBA Dialog Boxes," to find out more about these topics.

■ A big part of procedure control involves anticipating potential user errors. You'll learn more about this topic in Chapter 15, "Debugging VBA Procedures."

PART

Putting VBA to Work

IN THIS CHAPTER

- Specifying, opening, creating, saving, and closing documents
- Using the Range object to work with text
- Using VBA to manipulate characters, words, sentences, and paragraphs

7

PROGRAMMING WORD

Microsoft Word is a large, complex program, so it will come as no surprise that its list of objects is equally as big and complicated. Fortunately, just as most people use only a tiny subset of Word's features, so too will you probably only use just a few of Word's objects in your VBA programming. In fact, with Word there are only really three levels of objects you'll need to worry about most of the time: Word itself, which is represented by the Application object; Word documents, which are represented by the Document object; and the text within those documents, which is represented by various objects, including Character, Sentence, and Paragraph. In this chapter, you'll focus on programming these basic objects.

Working with Documents

In Word, the Document object appears directly below the Application object in the object hierarchy. As you'll see in the sections that follow, you can use VBA to create new documents, open or delete existing documents, save and close open documents, and much more.

Specifying a Document Object

If you need to do something with a document, or if you need to work with an object contained in a specific document (such as a section of text), you need to tell Word which document to use. VBA gives you three ways to do this:

Use the Documents object—The Documents object is the collection of all open document files. To specify a particular document, either use its index number (where 1 represents the first document opened) or enclose the document name in quotation marks. For example, if Memo.doc was the first document opened, the following two statements would be equivalent:

```
Documents("Memo.doc")
Documents(1)
```

Use the ActiveDocument object—The ActiveDocument object represents the document that currently has the focus.

Use the ThisDocument object—The ThisDocument object represents the document where the VBA code is executing. If your code deals only with objects residing in the same document as the code itself, you can use the ActiveDocument object. However, if your code deals with other documents, use ThisDocument whenever you need to make sure that the code affects only the document containing the procedure.

Opening a Document

To open a document file, use the Open method of the Documents collection. The Open method has a dozen arguments you can use to fine-tune your document openings, but only one of these is mandatory. Here's the simplified syntax showing the one required argument (for the rest of the arguments, look up the Open method in the VBA Help system):

```
Documents.Open(FileName)
```

FileName   The name of the document file, including the drive and folder that contain the file.

For example, to open a document named
`Letter.doc` in the C:\My Documents folder, you
would use the following statement:

`Documents.Open "C:\My Documents\Letter.doc"`

The `RecentFiles` **Object**

Another way to open Word documents is to use
the `RecentFiles` object, which is the collection of
the most recently-used files displayed near the
bottom of Word's File menu. Each item on this
list is a `RecentFile` object.

You specify a `RecentFile` object by using
`RecentFiles(Index)`, where *Index* is an integer that
specifies the file you want to work with. The
most-recently used file is 1, the second most
recently-used file is 2, and so on.

tip

The maximum value of
Index is given by the
`RecentFiles.Maximum` property. Note, too, that you can
set this property. For example, the following state-
ment sets the maximum
value to 9 (the highest Word
allows for this value):

`RecentFiles.Maximum = 9`

Here are some `RecentFile` object properties to consider:

`RecentFile.Name`—Returns the filename of the specified *RecentFile*.

`RecentFile.Path`—Returns the pathname of the specified *RecentFile*.

Here's some code that tells Word to open the most-recently used file:

```
With RecentFiles(1)
    Documents.Open .Path & "\" & .Name
End With
```

It would be handy to have Word open the most recently used file each time you start
the program. If you want Word to run some code each time it's started, follow these
steps:

1. Open the Normal project in the VBA Editor's Project Explorer.

2. Create a new module and rename it **AutoExec**.

3. In this module, create a Sub procedure named Main.

4. Enter your code in that procedure.

Listing 7.1 shows a sample Main procedure that opens the most-recently used file at
startup.

LISTING 7.1 A Procedure to Open the Most-Recently Used Document at Startup

```
Sub Main()
    With RecentFiles(1)
        Documents.Open .Path & "\" & .Name
    End With
End Sub
```

Creating a New Document

If you need to create a new document, use the Documents collection's Add method:

```
Documents.Add(Template, NewTemplate,
DocumentType, Visible)
```

<table>
<tr><td>Template</td><td>This optional argument specifies the template file to use as the basis for the new document. Enter a string that spells out the path and name of the .DOT file. If you omit this argument, Word creates the new document based on the Normal template.</td></tr>
<tr><td>NewTemplate</td><td>If you set this optional argument to True, Word creates a new template file.</td></tr>
<tr><td>DocumentType</td><td>This optional argument determines the type of document that's created. Use one of the following constants:</td></tr>
</table>

wdNewBlankDocument	Creates a new, blank Word document (this is the default).
wdNewEmailMessage	Creates a new email message.
wdNewFrameset	Creates a new Web frameset page.
wdNewWebPage	Creates a new Web page.
wdNewXMLDocument	Creates a new XML document.

| Visible | This is an optional Boolean value that determines whether Word displays the new document in a visible window. True is the default; use False to create the document without displaying it in a visible window. |

note

The code used in this chapter's listings can be found on my Web site at the following address:

http://www.mcfedries.com/ABGVBA/Chapter07.doc

Since all of the Add method's arguments are optional, you can create a basic Word document based on the Normal template with the following simple statement:

```
Documents.Add
```

Saving a Document

The worst nightmare of any Word user is a power failure or glitch that shuts down Word or even the computer itself while you have one or more documents open with unsaved changes. I know people who have lost *hours* of work when this has happened. We tell ourselves to save more often, but it's easy to forget in the heat of battle. Even Word's AutoRecover feature doesn't always work as advertised, so it can't be relied upon.

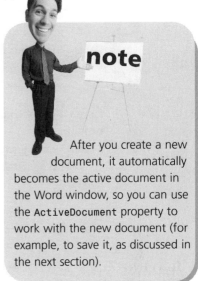

note

After you create a new document, it automatically becomes the active document in the Word window, so you can use the ActiveDocument property to work with the new document (for example, to save it, as discussed in the next section).

Using the Save Method

Fortunately, VBA proves very useful in solving this problem because it's easy to set up a procedure that takes the guesswork out of saving. Before we get to that, however, let's look at a few fundamental properties and methods of Document objects.

First up is the Save method:

Document.Save

> *Document*   This is a reference to the document you want to save.

For example, the following statement saves the active document:

```
ActiveDocument.Save
```

If you're dealing with a large document, you might not want to save it unnecessarily since the Save operation may take a while. You can avoid that by first checking the document's Saved property. If this returns False, it means the document has unsaved changes. Here's an example:

```
If ActiveDocument.Saved = False Then
    ActiveDocument.Save
End If
```

The Save method will fail if the document is a new one that has never been saved before. How can you tell? There are two ways:

■ If you've just created the document using the Add method.

■ Check the document's Path property. For a document that has been saved, Path returns the drive and folder in which the document is stored. (Note that the string returned by the Path property does not have a trailing backslash; for example, "C:\My Documents".) However, if the document has never been saved, the Path property returns an empty string ("").

Here's a bit of code that checks the Path property before trying to save the active document:

```
If ActiveDocument.Path <> "" Then
    ActiveDocument.Save
End If
```

Listing 7.2 presents a procedure named SafeSave that combines these two checks so that it avoids saving new or unchanged documents.

LISTING 7.2   A Procedure that Avoids Saving New or Unchanged Documents

```
Sub SafeSave()
    With ActiveDocument
        If .Path <> "" And .Saved = False Then
            .Save
        End If
    End With
End Sub
```

Using the SaveAs Method

If the document is new, use the SaveAs method instead.

Document.SaveAs(*FileName*, *FileFormat*)

Document	The Document object you want to save to a different file.
FileName	(optional) The full name of the new document file, including the drive and folder where you want the file to reside. If you don't specify this value, Word uses the current folder and a default named (such as Doc1.doc).
FileFormat	(optional) The file format to which the document should be saved. You can either use a predefined wdSaveFormat constant or an integer that specifies the format (wdWordDocument is the default):

File Format	Constant	Integer Value
Word Document	wdFormatDocument	0
Document Template	wdFormatTemplate	1
Text Only	wdFormatText	2
Text Only with Line Breaks	wdFormatTextLineBreaks	3
MS-DOS Text	wdFormatDOSText	4
MS-DOS Text with Line Breaks	wdFormatDOSTextLineBreaks	5
Rich Text Format	wdFormatRTF	6
Unicode Text	wdFormatUnicodeText	7
Web Page	wdFormatHTML	8
Web Archive	wdFormatWebArchive	9
XML Document	wdFormatXML	12

Both of the following statements are equivalent (that is, they both save the active document as a Web page):

```
ActiveDocument.Save "index.html",
wdFormatHTML
ActiveDocument.Save "index.html", 8
```

Closing a Document

When you no longer need a document, you can reduce clutter on the screen and within Word by closing the corresponding Document object using the Close method:

```
Document.Close(SaveChanges, OriginalFormat,
RouteDocument)
```

> **note**
>
> This is the simplified syntax for the SaveAs method. To see all 11 arguments in their full syntax, look up the SaveAs method in the VBA Help system.

Document	The Document object you want to close.
SaveChanges	(optional) If the document has been modified, this argument determines whether Word saves those changes:

wdSaveChanges	Saves changes before closing.
wdDoNotSaveChanges	Doesn't save changes.
wdPromptToSaveChanges	Asks the user if he or she wants to save changes (this is the default).

OriginalFormat	Specifies the format to use when saving the document:

wdOriginalFormat	Saves the document using its original format (this is the default).
wdWordDocument	Saves the document in Word format.
wdPromptUser	Asks the user if he wants to save the document in its original format.

RouteDocument	If set to True, this argument tells Word to route the document to the next recipient.

For example, the following statement closes the active document and saves any changes:

```
ActiveDocument.Close wdSaveChanges
```

Example: Making Document Backups

Let's put the Document object properties and methods you've learned so far to work by creating a procedure that not only saves a document, but also makes a backup copy to a floppy drive. Listing 7.3 shows a procedure named MakeBackup that does all this by using the SaveAs method, as well as a few other methods and properties of the Document object.

LISTING 7.3 A Procedure that Creates a Backup Copy of the Active Document on a Floppy Disk

```
Sub MakeBackup()
    Dim backupFile As String
    Dim currFile As String
    With ActiveDocument
        '
        ' Don't bother if the document is unchanged or new
        '
        If .Saved Or .Path = "" Then Exit Sub
        '
        ' Mark current position in document
        '
        .Bookmarks.Add Name:="LastPosition"
        '
        ' Turn off screen updating
        '
        Application.ScreenUpdating = False
```

LISTING 7.3 (continued)

```
    '
    ' Save the file
    '
    .Save
    '
    ' Store the current file path, construct the path for the
    ' backup file, and then save it to Drive A
    '
    currFile = .FullName
    backupFile = "A:\" + .Name
    .SaveAs FileName:=backupFile
End With
'
' Close the backup copy (which is now active)
'
ActiveDocument.Close
'
' Reopen the current file
'
Documents.Open FileName:=currFile
'
' Return to pre-backup position
'
Selection.GoTo What:=wdGoToBookmark, Name:="LastPosition"
'
' Turn screen updating back on
'
Application.ScreenUpdating = True
End Sub
```

After declaring a couple of variables, this procedure checks to see whether the backup operation is necessary. In other words, if the document has no unsaved changes (the Saved property returns True) or if it's a new, unsaved document (the Path property returns ""), bail out of the procedure (by running Exit Sub).

Otherwise, a new Bookmark object is created to save the current position in the document. (This ensures that when we reopen the document after running SaveAs later on, the user will be returned to his or her place in the document.) Bookmarks is a collection that holds all the defined bookmarks in a specified Document object. Each element of this collection is a Bookmark object. To add a bookmark, use the Add method, as follows:

```
Document.Bookmarks.Add Name:= BookmarkName
```

Document	The Document object you want to work with.
BookmarkName	A string that specifies the name of the bookmark.

Then the following statement turns off screen updating, which means the user won't see the opening and closing of files that occur later in the code:

```
Application.ScreenUpdating = False
```

Then the file is saved using the Save method. You're now ready to perform the backup. First, the currFile variable is used to store the document's full path name (that is, the document's drive, folder, and filename), which is given by the FullName property. Then the path name of the backup file is built with the following statement:

```
backupFile = "A:\" + .Name
```

This will be used to save the file to drive A. Note that this statement is easily customized to save the file to a different hard disk or even a network drive.

The actual backup takes place via the SaveAs method, which saves the document to the path given by backupFile. From there, the procedure closes the backup file, reopens the original file, and uses the GoTo method to return to the original position within the document.

Automating the Backup Procedure

Rather than running the MakeBackup procedure by hand, it would be better to schedule backups at specific times or at regular intervals. You can do this by using the Application object's OnTime method, which runs a procedure at a specified time, using the following syntax:

```
Application.OnTime(When, Name, Tolerance)
```

When	The time (and date, if necessary) you want the procedure to run. Enter a date/time serial number.
Name	The name (entered as text) of the procedure to run when the time given by *When* arrives.
Tolerance	If Word isn't ready to run the procedure at *When*, it will keep trying for the number of seconds specified by *Tolerance*. If you omit *Tolerance*, VBA waits until Word is ready.

The easiest way to enter a time serial number for the When argument is to use the TimeValue function:

```
TimeValue(Time)
```

> Time   A string representing the time you want to use (such as "5:00PM" or "17:00").

For example, the following formula runs the MakeBackup procedure at 5:00 PM:

```
Application.OnTime _
    When:=TimeValue("5:00PM"), _
    Name:="MakeBackup"
```

That's fine, but what we really want is for the OnTime method to run after a specified time interval (for example, a half hour from now). To make this happen, use Now + TimeValue(Time) for When (where Time is the interval you want to use). For example, the following statement schedules the MakeBackup procedure to run in five minutes:

```
Application.OnTime _
    When:=Now + TimeValue("00:05"), _
    Name:="MakeBackup"
```

More Useful Document Object Methods

Besides Open, Save, SaveAs, and Close, Document objects have dozens of other methods that let you do everything from activating a document to printing it. Here are some of the methods you'll use most often:

Document.Activate—Activates the specified open Document. For example, the following statement activates the Tirade.doc document:

```
Documents("Tirade.doc").Activate
```

Document.PrintOut—Prints the specified Document. The full syntax of this method has no fewer than 18 arguments (all of which are optional). Here are the first dozen:

```
Document.PrintOut(Background, Append, Range, OutputFileName, From, _
        To, Item, Copies, Pages, PageType, PrintToFile, Collate)
```

> Document   The Document object you want to print.
>
> Background   If True, the procedure continues while Word prints the document in the background. If False, the procedure waits until the document has spooled.
>
> Append   If True, the output is appended to the end of the file specified by the OutputFileName argument. If False, the output overwrites the contents of the file.

Range	Specifies the range of text to print, as follows:

wdPrintAllDocument	Prints the entire document.
wdPrintCurrentPage	Prints only the current page.
wdPrintFromTo	Prints a range of pages from a starting page number (see the *From* argument) to an ending page (see the *To* argument).
wdPrintRangeOfPages	Prints a range of pages (see the *Pages* argument).
wdPrintPrintSelection	Prints only the currently selected text.

OutPutFileName	The path and filename of the file to which you want the document printed. (Note that the *PrintToFile* argument must be set to True.)
From	If *Range* is wdPrintFromTo, this argument specifies the page number from which to start printing.
To	If *Range* is wdPrintFromTo, this argument specifies the page number of the last page to print.
Item	A constant that represents the item you want to print. Use one of the following values—wdPrintAutoTextEntries, wdPrintComments, wdPrintDocumentContent, wdPrintKeyAssignments, wdPrintProperties, or wdPrintStyles.
Copies	The number of copies to print. The default value is 1.
Pages	If *Range* is wdPrintRangeOfPages, this argument specifies the page range (for example, 4-8,10).
PageType	Specifies which pages to print using one of the following constants—wdPrintAllPages, wdPrintEvenPagesOnly, wdPrintOddPagesOnly.
PrintToFile	If True, Word prints the document to a file and prompts the user for a filename.
Collate	If True and *Copies* is greater than 1, prints the entire document, then prints the next copy. If False and *Copies* is greater than 1, prints multiple copies of the first page, then the second page, and so on.

Document.`PrintPreview`—Displays the specified *Document* in the Print Preview window.

Document.`Redo`—Redoes the last action that was (or actions that were) undone:

Document.`Redo(`*Times*`)`

Document	The `Document` object you want to work with.
Times	(optional) The number of actions that you want redone (the default is 1).

Document.`Select`—Selects all the text in the specified *Document*.

Document.`Undo`—Undoes the last action that was (or actions that were) performed:

Document.`Undo(`*Times*`)`

Document	The `Document` object you want to work with.
Times	(optional) The number of actions that you want undone (the default is 1) .

Working with Text

Although you can add lines, graphics, and other objects to a document, text is what Word is all about. So it won't come as any surprise to you that Word has a truckload of objects that give you numerous ways to work with text. The next few sections take you through a few of these objects.

The Range Object

If you've used VBA with Excel, you probably know that Excel has no separate object to represent a cell. Instead, a cell is considered to be just an instance of the generic `Range` class.

Along similar lines, Word has no separate objects for its most fundamental text units: the character and the word. Like Excel, Word considers these items to be instances of a generic class, which is also called the Range object. A `Range` object is defined as a continuous section of text in a document: a few characters in a row, a few words in a row, a few paragraphs in a row, or whatever. A range can be anything from a single character to an entire document, as long as the text within it is continuous.

There are two basic methods for returning a `Range` object: the Document object's `Range` method and the `Range` property.

The Range Method

The Document object has a Range method that lets you specify starting and ending points for a range. Here's the syntax:

```
Document.Range(Start,End)
```

Document	The Document object you want to work with.
Start	The starting character position. Note that the first character in a document is at position 0.
End	The ending character position. Note that this character is *not* included in the range.

For example, the following statements use the myRange object variable to store the first 100 characters (0 through 99) in the active document:

```
Dim myRange As Range
myRange = ActiveDocument.Range(0, 100)
```

The Range Property

Many Word objects have a Range property that returns a Range object, including the Paragraph and Selection objects (discussed later). This is important because these objects lack certain properties and methods that are handy for manipulating text. For example, the Paragraph object doesn't have an Italic property. The Range object does, however, so you format a paragraph's font as italic programmatically by referring to its Range property, like so:

```
ActiveDocument.Paragraphs(1).Range.Italic = True
```

This statement formats the first paragraph in the active document with italic text. (I discuss the Paragraphs collection in a moment.)

Reading and Changing Range Text

The Range object has a Text property that returns the text in the specified range. You can also use the Text property to set the text within the specified range. For example, the following code fragment checks the text in a document called letter.doc to see whether the first four characters equal the string "Dear"; if so, the text is replaced with "Greetings":

```
With Documents("letter.doc").Range.(0,4)
    If .Text = "Dear" Then
        .Text = "Greetings"
    End If
End With
```

Formatting Text

The Range object's properties also include many of the standard text formatting commands. Here's a brief review of just a few of these properties:

Range.Bold—Returns True if the specified *Range* is formatted entirely as bold, returns False if no part of the range is bold, and returns wdUndefined if only part of the range is formatted as bold. You can also set this property using True (for bolding), False (to remove bolding), or wdToggle (to toggle the current setting between True and False).

Range.Case—Returns or sets the case of the specified *Range*. This property uses various wdCharacterCase constants, including wdLowerCase, wdTitleSentence, wdTitleWord, wdToggleCase, and wdUpperCase.

Range.Font—Returns or sets a Font object that specifies the character formatting used in the *Range*.

Range.Italic—Returns True if the specified *Range* is formatted entirely as italic, returns False if no part of the range is italic, and returns wdUndefined if only part of the range is formatted as italic. You can also set this property using True (for italics), False (to remove italics), or wdToggle (to toggle the current setting between True and False).

For example, the following code fragment takes the Range object of the active document's first paragraph and then sets Bold to True, Italic to True, and the case to wdTitleWord:

```
With ActiveDocument.Paragraphs(1).Range
    .Bold = True
    .Italic = True
    .Case = wdTitleWord
End With
```

If you want maximum control over the character formatting in a range, use the Font property, which returns a Font object. From there you can manipulate not only the Bold and Italic properties, but also the type size (the Size property), the color (Color), strike through (StrikeThrough and DoubleStrikeThrough), small caps (SmallCaps), and much more. Here's an example:

```
With ActiveDocument.Range.Font
    .Color = RGB(0, 0, 255)
    .Size = 12
    .SmallCaps = True
End With
```

Some Useful Range Object Methods

Because it's the fundamental text object, it's not surprising that the Range object boasts a large number of methods that you can use to manipulate text. Here are a few of the ones you'll use most often:

Range.Copy—Copies the Range to the Clipboard.

Range.Cut—Cuts the Range from the document and places it on the Clipboard.

Range.Delete—If used without arguments, this method deletes the entire Range. However, you can fine-tune your deletions by using the following syntax:

Range.Delete(Unit,Count)

Range	The Range object containing the text you want to delete.
Unit	(optional) A constant that specifies whether you're deleting characters (use wdCharacter) or entire words (use wdWord). If you omit this argument, VBA assumes you're deleting characters.
Count	(optional) The number of units to delete. Use a positive number to delete forward; use a negative number to delete backward. (The default is 1.)

Range.InsertAfter—Inserts text after the specified Range:

Range.InsertAfter(Text)

Range	The Range object after which you want to insert the text.
Text	The text to insert.

Range.InsertBefore—Inserts text before the specified Range:

Range.InsertBefore(Text)

Range	The Range object before which you want to insert the text.
Text	The text to insert.

Range.InsertParagraph—Inserts a paragraph that replaces the specified Range.

Range.InsertParagraphAfter—Inserts a paragraph after the specified Range.

Range.InsertParagraphBefore—Inserts a paragraph before the specified Range.

Range.Paste—Pastes the contents of the Clipboard at the current Range position. To avoid overwriting the currently selected Range, use the Collapse method before pasting.

Range.Select—Selects the specified Range. See the next section to learn more about the resulting Selection object.

The `Selection` Object

The `Selection` object always references one of two things:

- The selected text.
- The position of the insertion point cursor.

Because much of what you do in Word involves one or the other of these items (formatting text, inserting text at the insertion point, and so on), the `Selection` object is one of the most important in Word. (I'm simplifying things a bit for this discussion because the `Selection` object can also refer to a selected shape, inline shape, or block. I'll deal only with text-related selections in this section.)

You reference the currently selected text or insertion point by using the `Selection` property without an object qualifier. For example, the following statement formats the selected text as bold:

```
Selection.Range.Bold = True
```

To specify a `Selection` object, use the `Select` method, which is available with a number of Word objects, including `Document`, `Range`, `Bookmark`, and `Table`. For example, the following statement selects the first paragraph in the active document:

```
ActiveDocument.Paragraphs(1).Range.Select
```

Checking the `Selection` Type

The `Selection` object has a number of properties, including many that you've seen already with the `Document` and `Range` objects. The few properties that are unique to the `Selection` object aren't particularly useful, so I won't discuss them here. The lone exception is the `Type` property:

`Type`—Returns the type of selection:

wdNoSelection	Nothing is selected.
wdSelectionColumn	A column in a table is selected.
wdSelectionIP	The selection is the insertion point.
wdSelectionNormal	Some text is selected.
wdSelectionRow	A row in a table is selected.

`Selection` Object Methods

Again, the `Selection` object offers many of the same methods as the `Range` object, including `Copy`, `Cut`, `Delete`, `InsertAfter`, `InsertBefore`, `InsertParagraphAfter`, `InsertParagraphBefore`, and `Paste`. Here's a look at a few methods that are either unique to the `Selection` object or are most often used with this object:

Collapse—Removes the selection and positions the insertion point according to the following syntax:

Selection.Collapse *Direction*

Direction	(optional) Specifies where you want the insertion point to end up. Use wdCollapseStart to position the cursor at the beginning of the Selection (this is the default). Use wdCollapseEnd to position the cursor at the end of the Selection.

EndKey—Extends the selection or moves the insertion point to the end of a specified unit (such as a line). In other words, this method is equivalent to pressing the End key. Note, too, that this method returns the number of characters that the selection was moved. Here's the syntax:

Selection.EndKey(*Unit, Extend*)

Unit	(optional) Specifies what the Selection is moved to the end of. For regular text, use wdLine (this is the default) or wdStory. In a table, use wdColumn or wdRow.
Extend	(optional) Specifies what happens to the Selection. To extend the selection to the end of the specified *Unit*, use wdExtend; to collapse the Selection to the insertion point, use wdMove (this is the default).

EndOf—Extends the selection or moves the insertion point to the end of a specified unit (such as a paragraph). This method returns the number of characters that the selection was moved. This method offers a bit more flexibility than the EndKey method. Here's the syntax:

Selection.EndOf(*Unit, Extend*)

Unit	(optional) Specifies the unit by which the Selection is moved. For regular text, use wdCharacter, wdWord (this is the default), wdLine, wdSentence, wdParagraph, wdSection, or wdStory. In a table, use wdCell, wdColumn, wdRow, or wdTable.
Extend	(optional) Specifies what happens to the Selection. To extend the selection to the end of the specified *Unit*, use wdExtend; to collapse the Selection to the insertion point at then end of the unit, use wdMove (this is the default) .

Expand—Expands the selection using the following syntax:

```
Selection.Expand Unit
```

Unit	(optional) Specifies how the Selection is expanded. For regular text, use wdCharacter, wdWord (this is the default), wdLine, wdSentence, wdParagraph, wdSection, or wdStory. In a table, use wdCell, wdColumn, wdRow, or wdTable.

For example, the following code selects the first word in the first paragraph. With the Selection object in place, it then changes the first word to uppercase, expands the selection to the entire paragraph, formats the new selection as bold, and then collapses the selection to put the insertion point after the paragraph:

```
ActiveDocument.Paragraphs(1).Range.Words(1).Select
With Selection
    .Range.Case = wdUpperCase
    .Expand wdParagraph
    .Range.Bold = True
    .Collapse wdCollapseEnd
End With
```

HomeKey—Extends the selection or moves the insertion point to the beginning of a specified unit (such as a line). This method is equivalent to pressing the Home key. As with the EndKey method, HomeKey returns the number of characters that the selection was moved. Use the following syntax:

```
Selection.Home(Unit, Extend)
```

Unit	(optional) Specifies what the Selection is moved to the beginning of. For regular text, use wdLine (this is the default) or wdStory. In a table, use wdColumn or wdRow.
Extend	(optional) Specifies what happens to the selection. To extend the Selection to the beginning of the specified *Unit*, use wdExtend; to collapse the selection to the insertion point, use wdMove (this is the default) .

Move—Collapses the current selection and moves the insertion point by a specified number of units. This method returns the number of units that the insertion point was moved. Here's the syntax:

```
Selection.Move(Unit, Count)
```

Unit	(optional) Specifies the unit by which the insertion point is moved. For regular text, use wdCharacter (this is the default), wdWord, wdLine, wdSentence, wdParagraph, wdSection, or wdStory. In a table, use wdCell, wdColumn, wdRow, or wdTable.

Count	(optional) The number of units by which the insertion point is moved (the default is 1).

StartOf—Extends the selection or moves the insertion point to the start of a specified unit (such as a paragraph). This method returns the number of characters that the selection was moved. This method offers a bit more flexibility than the HomeKey method. Here's the syntax:

Selection.StartOf(*Unit, Extend*)

Unit	(optional) Specifies the unit by which the Selection is moved. For regular text, use wdCharacter, wdWord (this is the default), wdLine, wdSentence, wdParagraph, wdSection, or wdStory. In a table, use wdCell, wdColumn, wdRow, or wdTable.
Extend	(optional) Specifies what happens to the Selection. To extend the selection to the start of the specified *Unit*, use wdExtend; to collapse the Selection to the insertion point at the start of the unit, use wdMove (this is the default).

> **note**
>
> If you don't want the current selection deleted when you insert a new paragraph, use the InsertParagraphAfter or InsertParagraphBefore methods. See "Some Useful Range Object Methods," earlier in this chapter.

TypeBackspace—Deletes the character to the left of the insertion point. If the current selection isn't collapsed, this method deletes the selected text. (This method is equivalent to pressing the Backspace key.)

TypeParagraph—Inserts a new paragraph at the insertion point. If the current selection isn't collapsed, this method deletes the selected text. (This method is equivalent to pressing the Enter key.)

TypeText—Inserts text at the insertion point. If the current selection isn't collapsed and the Options.ReplaceSelection property is True, this method replaces the selection with the specified text. Here's the syntax:

Selection.TypeText *Text*

Text	The string to be inserted.

Listing 7.4 shows a procedure that inserts text. It first checks to see whether the current selection is the insertion point or whether Options.ReplaceSelection is False. If either is true, the text is inserted. Otherwise, the user is asked if they want to replace the selected text. (See Chapter 12, "Interacting with the User," to learn about the MsgBox function.)

LISTING 7.4   A Procedure that Asks the User if the Selected Text Should Be Replaced

```
Sub AskToReplaceText()
    Dim result As Integer
    '
    ' Are we at the insertion point or is ReplaceSelection off?
    '
    If Selection.Type = wdSelectionIP Or _
       Not Options.ReplaceSelection Then
        '
        ' If so, just insert the text
        '
        Selection.TypeText "Howdy"
    Else
        '
        ' Otherwise, ask the user about replacing the text
        '
        result = MsgBox("Replace the selected text?", vbYesNo + vbQuestion)
        If result = vbNo Then
            '
            ' Turn off ReplaceSelection to insert without replacing
            '
            Options.ReplaceSelection = False
            Selection.TypeText "Howdy"
            Options.ReplaceSelection = True
        Else
            '
            ' Replace the selected text
            '
            Selection.TypeText "Howdy"
        End If
    End If
End Sub
```

The Characters Object

The Characters object is a collection that represents all the characters in whatever object is specified. For example, ActiveDocument.Paragraphs(1).Range.Characters is the collection of all the characters in the Range object given by ActiveDocument.Paragraphs(1).Range (the first paragraph in the active document). Other objects that have the Characters property are Document and Selection.

Because `Characters` is a collection, you refer to individual characters by including an index number—`Characters(50)`, for example. The following statement formats the first character in the active document to point size 20:

`ActiveDocument.Characters(1).Font.Size = 20`

To count the number of characters in the specified object, use the `Count` property:

`totalChars = Documents("Chaptr07.doc").Characters.Count`

This example sets the variable `totalChars` equal to the number of characters in the `Chaptr07.doc` file.

Listing 7.5 shows another example that uses the `Characters` object. In this case, the function procedure named `CountCharacters` takes on an `Object` argument named `countObject` and a `String` argument named `letter`. The procedure determines the number of instances of `letter` that occur within `countObject`.

LISTING 7.5   A Function that Counts the Number of Instances of a Specified Character in an Object

```
Function CountCharacters(countObject As Object, letter As String) As Long
    Dim i As Long, char As Range
    i = 0
    For Each char In countObject.Characters
        If char = letter Then i = i + 1
    Next 'char
    CountCharacters = i
End Function

Sub TestCountCharacters()
    MsgBox CountCharacters(ActiveDocument, "e")
End Sub
```

The Words Object

The `Words` object is a collection that represents all the words in whatever object is specified. For example, `ActiveDocument.Words` is the collection of all the words in the active document. Other objects that have the `Words` property are `Paragraph`, `Range`, and `Selection`.

You refer to individual words by using an index number with the `Words` collection. As I mentioned earlier, however, this doesn't return a "Word" object; there is no such thing in Microsoft Word's VBA universe. Instead, individual words are classified as `Range` objects (see "The `Range` Object" earlier in this chapter).

The following statement formats the first word in the active document as bold:

```
ActiveDocument.Words(1).Font.Bold = True
```

To count the number of words in the specified object, use the Count property:

```
totalWords = Documents("Article.doc").Words.Count
```

Note, however, that the Words object includes the punctuation and paragraph marks inside the object, which is certainly bizarre behavior, and serves to render the Words.Count property more or less useless. If you want to know the number of real words in an object, use the CountWords function shown in Listing 7.5.

LISTING 7.5 A Function that Counts the Number of "Real" Words in an Object, Ignoring Punctuation Marks and Paragraph Marks

```
Function CountWords(countObject As Object) As Long
    Dim i As Long, word As Range
    i = 0
    For Each word In countObject.Words
        Select Case Asc(Left(word, 1))
            Case 48 To 57, 65 To 90, 97 To 122
                i = i + 1
        End Select
    Next 'word
    CountWords = i
End Function


Sub TestCountWords()
    With ActiveDocument
        MsgBox "Words.Count reports " & .Words.Count & Chr(13) & _
                "CountWords reports " & CountWords(.Range)
    End With
End Sub
```

This function takes a generic object as an argument (because the function can work with a Document, Range, or Selection object). It then uses a For Each loop to run through each word in the object. With each loop, the ASCII value of the leftmost character is plugged into a Select Case statement. If that value is between 48 and 57, between 65 and 90, or between 97 and 122, it means the character is either a number or a letter. If so, the function counts the word as a "real" word and increments the counter i.

The Sentences Object

The next rung on Word's text object ladder is the Sentences object. This is a collection of all the sentences in whatever object you specify, be it a Document, Range, or Selection.

As with Words, you refer to specific members of the Sentences collection using an index number, and the resulting object is a Range. For example, the following statement stores the active document's first sentence in the firstSentence variable:

```
firstSentence = ActiveDocument.Sentences(1)
```

Again, the Count property can be used to return the total number of sentences in an object. In the following procedure fragment, the Count property is used to determine the last sentence in a document:

```
With Documents("Remarks.doc")
    totalSentences = .Sentences.Count
    lastSentence = .Sentences(.totalSentences)
End With
```

The Paragraph Object

From characters, words, and sentences, you make the next logical text leap: paragraphs. A Paragraph object is a member of the Paragraphs collection, which represents all the paragraphs in the specified Document, Range, or Selection. As with the other text objects, you use an index number with the Paragraphs object to specify an individual paragraph.

Some Useful Paragraph Object Properties

Word's various paragraph formatting options are well-represented in the large set of properties available for the Paragraph object. Here are a few useful ones:

Paragraph.LeftIndent—Returns or sets the left indent (in points) of the specified Paragraph.

Paragraph.LineSpacing—Returns or sets the line spacing setting (in points) for the specified Paragraph.

Paragraph.RightIndent—Returns or sets the right indent (in points) for the specified *Paragraph*.

Paragraph.SpaceAfter—Returns or sets the spacing (in points) after the specified *Paragraph*.

Paragraph.SpaceBefore—Returns or sets the spacing (in points) before the specified *Paragraph*.

Paragraph.Style—Returns or sets the style of the specified *Paragraph*. Word has a huge number of constants that represent its predefined styles. For example, to set the Heading 1 style, you would use the wdStyleHeading1 constant. To see the other constants, search for wdBuiltInStyle in the Object Browser.

The following procedure fragment applies several properties to the active paragraph (recall that the InchesToPoints function converts values expressed in inches to the equivalent value expressed in points):

```
With Selection.Range
    .LeftIndent=InchesToPoints(1)
    .LineSpacing=12
    .SpaceAfter=6
    .Style=wdStyleNormal
End With
```

Some Useful Paragraph Object Methods

To finish our look at the Paragraph object, here are a few methods you can wield in your code:

Paragraph.Indent—Indents the specified *Paragraph* to the next tab stop.

Paragraph.Outdent—Outdents the *Paragraph* to the previous tab stop.

Paragraph.Space1—Sets the specified *Paragraph* to single-spaced.

Paragraph.Space15—Sets the specified *Paragraph* to 1.5-line spacing.

Paragraph.Space2—Sets the specified *Paragraph* to double-spaced.

THE ABSOLUTE MINIMUM

This chapter took you on a tour of VBA in Word. You learned more about Word's Application object, including a few useful properties and methods. From there, we went through a number of Word-specific objects, including the Document, Range, Selection, Characters, Words, Sentences, and Paragraph objects.

Here's a list of chapters where you'll find related information:

- For a general discussion of VBA objects, see Chapter 5, "Working with Objects."

- I show you how to use MsgBox and other interaction functions in Chapter 12, "Interacting with the User."

- The MakeBackup procedure should probably check to see whether there is a disk in drive A for running the SaveAs method. I show you how to account for this type of error in Chapter 15, "Debugging VBA Procedures."

8

PROGRAMMING EXCEL

If you're using VBA in Excel, most of your procedures will eventually do *something* to the Excel environment. They might open a workbook, rename a worksheet, select a cell or range, enter a formula, or even set some of Excel's options. Therefore, knowing how VBA interacts with Excel is crucial if you ever hope to write useful routines. This chapter looks closely at that interaction. You learn how to work with all the most common Excel objects, including the Workbook, Worksheet, and Range objects.

Excel's Application Object

You begin, however, with the `Application` object. Recall that in Chapter 5, "Working with Objects," you learned a few `Application` object properties and methods that are common to all VBA applications. As you can imagine, though, each application has its own unique set of properties and methods for the `Application` object. Excel is no exception, as you'll see in this section.

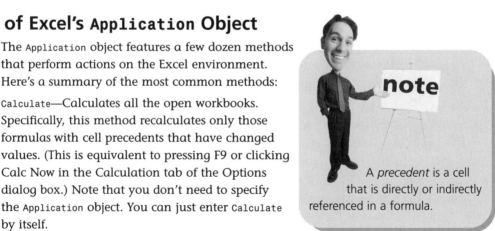

caution

The `WorksheetFunctions` object includes only those worksheet functions that don't duplicate an existing VBA function. For example, VBA has a `UCase` function that's equivalent to Excel's `UPPER()` worksheet function (both convert a string into uppercase). In this case, you must use VBA's `UCase` function in your code. If you try to use `Application.WorksheetFunctions.Upper`, you'll receive an error message. For a complete list of VBA functions, see Appendix B, "VBA Functions."

Accessing Worksheet Functions

VBA has dozens of functions of its own, but its collection is downright meager compared to the hundreds of worksheet functions available with Excel. If you need to access one of these worksheet functions, VBA makes them available via a property of the `Application` object called `WorksheetFunctions`. Each function works exactly as it does on a worksheet—the only difference being that you have to append "Application." to the name of the function.

For example, to run the `SUM()` worksheet function on the range named `Sales` and store the result in a variable named `totalSales`, you'd use the following statement:

```
totalSales = Application.WorksheetFunctions.Sum(Range("Sales"))
```

Methods of Excel's `Application` Object

The `Application` object features a few dozen methods that perform actions on the Excel environment. Here's a summary of the most common methods:

`Calculate`—Calculates all the open workbooks. Specifically, this method recalculates only those formulas with cell precedents that have changed values. (This is equivalent to pressing F9 or clicking Calc Now in the Calculation tab of the Options dialog box.) Note that you don't need to specify the `Application` object. You can just enter `Calculate` by itself.

note

A *precedent* is a cell that is directly or indirectly referenced in a formula.

`Application.CalculateFull`—Runs a full calculation of all the open workbooks. Specifically, this method recalculates every formula in each workbook, even those with cell precedents that haven't changed values. (This is equivalent to pressing Ctrl+Alt+F9.)

`Application.DoubleClick`—Equivalent to double-clicking the current cell. If in-cell editing is activated, running this method opens the cell for editing; otherwise, running this method opens the cell's comment (if it has one) for editing.

`Application.Evaluate`—Converts a string into an Excel object using the following syntax:

`Evaluate(Name)`

> Name   A string that specifies either a cell address, a range, or a defined name.

The code used in this chapter's examples can be found on my Web site at the following address:

`http://www.mcfedries.com/ABGVBA/Chapter08.xls`

For example, `Evaluate("A1")` returns a Range object (that is, a cell or groups of cells; see "Working with `Range` Objects," later in this chapter) that represents cell A1 in the active worksheet. Listing 8.1 shows a more elaborate example that takes the value in cell A1 (the value is "A") and the value in cell B1 (the value is "2"), concatenates them, and then uses `Evaluate` to display the value from cell A2.

LISTING 8.1   A Procedure that Tests the `Evaluate` Function

```
Sub EvaluateTest()
    Dim columnLetter As String
    Dim rowNumber As String
    Dim cellAddress As String
    '
    ' Activate the "Test Data" worksheet
    '
    Worksheets("Test Data").Activate
    '
    ' Get the value in cell A1
    '
    columnLetter = [A1].Value
    '
    ' Get the value in cell B1
    '
```

LISTING 8.1   (continued)

```
rowNumber = [B1].Value
'
' Concatenate the two values and then display the message
'
cellAddress = columnLetter & rowNumber
MsgBox "The value in cell " & cellAddress & " is " & _
                Application.Evaluate(cellAddress)
End Sub
```

`Application.Quit`—Quits Excel. If there are any open workbooks with unsaved changes, Excel will ask if you want to save the changes. To prevent this, either save the workbooks before running the Quit method (you learn how to save workbooks later in this chapter in the section titled "Manipulating `Workbook` Objects"), or set the `Application.DisplayAlerts` property to False. (In the latter case, note that Excel will *not* save changes to the workbooks.)

`Application.Wait`—Pauses a running macro until a specified time is reached. Here's the syntax:

`Application.Wait(Time)`

> `Time`   The time you want to macro to resume running.

For example, if you wanted your procedure to delay for about five seconds, you would use the following statement:

`Application.Wait Now + TimeValue("00:00:05")`

See "Running a Procedure at a Specific Time," later in this chapter, to learn more about the `TimeValue` function.

Some Event-Like Methods

Excel's `Application` object comes with several methods that are "event-like." In other words, they respond to outside influences such as the press of a key. This section looks at four of these methods: `OnKey`, `OnTime`, `OnRepeat`, and `OnUndo`.

Running a Procedure When the User Presses a Key

When recording a macro, Excel enables you to assign a Ctrl+*key* shortcut to a procedure. However, there are two major drawbacks to this method:

- Excel uses some Ctrl+*key* combinations internally, so your choices are limited.
- It doesn't help if you would like your procedures to respond to "meaningful" keys such as Delete and Esc.

To remedy these problems, use the Application object's OnKey method to run a procedure when the user presses a specific key or key combination:

Application.OnKey(*Key*, *Procedure*)

Key	The key or key combination that runs the procedure. For letters, numbers, or punctuation marks, enclose the character in quotes (for example, "a"). For other keys, see Table 8.1.
Procedure	The name (entered as text) of the procedure to run when the user presses a key. If you enter the null string ("") for *Procedure*, a key is disabled. If you omit *Procedure*, Excel resets the key to its normal state.

TABLE 8.1   Key Strings to Use with the OnKey Method

Key	What to Use
Backspace	"{BACKSPACE}" or "{BS}"
Break	"{BREAK}"
Caps Lock	"{CAPSLOCK}"
Delete	"{DELETE}" or "{DEL}"
Down arrow	"{DOWN}"
End	"{END}"
Enter (keypad)	"{ENTER}"
Enter	"~" (tilde)
Esc	"{ESCAPE}" or "{ESC}"
Help	"{HELP}"
Home	"{HOME}"
Insert	"{INSERT}"
Left arrow	"{LEFT}"
Num Lock	"{NUMLOCK}"
Page Down	"{PGDN}"
Page Up	"{PGUP}"
Right arrow	"{RIGHT}"
Scroll Lock	"{SCROLLLOCK}"
Tab	"{TAB}"
Up arrow	"{UP}"
F1 through F15	"{F1}" through "{F15}"

You also can combine these keys with the Shift, Ctrl, and Alt keys. You just precede these codes with one or more of the codes listed in Table 8.2.

TABLE 8.2   Symbols that Represent Alt, Ctrl, and Shift in OnKey

Key	What to Use
Alt	% (percent)
Ctrl	^ (caret)
Shift	+ (plus)

For example, pressing Delete normally wipes out only a cell's contents. If you would like a quick way of deleting everything in a cell (contents, formats, comments, and so on), you could set up (for example) Ctrl+Delete to do the job. Listing 8.2 shows three procedures that accomplish this:

SetKey— This procedure sets up the Ctrl+Delete key combination to run the DeleteAll procedure. Notice how the *Procedure* argument includes the name of the workbook where the DeleteAll procedure is located; therefore, this key combination will operate in any workbook.

DeleteAll— This procedure runs the Clear method on the currently selected cells. (See "More Range Object Methods," later in this chapter to learn about the Clear method.)

ResetKey— This procedure resets Ctrl+Delete to its default behavior.

LISTING 8.2   Procedures that Set and Reset a Key Combination Using the OnKey Method

```
Sub SetKey()
    Application.OnKey _
        Key:="^{Del}", _
        Procedure:="Chaptr08.xls!DeleteAll"
End Sub

Sub DeleteAll()
    Selection.Clear
End Sub

Sub ResetKey()
    Application.OnKey _
        Key:="^{Del}"
End Sub
```

Running a Procedure at a Specific Time

If you need to run a procedure at a specific time, use the OnTime method:

```
Application.OnTime(EarliestTime, Procedure, LatestTime, Schedule)
```

EarliestTime	The time (and date, if necessary) you want the procedure to run. Enter a date/time serial number.
Procedure	The name (entered as text) of the procedure to run when the *EarliestTime* arrives.
LatestTime	If Excel isn't ready to run the procedure at *EarliestTime* (in other words, if it's not in Ready, Cut, Copy, or Find mode), it will keep trying until *LatestTime* arrives. If you omit *LatestTime*, VBA waits until Excel is ready. Enter a date/time serial number.
Schedule	A logical value that determines whether the procedure runs at *EarliestTime* or not. If *Schedule* is True or omitted, the procedure runs. Use False to cancel a previous OnTime setting.

The easiest way to enter the time serial numbers for *EarliestTime* and *LatestTime* is to use the TimeValue function:

```
TimeValue(Time)
```

Time	A string representing the time you want to use (such as "5:00PM" or "17:00").

For example, the following formula runs a procedure called Backup at 5:00 PM:

```
Application.OnTime _
    EarliestTime:=TimeValue("5:00PM"), _
    Procedure:="Backup"
```

> **tip**
>
> If you want the OnTime method to run after a specified time interval (for example, an hour from now), use Now + TimeValue(*Time*) for *EarliestTime* (where *Time* is the interval you want to use). For example, the following statement schedules a procedure to run in 30 minutes:
>
> ```
> Application.OnTime _
>     EarliestTime:=Now +
> TimeValue("00:30"), _
>     Procedure:="Backup"
> ```

Running a Procedure When the User Selects Repeat or Undo

Excel has a couple of event-like methods that run procedures when the user selects Edit, Repeat or Edit, Undo.

The `OnRepeat` method customizes the name of the Edit, Repeat menu item and specifies the procedure that runs when the user selects Edit, Repeat. Set this property at the end of a procedure so the user can easily repeat the procedure just by selecting Edit, Repeat. Here's the syntax:

```
Application.OnRepeat(Text, Procedure)
```

Text	The name of the Edit, Repeat menu item. This command normally uses R as its accelerator key, so make sure that the *Text* argument has an ampersand (&) before the R (for example, &Repeat Formatting).
Procedure	The procedure to run when the user selects Edit, Repeat (this will usually be the name of the procedure that contains the `OnRepeat` statement).

The `OnUndo` method is similar to `OnRepeat`, except that it sets the name of the Edit, Undo menu item and specifies the procedure that runs when the user selects Edit, Undo:

```
Application.OnUndo(Text, Procedure)
```

Text	The name of the Edit, Undo menu item. Note that the Undo command uses the letter U as its accelerator key.
Procedure	The procedure to run when the user selects Edit, Undo.

Listing 8.3 shows an example that uses both `OnRepeat` and `OnUndo`. The `currCell` variable stores the address of the active cell. Notice that it's declared at the module-level to make it available to all the procedures in the module (see Chapter 3, "Understanding Program Variables"). The `BoldAndItalic` procedure makes the font of the active cell bold and italic and then sets the `OnRepeat` property (to run `BoldAndItalic` again) and the `OnUndo` property (to run the procedure named `UndoBoldAndItalic`).

LISTING 8.3   Procedures that Set the `OnRepeat` and `OnUndo` Properties

```
Dim currCell As String  ' The module-level variable
Sub BoldAndItalic()
    With ActiveCell
        .Font.Bold = True
        .Font.Italic = True
        currCell = .Address
    End With
    Application.OnRepeat _
```

LISTING 8.3   Procedures that Set the `OnRepeat` and `OnUndo` Properties

```
        Text:="&Repeat Bold and Italic", _
        Procedure:="BoldAndItalic"
    Application.OnUndo _
        Text:="&Undo Bold and Italic", _
        Procedure:="UndoBoldAndItalic"
End Sub

Sub UndoBoldAndItalic()
    With Range(currCell).Font
        .Bold = False
        .Italic = False
    End With
End Sub
```

Manipulating Workbook Objects

`Workbook` objects appear directly below the `Application` object in Excel's object hierarchy. You can use VBA to create new workbooks, open or delete existing workbooks, save and close open workbooks, and much more. The next section takes you through various techniques for specifying workbooks in your VBA code; then you'll look at some `Workbook` object properties, methods, and events.

Specifying a `Workbook` Object

If you need to perform some action on a workbook, or if you need to work with an object contained in a specific workbook (such as a worksheet), you need to tell Excel which workbook you want to use. VBA gives you no fewer than three ways to do this:

Use the `Workbooks` object—The `Workbooks` object is the collection of all the open workbook files. To specify a workbook, either use its index number (where 1 represents the first workbook opened) or enclose the workbook name in quotation marks. For example, if the `Budget.xls` workbook was the first workbook opened, the following two statements would be equivalent:

```
Workbooks(1)
Workbooks("Budget.xls")
```

Use the `ActiveWorkbook` object—The `ActiveWorkbook` object represents the workbook that currently has the focus.

Use the `ThisWorkbook` object The `ThisWorkbook` object represents the workbook where the VBA code is executing. If your code only deals with objects residing in the same workbook as the code itself, you can use the `ActiveWorkbook` object. However, if your code deals with other workbooks, use `ThisWorkbook` whenever you need to make sure that the code affects only the workbook containing the procedure.

Opening a Workbook

To open a workbook file, use the `Open` method of the `Workbooks` collection. The `Open` method has a dozen arguments you can use to fine-tune your workbook openings, but only one of these is mandatory. Here's the simplified syntax showing the one required argument (for the rest of the arguments, look up the `Open` method in the VBA Help system):

`Workbooks.Open(FileName)`

> *FileName* The full name of the workbook file, including the drive and folder that contain the file.

For example, to open a workbook named `Data.xls` in the C:\My Documents folder, you would use the following statement:

`Workbooks.Open "C:\My Documents\Data.xls"`

Creating a New Workbook

If you need to create a new workbook, use the `Workbooks` collection's `Add` method:

`Workbooks.Add(Template)`

Template is an optional argument that determines how the workbook is created. If *Template* is a string specifying an Excel file, VBA uses the file as a template for the new workbook. You also can specify one of the following constants:

> `xlWBATWorksheet` Creates a workbook with a single worksheet.
>
> `xlWBATChart` Creates a workbook with a single chart sheet.

Here's a sample statement that uses the `Add` method to open a new workbook based on Excel's `Invoice.xlt` template file:

```
Workbooks.Add "C:\Program Files\Microsoft Office" & _
    "\Templates\Spreadsheet Solutions\Invoice.xlt"
```

Workbook Object Properties

Here's a rundown of some common properties associated with `Workbook` objects:

`Workbook.ActiveSheet`—Returns a `Worksheet` object
that represents the worksheet in `Workbook` that currently has the focus.

`Workbook.FullName`—Returns the full pathname of
the `Workbook`. The full pathname includes the workbook's path (the drive and folder in which the file
resides) and the filename.

`Workbook.Name`—Returns the filename of the `Workbook`.

`Workbook.Path`—Returns the path of the `Workbook` file.
Note, however, that there is no trailing backslash (\) in the returned value (for
example, C:\My Documents).

`Workbook.Saved`—Determines whether or not changes have been made to the `Workbook`
since it was last saved. If changes have been made, Saved returns False.

A new, unsaved
workbook's `Path` property
returns an empty string ("").

Workbook Object Methods

`Workbook` objects have dozens of methods that let you do everything from saving a
workbook to closing a workbook. Here are a few methods that you'll use most often:

`Workbook.Activate`—Activates the specified open `Workbook`. For example, the following
statement activates the `Finances.xls` workbook:

```
Workbooks("Finances.xls").Activate
```

`Workbook.Close`—Closes the specified `Workbook`. This method uses the following syntax:

```
Workbook.Close(SaveChanges, FileName, RouteWorkbook)
```

Workbook	The `Workbook` object you want to close.
SaveChanges	If the workbook has been modified, this argument deter- mines whether or not Excel saves those changes:

SaveChanges	*Action*
True	Saves changes before closing.
False	Doesn't save changes.
Omitted	Asks the user if she wants to save changes.

FileName	Save the workbook under this filename.

RouteWorkbook	Routes the workbook according to the following values:

RouteWorkbook	*Action*
True	Sends the workbook to the next recipient.
False	Doesn't send the workbook.
Omitted	Asks the user if she wants to send the workbook.

Workbook.PrintOut—Prints the specified *Workbook* using the following syntax:
Workbook.PrintOut(*From, To, Copies, Preview, ActivePrinter,*
➥*PrintToFile, Collate, PrToFileName*)

Workbook	The Workbook object you want to print.
From	The page number from which to start printing.
To	The page number of the last page to print.
Copies	The number of copies to print. The default value is 1.
Preview	If True, Excel displays the Print Preview window before printing. The default value is False.
ActivePrinter	Specifies the printer to use.
PrintToFile	If True, Excel prints the workbook to a file and prompts the user for a filename.
Collate	If True, and *Copies* is greater than 1, Excel collates the copies.
PrToFileName	The name of the file to which you want to print (*PrintToFile* must be True) .

Workbook.PrintPreview—Displays the specified *Workbook* in the Print Preview window.

Workbook.Save—Saves the specified *Workbook*. If the workbook is new, use the SaveAs method instead.

Workbook.SaveAs—Saves the specified *Workbook* to a different file. Here's the simplified syntax for the SaveAs method (to see all 11 arguments in the full syntax, look up the SaveAs method in the VBA Help system):
Workbook.SaveAs(*FileName*)

Workbook	The Workbook object you want to save to a different file.
FileName	The full name of the new workbook file, including the drive and folder where you want the file to reside.

Dealing with Worksheet Objects

Worksheet objects contain a number of properties and methods you can exploit in your code. These include options for activating and hiding worksheets, adding new worksheets to a workbook, and moving, copying, and deleting worksheets. The next few sections discuss these and other worksheet operations.

Specifying a Worksheet Object

If you need to deal with a worksheet in some way, or if your code needs to specify an object contained in a specific worksheet (such as a range of cells), you need to tell Excel which worksheet you want to use. To do this, use the Worksheets object. Worksheets is the collection of all the worksheets in a particular workbook. To specify a worksheet, either use its index number (where 1 represents the first worksheet tab, 2 the second worksheet tab, and so on) or enclose the worksheet name in quotation marks. For example, if Sheet1 is the first worksheet, the following two statements would be equivalent:

```
Worksheets(1)
Worksheets("Sheet1")
```

Alternatively, if you want to work with whichever worksheet is currently active in a specified Workbook object, use the ActiveSheet property, as in this example:

```
currentWorksheet = Workbooks("Budget").ActiveSheet
```

If you need to work with multiple worksheets (say, to set up a 3D range), use VBA's Array function with the Worksheets collection. For example, the following statement specifies the Sheet1 and Sheet2 worksheets:

```
Worksheets(Array("Sheet1","Sheet2"))
```

Creating a New Worksheet

The Worksheets collection has an Add method you can use to insert new worksheets into the workbook. Here's the syntax for this method:

```
Worksheets.Add(Before, After, Count, Type)
```

Before	The sheet before which the new sheet is added. If you omit both *Before* and *After,* the new worksheet is added before the active sheet.
After	The sheet after which the new sheet is added. Note that you can't specify both the *Before* and *After* arguments.
Count	The number of new worksheets to add. VBA adds one worksheet if you omit *Count*.

Type   The type of worksheet. You have three choices—xlWorksheet (the default) and two constants that create Excel 4 sheets (which, therefore, you'll never use): xlExcel4MacroSheet and xlExcel4IntlMacroSheet.

In the following statement, a new worksheet is added to the active workbook before the Sales sheet:

```
Worksheets.Add Before:=Worksheets("Sales")
```

Properties of the Worksheet Object

Let's take a tour through some of the most useful properties associated with Worksheet objects:

Worksheet.Name—Returns or sets the name of the specified Worksheet. For example, the following statement renames the Sheet1 worksheet to 2004 Budget:

```
Worksheets("Sheet1").Name = "2004 Budget"
```

Worksheet.StandardHeight—Returns the standard height of all the rows in the specified Worksheet.

Worksheet.StandardWidth—Returns the standard width of all the columns in the specified Worksheet.

UsedRange—Returns a Range object that represents the used range in the specified Worksheet.

Worksheet.Visible—Controls whether or not the user can see the specified Worksheet. Setting this property to False is equivalent to selecting Format, Sheet, Hide. For example, to hide a worksheet named Expenses, you would use the following statement:

```
Worksheets("Expenses").Visible = False
```

To unhide the sheet, set its Visible property to True.

Methods of the Worksheet Object

Here's a list of some common Worksheet object methods:

Worksheet.Activate—Makes the specified Worksheet active (so that it becomes the ActiveSheet property of the workbook). For example, the following statement activates the Sales worksheet in the Finance.xls workbook:

```
Workbooks("Finance.xls").Worksheets("Sales").Activate
```

Worksheet.Calculate—Calculates the specified Worksheet. For example, the following statement recalculates the Budget 2004 worksheet:

```
Worksheets("Budget 2004").Calculate
```

Worksheet.Copy—Copies the specified *Worksheet* using the following syntax:
Worksheet.Copy(*Before, After*)

Worksheet	The worksheet you want to copy.
Before	The sheet before which the sheet will be copied. If you omit both *Before* and *After*, VBA creates a new workbook for the copied sheet.
After	The sheet after which the new sheet is added. You can't specify both the *Before* and *After* arguments.

In the following statement, the Budget 2004 worksheet is copied to a new workbook:
Worksheets("Budget 2004").Copy

Worksheet.Delete—Deletes the specified *Worksheet*. For example, the following statement deletes the active worksheet:
ActiveSheet.Delete

Worksheet.Move—Moves the specified *Worksheet* using the following syntax:
Worksheet.Move(*Before, After*)

Worksheet	The worksheet you want to move.
Before	The sheet before which the sheet will be moved. If you omit both *Before* and *After,* VBA creates a new workbook for the moved sheet.
After	The sheet after which the new sheet is added. You can't specify both the *Before* and *After* arguments.

In the following statement, the Budget 2004 worksheet is moved before the Budget 2003 worksheet:
Worksheets("Budget 2004").Move Before:=Worksheets("Budget 2003")

Worksheet.Select—Selects the specified *Worksheet*.

Working with Range Objects

Mastering cell and range references is perhaps the most fundamental skill to learn when working with spreadsheets. After all, most worksheet chores involve cells, ranges, and range names. However, this skill takes on added importance when you're dealing with VBA procedures. When you're editing a worksheet directly, you can easily select cells and ranges with the mouse or the keyboard, or you can paste range names into formulas. In a procedure, though, you always have to describe—or even calculate—the range you want to work with.

What you describe is the most common of all Excel VBA objects: the Range object. A Range object can be a single cell, a row or column, a selection of cells, or a 3D range. The following sections look at various techniques that return a Range object, as well as a number of Range object properties and methods.

Returning a Range Object

Much of your VBA code will concern itself with Range objects of one kind or another. Therefore, you need to be well-versed in the various techniques that are available for returning range objects, whether they're single cells, rectangular ranges, or entire rows and columns. This section takes you through each of these techniques.

Using the Range Method

The Range method is the most straightforward way to identify a cell or range. It has two syntaxes. The first requires only a single argument:

```
Worksheet.Range(Name)
```

> *Worksheet*   The Worksheet object to which the Range method applies. If you omit *Worksheet*, VBA assumes the method applies to the ActiveSheet object.
>
> *Name*   A range reference or name entered as text.

For example, the following statements enter a date in cell B2 and then create a data series in the range B2:B13 of the active worksheet (I'll discuss the Formula and DataSeries methods in more detail later):

```
Range("B2").Value = #01/01/95#
Range("B2:B13").DataSeries Type:=xlDate, Date:=xlMonth
```

The Range method also works with named ranges. For example, the following statement clears the contents of a range named Criteria in the Data worksheet:

```
Worksheets("Data").Range("Criteria").ClearContents
```

The second syntax for the Range method requires two arguments:

```
Worksheet.Range(Cell1, Cell2)
```

> *Worksheet*   The Worksheet object to which the Range method applies. If you omit *Worksheet*, VBA assumes that the method applies to the ActiveSheet object.
>
> *Cell1, Cell2*   The cells that define the upper-left corner (*Cell1*) and lower-right corner (*Cell2*) of the range. Each can be a cell address as text, a Range object consisting of a single cell, or an entire column or row.

The advantage of this syntax is that it separates the range corners into individual arguments. This lets you modify each corner under procedural control. For example, you could set up variables named upperLeft and lowerRight and then return Range objects of different sizes:

```
Range(upperLeft,lowerRight)
```

Using the Cells Method

The Cells method returns a single cell as a Range object. Here's the syntax:

```
Object.Cells(RowIndex, ColumnIndex)
```

Object	A Worksheet or Range object. If you omit *Object*, the method applies to the ActiveSheet object.
RowIndex	The row number of the cell. If *Workbook* is a worksheet, a *RowIndex* of 1 refers to row 1 on the sheet. If *Object* is a range, *RowIndex* 1 refers to the first row of the range.
ColumnIndex	The column of the cell. You can enter a letter as text or a number. If *Object* is a worksheet, a *ColumnIndex* of "A" or 1 refers to column A on the sheet. If *Object* is a range, *ColumnIndex* "A" or 1 refers to the first column of the range.

tip

You also can refer to a cell by enclosing an A1-style reference in square brackets ([]). For example, the following statement clears the comments from cell C4 of the active worksheet:

```
ActiveSheet.[C4].ClearComments
```

For example, the following procedure fragment loops five times and enters the values Field1 through Field5 in cells A1 through E1:

```
For colNumber = 1 To 5
    Cells(1, colNumber).Value = "Field" & colNumber
Next colNumber
```

Returning a Row

If you need to work with entire rows or columns, VBA has several methods and properties you can use. In each case, the object returned is a Range.

The most common way to refer to a row in VBA is to use the Rows method. This method uses the following syntax:

Object.Rows(*Index*)

Object	The Worksheet or Range object to which the method applies. If you omit *Object*, VBA uses the ActiveSheet object.
Index	The row number. If *Object* is a worksheet, an *Index* of 1 refers to row 1 on the sheet. If *Object* is a range, an *Index* of 1 refers to the first row of the range. If you omit *Index*, the method returns a collection of all the rows in *Object*.

For example, Listing 8.4 shows a procedure named InsertRangeRow. This procedure inserts a new row before the last row of whatever range is passed as an argument (rangeObject). This would be a useful subroutine in programs that need to maintain ranges (such as an Excel list).

LISTING 8.4   A Procedure that Uses the Rows Method to Insert a Row Before the Last Row of a Range

```
Sub InsertRangeRow(rangeObject As Range)
    Dim totalRows As Integer, lastRow As Integer
    With rangeObject
        totalRows = .Rows.Count              ' Total rows in the range
        lastRow = .Rows(totalRows).Row       ' Last row number
        .Rows(lastRow).Insert                ' Insert before last row
    End With
End Sub


Sub InsertTest()
    InsertRangeRow ThisWorkbook.Worksheets("Sheet1").Range("Test")
End Sub
```

After declaring the variables, the first statement uses the Rows method without the *Index* argument to return a collection of all the rows in rangeObject and uses the Count property to get the total number of rangeObject rows:

totalRows = rangeObject.Rows.Count

The second statement uses the totalRows variable as an argument in the Rows method to return the last row of rangeObject, and then the Row property returns the row number:

lastRow = rangeObject.Rows(totalRows).Row

Finally, the last statement uses the Insert method to insert a row before lastRow. (You'll learn about the Insert method a bit later in the section titled "More Range Object Methods.")

To use InsertRangeRow, you need to pass a Range object to the procedure. For example, the InsertRange procedure shown at the end of Listing 8.4 inserts a row into a range named Test.

Returning a Column

To return a column, use the Columns method. The syntax for this method is almost identical to the Rows method:

Object.Columns(Index)

Object | The Worksheet or Range object to which the method applies. If you omit Object, VBA uses the ActiveSheet object.

Index | The column number. If Object is a worksheet, an Index of "A" or 1 refers to column A on the sheet. If Object is a range, Index "A" or 1 refers to the first column of the range. If you omit Index, the method returns a collection of all the columns in Object.

For example, the following statement sets the width of column B on the active worksheet to 20:

Columns("B").ColumnWidth = 20

Using the Offset Method

When defining your Range objects, you often won't know the specific range address to use. For example, you might need to refer to the cell that's two rows down and one column to the right of the active cell. You could find out the address of the active cell and then calculate the address of the other cell, but VBA gives you an easier (and more flexible) way: the Offset method. Offset returns a

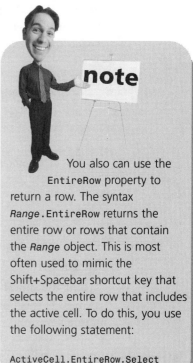

You also can use the EntireRow property to return a row. The syntax Range.EntireRow returns the entire row or rows that contain the Range object. This is most often used to mimic the Shift+Spacebar shortcut key that selects the entire row that includes the active cell. To do this, you use the following statement:

ActiveCell.EntireRow.Select

The syntax Range.EntireColumn returns the entire column or columns that contain the specified Range object.

`Range` object that is offset from a specified range by a certain number of rows and columns. Here is its syntax:

`Range.Offset(RowOffset, ColumnOffset)`

Range	The original `Range` object.
RowOffset	The number of rows to offset *Range*. You can use a positive number (to move down), a negative number (to move up), or 0 (to use the same rows). If you omit *RowOffset*, VBA uses 0.
ColumnOffset	The number of columns to offset *Range*. Again, you can use a positive number (to move right), a negative number (to move left), or 0 (to use the same columns). If you omit *ColumnOffset*, VBA uses 0.

For example, the following statement formats the range B2:D6 as bold:

`Range("A1:C5").Offset(1,1).Font.Bold = True`

Listing 8.5 shows a procedure called `ConcatenateStrings` that concatenates two text strings. This is handy, for instance, if you have a list with separate first and last name fields and you want to combine them.

LISTING 8.5   A Procedure that Uses the `Offset` Method to Concatenate Two Text Strings

```
Sub ConcatenateStrings()
    Dim string1 As String, string2 As String
    '
    ' Store the contents of the cell 2 to the left of the active cell
    '
    string1 = ActiveCell.Offset(0, -2)
    '
    ' Store the contents of the cell 1 to the left of the active cell
    '
    string2 = ActiveCell.Offset(0, -1)
    '
    ' Enter combined strings (separated by a space) into active cell
    '
    ActiveCell.Value = string1 & " " & string2
End Sub
```

The procedure begins by declaring `string1` and `string2`. The next statement stores in `string1` the contents of the cell two columns to the left of the active cell by using the

`Offset` method as follows:

```
String1 = ActiveCell.Offset(0, -2)
```

Similarly, the next statement stores in `String2` the contents of the cell one column to the left of the active cell. Finally, the last statement combines `String1` and `String2` (with a space in between) and stores the new string in the active cell.

Selecting a Cell or Range

VBA lets you access objects directly without having to select them first. This means that your VBA procedures rarely have to select a range. For example, even if, say, cell A1 is currently selected, the following statement will set the font in the range B1:B10 without changing the selected cell:

```
Range("B1:B10").Font.Name = "Times New
Roman"
```

However, there are times when you do need to select a range. For example, you might need to display a selected range to the user. To select a range, use the `Select` method:

```
Range.Select
```

> *Range*   The `Range` object you want to select.

For example, the following statement selects the range A1:E10 in the Sales worksheet:

```
Worksheets("Sales").Range("A1:E10").Select
```

> **tip**
>
> To return a `Range` object that represents the currently selected range, use the `Selection` property. For example, the following statement applies the Times New Roman font to the currently selected range:
>
> ```
> Selection.Font.Name = "Times
> New Roman"
> ```

Defining a Range Name

In Excel VBA, range names are `Name` objects. To define them, you use the `Add` method for the `Names` collection (which is usually the collection of defined names in a workbook). Here is an abbreviated syntax for the `Names` collection's `Add` method (this method has 11 arguments; see the VBA Reference in the Help system):

```
Names.Add(Text, RefersTo)
```

> *Text*   The text you want to use as the range name.
>
> *RefersTo*   The item to which you want the name to refer. You can enter a constant, a formula as text (such as "=Sales-Expenses"), or a worksheet reference (such as "Sales!A1:C6").

For example, the following statement adds the range name `SalesRange` to the `Names` collection of the active workbook:

```
ActiveWorkbook.Names.Add _
    Text:="SalesRange", _
    RefersTo:="=Sales!$A$1$C$6"
```

More Range Object Properties

Some of the examples you've seen in the last few sections have used various `Range` object properties. Here's a review of a few more properties you're likely to use most often in your VBA code:

Range.`Address`—Returns the address, as text, of the specified *Range*.

Range.`Column`—Returns the number of the first column in the specified *Range*.

Range.`Count`—Returns the number of cells in the specified *Range*.

Range.`CurrentRegion`—Returns a `Range` object that represents the entire region in which the specified *Range* resides. A range's "region" is the area surrounding the range that is bounded by at least one empty row above and below and at least one empty column to the left and the right.

Range.`Formula`—Returns or sets a formula for the specified *Range*.

Range.`FormulaArray`—Returns or sets an array formula for the specified *Range*.

Range.`NumberFormat`—Returns or sets the numeric format in the specified *Range*. Enter the format you want to use as a string, as shown in the following statement:

```
Worksheets("Analysis").Range("Sales").NumberFormat = _
    "$#,##0.00_);[Red]($#,##0.00)"
```

Range.`Row`—Returns the number of the first row in the specified *Range*.

Range.`Value`—Returns or sets the value in the specified *Range*.

More Range Object Methods

Here's a look at a few more methods that should come in handy in your VBA procedures:

Range.`Cut`—Cuts the specified *Range* to the Clipboard or to a new destination. The `Cut` method uses the following syntax:

```
Range.Cut(Destination)
```

Range	The `Range` object to cut.
Destination	The cell or range where you want the cut range to be pasted.

For example, the following statement cuts the range A1:B3 and moves it to the range B4:C6:

```
Range("A1:B3").Cut Destination:=Range("B4")
```

*Range.*Copy—Copies the specified *Range* to the Clipboard or to a new destination. Copying a range is similar to cutting a range. Here's the syntax for the Copy method:

```
Range.Copy(Destination)
```

Range	The range to copy.
Destination	The cell or range where you want the copied range to be pasted.

*Range.*Clear—Removes everything from the specified *Range* (contents, formats, and comments).

*Range.*ClearComments—Removes the cell comments for the specified *Range.*

*Range.*ClearContents—Removes the contents of the specified *Range.*

*Range.*ClearFormats—Removes the formatting for the specified *Range.*

*Range.*DataSeries—Creates a data series in the specified *Range.* The DataSeries method uses the following syntax:

```
Range.DataSeries(Rowcol, Type, Date, Step, Stop, Trend)
```

Range	The range to use for the data series.
Rowcol	Use xlRows to enter the data in rows, or xlColumns to enter the data in columns. If you omit *Rowcol*, Excel uses the size and shape of *Range.*
Type	The type of series. Enter xlLinear (the default), xlGrowth, xlChronological, or xlAutoFill.
Date	The type of date series, if you used xlChronological for the *Type* argument. Your choices are xlDay (the default), xlWeekday, xlMonth, or xlYear.
Step	The step value for the series (the default value is 1).
Stop	The stop value for the series. If you omit *Stop,* Excel fills the range.
Trend	Use True to create a linear or growth trend series. Use False (the default) to create a standard series.

*Range.*FillDown—Uses the contents and formatting from the top row of the specified *Range* to fill down into the rest of the range.

*Range.*FillLeft—Uses the contents and formatting from the rightmost column of the specified *Range* to fill left into the rest of the range.

Range.FillRight—Uses the contents and formatting from the leftmost column of the specified *Range* to fill right into the rest of the range.

Range.FillUp—Uses the contents and formatting from the bottom row of the specified *Range* to fill up into the rest of the range.

Range.Insert—Inserts cells into the specified *Range* using the following syntax:

Range.Insert(*Shift*)

Range	The range into which you want to insert the cells.
Shift	The direction you want to shift the existing cells. Use either xlShiftToRight or xlShiftDown. If you omit this argument, Excel determines the direction based on the shape of *Range*.

Range.Resize—Resizes the specified *Range*. Here's the syntax for this method:

Range.Resize(*RowSize*, *ColSize*)

Range	The range to resize.
RowSize	The number of rows in the new range.
ColSize	The number of columns in the new range.

For example, suppose you use the InsertRangeRow procedure from Listing 8.4 to insert a row into a named range. In most cases, you'll want to redefine the range name so that it includes the extra row you added. Listing 8.6 shows a procedure that calls InsertRangeRow and then uses the Resize method to adjust the named range.

LISTING 8.6   A Procedure that Uses Resize to Adjust a Named Range

```
Sub InsertAndRedefineName()
    With ThisWorkbook.Worksheets("Test Data")
        InsertRangeRow .Range("Test")
        With .Range("Test")
            Names.Add _
                Name:="Test", _
                RefersTo:=.Resize(.Rows.Count + 1)
        End With
        .Range("Test").Select
End Sub
```

In the Names.Add method, the new range is given by the expression .Resize(.Rows.Count + 1). Here, the Resize method returns a range that has one more row than the Test range.

THE ABSOLUTE MINIMUM

This chapter showed you how to use VBA to manipulate Excel. You began by examining the Application object, where you learned how to access Excel's worksheet functions and saw a few useful Application object methods. Next you learned about Workbook objects, from specifying them to opening them to creating new ones. From there you tackled a few Workbook properties and methods. Worksheet objects came next, and you saw how to specify them and create them, as well as use their more common properties and methods. Finally, you learned about the most common Excel object, the Range, where you saw various methods for specifying ranges as well as numerous properties and methods that should prove useful.

Here are some chapters to check out for related information:

- For a general discussion of VBA objects, see Chapter 5, "Working with Objects."

- Some VBA functions perform the same tasks as some Excel worksheet functions. To find out which ones, see Appendix B, "VBA Functions."

9

PROGRAMMING POWERPOINT

This chapter shows you how to leverage your VBA knowledge in the PowerPoint environment by examining a few PowerPoint objects and their associated properties, methods, and events. To illustrate these items, I'll build an example presentation strictly by using VBA code.

PowerPoint's Application Object

Chapter 5, "Working with Objects," ran through some Application object properties and methods that are common to all VBA-enabled applications. You've also seen in the last two chapters how Word and Excel have a few unique Application object members. PowerPoint's Application object has just a few unique properties and no unique methods. Here's a list of some of PowerPoint's unique properties:

ActivePresentation—Returns a Presentation object that represents the presentation file that currently has the focus within PowerPoint. See "PowerPoint's Presentation Object" later in this chapter to learn about the properties and methods of the Presentation object.

ActivePrinter—Returns or sets the name of the active printer. (Note that to set the active printer, you must specify the name of an existing Windows printer.) The following statement sets the active printer:

```
ActivePrinter = "HP LaserJet 5P/5MP PostScript local on LPT1:"
```

Presentations—Returns the Presentations object, which is the collection of all open presentations.

SlideShowWindows—Returns the SlideShowWindows object, which is the collection of all open slide show windows.

PowerPoint's Presentation Object

In PowerPoint, the Presentation object represents a presentation file (.PPT) that is open in the PowerPoint application window. You can use VBA to create new presentations, open or delete existing presentations, save and close presentations, and more. The next section takes you through various techniques for specifying presentations in your VBA code; then we'll look at some Presentation object properties and methods.

Specifying a Presentation Object

If you need to do something with a presentation, or if you need to work with an object contained in a specific presentation (such as a slide), you need to tell PowerPoint which presentation you want to use. VBA gives you three ways to do this:

Use the Presentations object—The Presentations object is the collection of all open presentation files. To specify a particular presentation, either use its index number (where 1 represents the first presentation opened) or enclose the presentation filename in quotation marks. For example, if `Proposal.ppt` were the first presentation opened, the following two statements would be equivalent:

```
Presentations(1)
Presentations("Proposal.ppt")
```

Use the `ActivePresentation` object—The `ActivePresentation` object represents the presentation that currently has the focus.

Use the `Presentation` property—Open slide show windows have a `Presentation` property that returns the name of the underlying presentation. For example, the following statement uses the `currPres` variable to store the name of the presentation in the first slide show window:

```
currPres = SlideShowWindows(1).Presentation
```

Opening a Presentation

To open a presentation file, use the `Open` method of the `Presentations` collection. The `Open` method has several arguments you can use to fine-tune your presentation openings, but only one of these is mandatory. Here's the simplified syntax showing the one required argument (for the rest of the arguments, look up the `Open` method in the VBA Help system):

```
Presentations.Open(FileName)
```

> *FileName* The full name of the presentation file, including the drive and folder that contain the file.

For example, to open a presentation named `Proposal.ppt` in the C:\My Documents folder, you would use the following statement:

```
Presentations.Open "C:\My Documents\Proposal.ppt"
```

Creating a New Presentation

If you need to create a new presentation, use the `Presentations` collection's `Add` method:

```
Presentations.Add(WithWindow)
```

WithWindow is a Boolean value that determines whether or not the presentation is created in a visible window. Use True for a visible window (this is the default); use False to hide the window.

Presentation Object Properties

Here's a list of a few common properties associated with `Presentation` objects:

`Presentation.FullName`—Returns the full pathname of the specified `Presentation`. The full pathname includes the presentation's path (the drive and folder in which the file resides) and the filename.

`Presentation.Name`—Returns the filename of the `Presentation`.

`Presentation.Path`—Returns the path of the `Presentation` file.

NO PATH?

A new, unsaved presentation's `Path` property returns an empty string (" ").

`Presentation.Saved`—Determines whether changes have been made to the specified `Presentation` since it was last saved.

`Presentation.SlideMaster`—Returns a `Master` object that represents the slide master for the specified `Presentation`.

`Presentation.Slides`—Returns a `Slides` object that represents the collection of `Slide` objects contained in the specified `Presentation`.

`Presentation.SlideShowSettings`—Returns a `SlideShowSettings` object that represents the slide show setup options for the specified `Presentation`.

`Presentation.TitleMaster`—Returns a `Master` object that represents the title master for the specified `Presentation`.

Presentation Object Methods

A `Presentation` object has methods that let you save the presentation, close it, print it, and more. Here are the methods you'll use most often:

`Presentation.ApplyTemplate`—Applies a design template to the specified `Presentation`. This method uses the following syntax:

`Presentation.ApplyTemplate(FileName)`

Presentation	The `Presentation` object to which you want to apply the template.
FileName	The full name of the template (.POT) file.

For example, the following statement applies the Dads Tie template to the active presentation:

```
ActivePresentation.ApplyTemplate _
    "C:\Microsoft Office\Templates\Presentation Designs\Dads Tie.pot"
```

Presentation.Close—Closes the specified *Presentation*. If the file has unsaved changes, PowerPoint will ask the user if he or she wants to save those changes.

Presentation.NewWindow—Opens a new window for the specified *Presentation*.

Presentation.PrintOut—Prints the specified *Presentation* using the following syntax:
Presentation.PrintOut(*From, To, PrintToFile, Copies, Collate*)

Presentation	The Presentation object you want to print.
From	The page number from which to start printing.
To	The page number of the last page to print.
PrintToFile	The name of a file to which you want the presentation printed.
Copies	The number of copies to print. The default value is 1.
Collate	If this argument is True and *Copies* is greater than 1, VBA collates the copies.

Presentation.Save—Saves the specified *Presentation*. If the presentation is new, use the SaveAs method instead.

Presentation.SaveAs—Saves the specified *Presentation* to a different file. Here's the syntax for the SaveAs method:
Presentation.SaveAs(*FileName, FileFormat, EmbedTrueTypeFonts*)

Presentation	The Presentation object you want to save to a different file.
FileName	The full name of the new presentation file, including the drive and folder where you want the file to reside.
FileFormat	The PowerPoint format to use for the new file. Use one of the predefined ppSaveAs constants (such as ppSaveAsPresentation or ppSaveAsHTML).
EmbedTrueTypeFonts	If True, PowerPoint embeds the presentation's TrueType fonts in the new file.

The Juggling Application

Throughout this chapter, I'll put the PowerPoint objects, methods, and properties that we talk about to good use in an application that builds an entire presentation from scratch. This presentation will consist of a series of slides that provide instructions on how to juggle.

The code for the application consists of six procedures:

Main—This procedure ties the entire application together by calling each of the other procedures in the module.

CreateJugglingPresentation—This procedure creates a new Presentation object and saves it.

AddJugglingSlides—This procedure adds the slides to the presentation and then formats them.

SetUpStartPage—This procedure adds and formats text for the presentation title page.

SetUpJugglingPages—This procedure adds and formats a title, picture, and instruction text for each of the four pages that explain how to juggle.

RunJugglingSlideShow—This procedure asks the user if he or she wants to run the slide show and then runs it if Yes is chosen.

To get started, Listing 9.1 shows the Main procedure.

LISTING 9.1 This Procedure Ties Everything Together by Calling Each of the Code Listings Individually

```
' Global variable
Dim pres As Presentation

Sub Main()
    '
    ' Create the presentation file
    '
    CreateJugglingPresentation
    '
    ' Add the slides
    '
    AddJugglingSlides
    '
    ' Set up the title page
    '
    SetUpStartPage
    '
```

LISTING 9.1 (continued)

```
' Set up the Juggling pages
'
SetUpJugglingPages
'
' Save it and then run it
'
pres.Save
RunJugglingSlideShow
End Sub
```

First, the pres variable is declared as a Presentation object. Notice that this variable is defined at the top of the module, *before* any of the procedures. When you define a variable like this, it means that it can be used in all the procedures in the module. Then Main begins by calling the CreateJugglingPresentation procedure, shown in Listing 9.2. From there, the other procedures (discussed later in this chapter) are called, and the presentation is saved.

LISTING 9.2 This Procedure Creates a New Presentation and then Saves It

```
Sub CreateJugglingPresentation()
    Dim p As Presentation
    '
    ' If the old one is still open, close it without saving
    '
    For Each p In Presentations
        If p.Name = "Juggling" Then
            p.Saved = True
            p.Close
        End If
    Next p
    '
    ' Create a new Presentation object and store it in pres
    '
    Set pres = Presentations.Add
    pres.SaveAs FileName:="Juggling.ppt"
End Sub
```

A `For Each...Next` loop runs through each open presentation and checks the `Name` property. If it equals `Juggling.ppt`, we know the file is already open. If it's open (say, from running the application previously), the procedure closes it without saving it. The `pres` variable is `Set` and then the presentation is saved using the `SaveAs` method.

Working with PowerPoint `Slide` Objects

The presentation and code used in this chapter's sample application can be found on my Web site at the following address:

```
http://www.mcfedries.com/ABGVBA/
Chapter09.ppt
```

PowerPoint presentations consist of a series of slides. In PowerPoint VBA, a slide is a `Slide` object that contains a number of properties and methods that you can wield in your code. These include options for setting the slide's layout, specifying the transition effect, and copying and deleting slides. The next few sections discuss these and other slide techniques.

Specifying a Slide

To work with a slide, you need to specify a `Slide` object. For a single slide, the easiest way to do this is to use the `Slides` object. `Slides` is the collection of all the slides in a particular presentation. To specify a slide, either use the slide's index number (where 1 represents the first slide in the presentation, 2 the second slide, and so on), or enclose the slide name in quotation marks. For example, if Slide1 is the first slide, the following two statements would be equivalent:

```
ActivePresentation.Slides(1)
ActivePresentation.Slides("Slide1")
```

If you need to work with multiple slides (say, to apply a particular layout to all the slides), use the `Range` method of the `Slides` object:

Presentation`.Slides.Range(`*Index*`)`

Presentation	The `Presentation` object that contains the slides.
Index	An array that specifies the slides.

For the *Index* argument, use VBA's `Array` function with multiple instances of slide index numbers or slide names. For example, the following statement specifies the slides named Slide1 and Slide2:

```
ActivePresentation.Slides.Range
(Array("Slide1","Slide2"))
```

Creating a New Slide

After you've created a presentation, you need to populate it with slides. To insert a new `Slide` object into a presentation, use the `Add` method of the `Slides` collection:

```
Presentation.Slides.Add(Index, Layout)
```

> **tip**
>
> To work with every slide in the presentation, use the `Range` method without an argument, as in this example:
>
> ```
> ActivePresentation.
> Slides.Range
> ```
>
> You can also use the `Presentation` object's `SlideMaster` property to work with the slide master. This will change the default settings for every slide in the presentation.

Presentation	The `Presentation` object in which you want to add the slide.
Index	The index number of the new slide within the `Slides` object. Use 1 to make this the first slide; use `Slides.Count + 1` to make this the last slide.
Layout	A constant that specifies the layout of the new slide. PowerPoint defines over two dozen constants, including `ppLayoutText` (for a text-only slide), `ppLayoutChart` (for a chart slide), `ppLayoutBlank` (for a blank slide). Look up the `Add` method in the VBA Help system to see the full list of constants.

The following statements add an organization chart slide to the end of the active presentation:

```
With ActivePresentation.Slides
    .Add Index:=.Count + 1, Layout:=ppLayoutOrgchart
End With
```

Inserting Slides from a File

Instead of creating slides from scratch, you might prefer to pilfer one or more slides from an existing presentation. The `InsertFromFile` method lets you do this. It uses the following syntax:

Presentation.Slides.InsertFromFile(*FileName*, *Index*, *SlideStart*, *SlideEnd*)

Presentation	The Presentation object in which you want to add the slides.
FileName	The name of the file (including the drive and folder) that contains the slides you want to insert.
Index	The index number of an existing slide in *Presentation*. The slides from *FileName* will be inserted after this slide.
SlideStart	The index number of the first slide in *FileName* that you want to insert.
SlideEnd	The index number of the last slide in *FileName* that you want to insert.

For example, the following procedure fragment inserts the first five slides from Budget.ppt at the end of the active presentation:

```
With ActivePresentation.Slides
    .InsertFromFile _

FileName:="C:\Presentations\Budget.ppt", _
        Index:=.Count, _
        SlideStart:=1, _
        SlideEnd:=5
End With
```

Slide **Object Properties**

To let you change the look and feel of your slides, PowerPoint VBA offers a number of Slide object properties. These properties control the slide's layout, background, color scheme, name, and more. This section runs through a few of the more useful Slide object properties.

note

If you specify multiple slides using the Range method described earlier, PowerPoint returns a SlideRange object that references the slides. This object has the same properties and methods as a Slide object, so you can work with multiple slides the same way that you work with a single slide.

Slide.Background—Returns or sets the background of the specified Slide. Note that this property actually returns a ShapeRange object. (See "Dealing with Shape Objects" later in this chapter.)

You normally use this property with the slide master to set the background for all the slides in the presentation. For example, the following statements store the slide master background in a variable and then use the Shape object's Fill property to change the background pattern for all the slides in the active presentation:

```
Set slideBack = ActivePresentation.SlideMaster.Background
slideBack.Fill.PresetGradient _
    Style:=msoGradientHorizontal, _
    Variant:=1, _
    PresetGradientType:=msoGradientFire
```

If you just want to change the background for a single slide, you must first set the slide's FollowMasterBackground property to False, like so:

```
With ActivePresentation.Slides(1)
    .FollowMasterBackground = False
    .Background.Fill.PresetGradient _
        Style:=msoGradientHorizontal, _
        Variant:=1, _
        PresetGradientType:=msoGradientFire
End With
```

Slide.FollowMasterBackground—As mentioned earlier, this property returns or sets whether or not the specified *Slide* uses the same Background property as the slide master. Set this property to False to set a unique background for an individual slide.

Slide.Layout—Returns or sets the layout for the specified *Slide*. Again, see the VBA Help system for the full list of layout constants.

Slide.Master—Returns the slide master for the specified *Slide*. The following two statements are equivalent:

```
ActivePresentation.SlideMaster
ActivePresentation.Slides(1).Master
```

Slide.Name—Returns or sets the name of the specified *Slide*.

Slide.Shapes—Returns a Shapes collection that represents all the Shape objects on the specified *Slide*.

Slide.SlideShowTransition—Returns a SlideShowTransition object that represents the transition special effects used for the specified *Slide* during a slide show.

The Juggling Application: Creating the Slides

Listing 9.3 shows the AddJugglingSlides procedure, which adds four slides to the Juggling presentation (represented, remember, by the pres variable) and then uses the SlideMaster object to set the default background for the slides.

LISTING 9.3   A Procedure That Adds the Slides to the Juggling Presentation and Formats Them

```
Sub AddJugglingSlides()
    Dim i As Integer

    With pres
        With .Slides
            '
            ' Add the opening slide
            '
            .Add(Index:=1, Layout:=ppLayoutTitle).Name = "Opener"
            '
            ' Now add the slides for each step
            '
            For i = 1 To 4
                .Add(Index:=i + 1, Layout:=ppLayoutTitle).Name = _
                               "Juggling" & i
            Next i
        End With
        '
        ' Set the background for all the slides
        '
        .SlideMaster.Background.Fill.PresetGradient _
            Style:=msoGradientHorizontal, _
            Variant:=1, _
            PresetGradientType:=msoGradientNightfall
    End With
End Sub
```

`Slide` Object Methods

PowerPoint VBA defines a few `Slide` object methods that let you cut, copy, paste, duplicate, export, select, and delete slides. I don't expect that you'll use these methods very often, so I won't discuss them in detail here. All are straightforward, however, so you should be able to figure them out from the VBA Help system.

Dealing with Shape Objects

PowerPoint slides are really just a collection of objects: titles, text boxes, pictures, labels, lines, curves, and so on. In PowerPoint VBA, each of these items is a `Shape` object. Therefore, in order to get full slide control in your VBA procedures, you must know how to add, edit, format, and otherwise manipulate these objects. That's the goal of this section.

Specifying a Shape

You have to specify a `Shape` object before you can work with it. The techniques you use for this are similar to those I outlined earlier for `Slide` objects.

For a single shape, use the `Shapes` object, which is the collection of all `Shape` objects on a particular slide. To specify a shape, either use the shape's index number (where 1 represents the first shape added to the slide, 2 is the second shape, and so on), or enclose the shape name in quotation marks. For example, if Rectangle 1 is the first shape, the following two statements would be equivalent:

```
ActivePresentation.Shapes(1)
ActivePresentation.Shapes("Rectangle 1")
```

If you need to work with multiple shapes, use the `Range` method of the `Shapes` object:

Slide`.Shapes.Range(`*Index*`)`

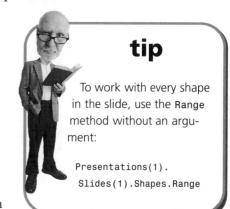

<table>
<tr><td>*Slide*</td><td>The `Slide` object that contains the shapes.</td></tr>
<tr><td>*Index*</td><td>An array that specifies the shapes.</td></tr>
</table>

tip

To work with every shape in the slide, use the `Range` method without an argument:

```
Presentations(1).
Slides(1).Shapes.Range
```

As with multiple slides, use VBA's `Array` function for the *Index* argument, like so:

```
Presentations(1).Slides(1).Shapes.Range(Array("Oval 1","TextBox 2"))
```

Adding Shapes to a Slide

The `Slides` object has 14 different methods you can use to insert shapes into a slide. Many of these methods use similar arguments, so before listing the methods, let's take a quick tour of the common arguments:

<table>
<tr><td>*BeginX*</td><td>For connectors and lines, the distance (in points) from the shape's starting point to the left edge of the slide window.</td></tr>
<tr><td>*BeginY*</td><td>For connectors and lines, the distance (in points) from the shape's starting point to the top edge of the slide window.</td></tr>
</table>

EndX	For connectors and lines, the distance (in points) from the shape's ending point to the left edge of the slide window.
EndY	For connectors and lines, the distance (in points) from the shape's ending point to the top edge of the slide window.
FileName	The path and name of the file used to create the shape (such as a picture or an OLE object).
Height	The height of the shape (in points).
Left	The distance (in points) of the left edge of the shape from the left edge of the slide window.
Orientation	The orientation of text within a label or text box. For horizontal text use the constant `msoTextOrientationHorizontal`; for vertical text use the constant `msoTextOrientationVerticalFarEast`.
SafeArrayOfPoints	For curves and polylines, this is an array of coordinate pairs that specifies the vertices and control points for the object.
Top	The distance (in points) of the top edge of the shape from the top edge of the slide window.
Width	The width of the shape (in points).

Here's a list of the `Shapes` object methods and arguments that you can use to create shapes:

`Slide.Shapes.AddComment`—Adds a comment to the specified `Slide` using the following syntax:

`Slide.Shapes.AddComment(Left, Top, Width, Height)`

`Slide.Shapes.AddConnector`—Adds a connector to the specified `Slide` using the following syntax:

`Slide.Shapes.AddConnector(Type, BeginX, BeginY, EndX, EndY)`

Type	A constant that specifies the connector type:

Type	Connector
`msoConnectorCurve`	A curved connector
`msoConnectorElbow`	A connector with an elbow
`msoConnectorStraight`	A straight connector

Slide.Shapes.AddCurve—Adds a curved line to the specified *Slide* using the following syntax:

Slide.Shapes.AddCurve(*SafeArrayOfPoints*)

Slide.Shapes.AddLabel—Adds a label to the specified *Slide* using the following syntax:

Slide.Shapes.AddLabel(*Orientation, Left, Top, Width, Height*)

Slide.Shapes.AddLine—Adds a straight line to the specified *Slide* using the following syntax:

Slide.Shapes.AddLine(*BeginX, BeginY, EndX, EndY*)

Slide.Shapes.AddMediaObject—Adds a multimedia file to the specified *Slide* using the following syntax:

Slide.Shapes.AddMediaObject(*FileName, Left, Top, Width, Height*)

Slide.Shapes.AddPicture—Adds a graphic to the specified *Slide* using the following syntax:

Slide.Shapes.AddPicture(*FileName, LinkToFile, SaveWithDocument, Left, Top, Width, Height*)

Here's a summary of the extra arguments used in this method:

LinkToFile	Set this argument to True to set up a link to the original file. If this argument is False, an independent copy of the picture is stored in the slide.
SaveWithDocument	Set this argument to True to save the picture with the presentation. Note that this argument must be True if *LinkToFile* is False.

The AddConnector method returns a Shape object that represents the new connector. You use this object's ConnectorFormat property to set up the beginning and ending points of the connector. In other words, you use the ConnectorFormat.BeginConnect and ConnectorFormat.EndConnect methods to specify the shapes attached to the connector.

I'll show you how to add text to a label and text box when we look at Shape object properties (see "Some Shape Object Properties").

`Slide.Shapes.AddPolyline`—Adds an open polyline or a closed polygon to the specified `Slide` using the following syntax:

`Slide.Shapes.AddPolyline(SafeArrayOfPoints)`

`Slide.Shapes.AddShape`—Adds an AutoShape to the specified `Slide` using the following syntax:

`Slide.Shapes.AddShape(Type, Left, Top, Width, Height)`

Here, the `Type` argument is a constant that specifies the AutoShape you want to add. PowerPoint VBA defines dozens of these constants. To see the full list, look up the `AutoShapeType` property in the VBA Help system.

`Slide.Shapes.AddTextbox`—Adds a text box to the specified *Slide* using the following syntax:

`Slide.Shapes.AddTextbox(Left, Top, Width, Height)`

`Slide.Shapes.AddTextEffect`—Adds a WordArt text effect to the specified `Slide` using the following syntax:

`Slide.Shapes.AddTextEffect(PresetTextEffect, Text, FontName,`
`➥FontSize, FontBold, FontItalic, Left, Top)`

Here's a summary of the extra arguments used in this method:

`PresetTextEffect`	A constant that specifies one of WordArt's preset text effects. Look up this method in the VBA Help system to see the few dozen constants that are available.
`Text`	The WordArt text.
`FontName`	The font applied to `Text`.
`FontSize`	The font size applied to `Text`.
`FontBold`	Set to True to apply bold to `Text`.
`FontItalic`	Set to True to apply italics to `Text`.

`Slide.Shapes.AddTitle`—Adds a title to the specified `Slide`. This method takes no arguments. However, be aware that the `AddTitle` method will raise an error if the slide already has a title. To check in advance, use the `HasTitle` property, as shown in the following example:

```
With ActivePresentation.Slides(1).Shapes
    If Not .HasTitle Then
        .AddTitle.TextFrame.TextRange.Text = "New Title"
    End If
End With
```

Some Shape Object Properties

PowerPoint VBA comes equipped with more than three dozen `Shape` object properties that control characteristics such as the dimensions and position of a shape, whether or not a shape displays a shadow, and the shape name. Let's take a quick look at a few of these properties:

`Shape.AnimationSettings`—This property returns an `AnimationSettings` object that represents the animation effects applied to the specified `Shape`. `AnimationSettings` contains various properties that apply special effects to the shape. Here's a sampler (see the VBA Help system for the complete list as well as the numerous constants that work with these properties):

- `AdvanceMode`—A constant that determines how the animation advances. There are two choices—automatically (in other words, after a preset amount of time; use `ppAdvanceOnTime`), or when the user clicks the slide (use `ppAdvanceOnClick`). For the latter, you can specify the amount of time by using the `AdvanceTime` property.

- `AfterEffect`—A constant that determines how the shape appears after the animation is complete.

- `Animate`—A Boolean value that turns the shape's animation on (True) or off (False).

- `AnimateTextInReverse`—When this Boolean value is True, PowerPoint builds the text animation in reverse order. For example, if the shape is a series of bullet points and this property is True, the animation displays the bullet points from last to first.

- `EntryEffect`—A constant that determines the special effect applied initially to the shape's animation. For example, you can make the shape fade in by using the `ppEffectFade` constant.

- `TextLevelEffect`—A constant that determines the paragraph level that gets animated.

- `TextUnitEffect`—A constant that determines how PowerPoint animates text: by paragraph, by word, or by letter.

`Shape.AutoShapeType`—For an `AutoShape` object, this property returns or sets the shape type for the specified `Shape`.

`Shape.Fill`—This property returns a `FillFormat` object that represents the fill formatting for the specified `Shape`. The `FillFormat` object defines numerous methods you can wield to apply a fill to a shape:

- `Background`—Sets the fill to match the slide's background.

- `OneColorGradient`—Sets the fill to a one-color gradient.

- `Patterned`—Sets the fill to a pattern.
- `PresetGradient`—A constant that sets the fill to one of PowerPoint's preset gradients.
- `PresetTextured`—A constant that sets the fill to one of PowerPoint's preset textures.
- `Solid`—Sets the fill to a solid color. After running this method, use the `Fill.ForeColor` property to set the fill color.
- `TwoColorGradient`—Sets the fill to a two-color gradient.
- `UserPicture`—Sets the fill to a graphics file that you specify.
- `UserTexture`—Sets the fill to a specified graphics image that gets tiled to cover the entire shape.

note

PowerPoint's color properties (such as `ForeColor`) return a `ColorFormat` object. This object represents either the color of a one-color object or the background or foreground color of an object with a pattern or gradient. To set a color, use the `ColorFormat` object's RGB property and VBA's RGB function to set a red-green-blue value, as in this example:

```
Shapes(1).Fill.Solid.ForeColor.
RGB = RGB(255,0,0)
```

Shape`.HasTextFrame`—A Boolean value that tells you if the specified *Shape* has a text frame (True) or not (False). See the `TextFrame` property, discussed later.

Shape`.Height`—Returns or sets the height, in points, for the specified *Shape*.

Shape`.Left`—Returns or sets the distance, in points, between the left edge of the bounding box of the specified *Shape* and the left edge of the presentation window.

Shape`.Name`—This property returns or sets the name for the specified *Shape*.

Shape`.Shadow`—This property returns a `ShadowFormat` object that represents the shadow for the specified *Shape*. The `ShadowFormat` object contains various properties that control the look of the shadow. For example, `Shadow.ForeColor` controls the shadow color and `Shadow.Visible` is a Boolean value that turns the shadow on (True) or off (False).

Shape`.TextEffectFormat`—For a WordArt object, this property returns a `TextEffectFormat` object that represents the text effects of the specified *Shape*.

Shape`.TextFrame`—This property returns a `TextFrame` object for the specified *Shape*. A text frame is an area within a shape that can hold text. The frame's text, as a whole, is represented by the `TextRange` object, and the actual text is given by the `Text` property of the `TextRange` object. This rather convoluted state of affairs means that you need to use the following property to a refer to a shape's text:

Shape`.TextFrame.TextRange.Text`

For example, the following statements add to the active presentation a new slide that contains only a title, and then they set the title text to 2004 Budget Proposal:

```
With ActivePresentation.Slides
    With .Add(1, ppLayoutTitleOnly).Shapes(1)
        .TextFrame.TextRange.Text = "2004 Budget Proposal"
    End With
End With
```

Also note that the `TextFrame` object has a number of other properties that control the text margins, orientation, word wrap, and more.

`Shape.Top`—Returns or sets the distance, in points, between the top edge of the bounding box of the specified `Shape` and the top edge of the presentation window.

`Shape.Visible`—A Boolean value that makes the specified `Shape` either visible (True) or invisible (False).

`Shape.Width`—Returns or sets the width, in points, for the specified `Shape`.

The Juggling Application: Creating the Title Page

To put some of these properties through their paces, Listing 9.4 shows the Juggling application's `SetUpStartPage` procedure.

LISTING 9.4   A Procedure That Sets Up the Text and Animation Settings for the First Page of the Juggling Presentation

```
Sub SetUpStartPage()
    Dim shapeTitle As Shape
    Dim shapeSubTitle As Shape

    With pres.Slides("Opener")
        Set shapeTitle = .Shapes(1)      ' The title
        Set shapeSubTitle = .Shapes(2)   ' The subtitle
        '
        ' Add the title text
        '
        With shapeTitle.TextFrame.TextRange
            .Text = "Juggling"
            With .Font
                .Name = "Arial"
                .Size = 44
                .Bold = True
                .Color.RGB = RGB(255, 255, 255)
```

LISTING 9.4 (continued)

```
            End With
        End With
        '
        ' Set the title animation
        '
        With shapeTitle.AnimationSettings
            .Animate = True
            .AdvanceMode = ppAdvanceOnTime
            .AdvanceTime = 0
            .TextUnitEffect = ppAnimateByCharacter
            .EntryEffect = ppEffectFlyFromLeft
        End With
        '
        ' Add the subtitle text
        '
        With shapeSubTitle.TextFrame.TextRange
            .Text = "A Step-By-Step Course"
            With .Font
                .Name = "Arial"
                .Size = 36
                .Bold = True
                .Color.RGB = RGB(255, 255, 255)
            End With
        End With
        '
        ' Set the subtitle animation
        '
        With shapeSubTitle.AnimationSettings
            .Animate = True
            .AdvanceMode = ppAdvanceOnTime
            .AdvanceTime = 0
            .TextUnitEffect = ppAnimateByWord
            .EntryEffect = ppEffectFlyFromBottom
        End With
    End With
End Sub
```

The first slide is named Opener, and this is the object used through most of the procedure. The shapeTitle variable is Set to the slide's title—Shapes(1)—and the shapeSubTitle variable is Set to the subtitle text box—Shapes(2).

From there, the title's `TextFrame` property is used to add and format the title text. Then its `AnimationSettings` property is used to animate the text. A similar sequence of code adds text, formatting, and animation to the subtitle.

Some `Shape` Object Methods

The `Shape` object comes with a number of methods that let you perform standard actions such as cutting, copying, pasting, and deleting. Here's a list of some other useful methods:

`Shape.Apply`—This method applies to the specified `Shape` the formatting that was captured from another shape using the `PickUp` method (described later).

`Shape.Duplicate`—This method makes a copy of the specified `Shape` in the same slide. The new shape is added to the `Shapes` object immediately after the specified `Shape`. Note, too, that this method returns a `Shape` object that refers to the new shape.

`Shape.Flip`—This method flips the specified `Shape` around its horizontal or vertical axis. Here's the syntax:

`Shape.Flip(FlipCmd)`

Shape	The `Shape` object you want to flip.
FlipCmd	A constant that determines how the shape is flipped. Use either `msoFlipHorizontal` or `msoFlipVertical`.

`Shape.IncrementLeft`—Moves the specified `Shape` horizontally using the following syntax:

`Shape.IncrementLeft(Increment)`

Shape	The `Shape` object you want to move.
Increment	The distance, in points, that you want the shape moved. Use a positive number to move the shape to the right; use a negative number to move the shape to the left.

`Shape.IncrementRotation`—Rotates the specified `Shape` around its z-axis using the following syntax:

`Shape.IncrementRotation(Increment)`

Shape	The `Shape` object you want to move.
Increment	The number of degrees you want the shape rotated. Use a positive number to rotate the shape clockwise; use a negative number to rotate the shape counterclockwise.

Shape.IncrementTop—Moves the specified *Shape* vertically using the following syntax:
Shape.IncrementTop(*Increment*)

Shape	The *Shape* object you want to move.
Increment	The distance, in points, that you want the shape moved. Use a positive number to move the shape down; use a negative number to move the shape up.

Shape.PickUp—Copies the formatting of the specified *Shape*. Use the *Apply* method (discussed earlier) to apply the copied formatting to a different object.

Shape.Select—This method selects the specified *Shape* using the following syntax:
Shape.Select(*Replace*)

Shape	The *Shape* object you want to select.
Replace	A Boolean value that either adds the shape to the current selection (False) or replaces the current selection (True). True is the default.

The Juggling Application: Creating the Instructions

To continue the Juggling application, the SetUpJugglingPages procedure, shown in Listing 9.5, is run. This procedure serves to set up the title, picture, and instruction text for each of the four instruction slides.

LISTING 9.5   A Procedure That Sets Up the Titles, Pictures, and Text Instructions for Each of the Juggling Slides

```
Sub SetUpJugglingPages()
    Dim thisPres As Presentation
    Dim slideTitle As Shape
    Dim slidePicture As Shape
    Dim slideText As Shape
    Dim i As Integer

    For i = 1 To 4
        With pres.Slides("Juggling" & i)
            '
            ' Get pictures from Chaptr09.ppt
            '
            Set thisPres = Presentations("Chaptr09.ppt")
            thisPres.Slides(1).Shapes(i + 1).Copy
            .Shapes.Paste
```

LISTING 9.5 (continued)

```
'
' Adjust the layout and then set the Shape variables
'
.Layout = ppLayoutObjectOverText
Set slideTitle = .Shapes(1)
Set slidePicture = .Shapes(2)
Set slideText = .Shapes(3)
'
' Add the title text
'
With slideTitle.TextFrame.TextRange
    Select Case i
        Case 1
            .Text = "Step 1: The Home Position"
        Case 2
            .Text = "Step 2: The First Throw"
        Case 3
            .Text = "Step 3: The Second Throw"
        Case 4
            .Text = "Step 4: The Third Throw"
    End Select
    With .Font
        .Name = "Arial"
        .Size = 44
        .Bold = True
        .Color.RGB = RGB(255, 255, 255)
    End With
End With
'
' Set the picture animation and shadow
'
With slidePicture
    With .AnimationSettings
        .Animate = True
        .AdvanceMode = ppAdvanceOnTime
        .AdvanceTime = 0
        .EntryEffect = ppEffectFade
    End With
    With .Shadow
        .ForeColor.RGB = RGB(0, 0, 0)
        .OffsetX = 10
        .OffsetY = 10
```

LISTING 9.5 (continued)

```
                .Visible = True
        End With
    End With
    '
    ' Add the instruction text
    '
    With slideText.TextFrame.TextRange
        Select Case i
        Case 1
        .Text = "Place two balls in your dominant hand, " & _
            "one in front of the other." & Chr(13) & _
            "Hold the third ball in your other hand." & _
            Chr(13) & _
            "Let your arms dangle naturally and bring " & _
            "your forearms parallel to the ground (as " & _
            "though you were holding a tray.)" & Chr(13) & _
            "Relax your shoulders, arms, and hands."
        Case 2
        .Text = "Of the two balls in your dominant hand, " & _
            "toss the front one towards your other hand " & _
            "in a smooth arc." & Chr(13) & _
            "Make sure the ball doesn't spin too much." & _
            Chr(13) & _
            "Make sure the ball goes no higher than " & _
            "about eye level."
        Case 3
        .Text = "Once the first ball reaches the top of " & _
            "its arc, toss the ball in your other hand." & _
            Chr(13) & _
            "Throw the ball towards your dominant hand, " & _
            "making sure it flies UNDER the first ball." & _
            Chr(13) & _
            "Again, try not to spin the ball and make " & _
            "sure it goes no higher than eye level."
        Case 4
        .Text = "Now for the tricky part (!). Soon " & _
            "after you release the second ball, the " & _
            "first ball will approach your hand. Go " & _
            "ahead and catch the first ball." & Chr(13) & _
            "When the second ball reaches its apex, " & _
            "throw the third ball (the remaining ball " & _
            "in your dominant hand) under it." & Chr(13) & _
```

LISTING 9.5 (continued)

```
                "At this point, it just becomes a game of " & _
                "catch-and-throw-under, catch-and-throw-" & _
                "under. Have fun!"
            End Select
            With .Font
                .Name = "Times New Roman"
                .Size = 24
                .Bold = False
                .Color.RGB = RGB(255, 255, 255)
            End With
        End With
    End With
    Next i

End Sub
```

A `For...Next` loop runs through each of the four instructional slides. (Recall that ear-lier, the `CreateJugglingSlides` procedure gave these slides the names Juggle1 through Juggle4.) Here's a summary of the various chores that are run within this loop:

- The first task is to load the pictures that illustrate each step. These pictures can be found on the slide in `Chaptr09.ppt`. To get them into the Juggling pres-entation, the code uses the `Copy` method to copy each one from `Chaptr09.ppt` to the Clipboard, and then it uses the `Paste` method to add the picture to the Juggling slide. When that's done, the slide's `Layout` property is set to `ppLayoutObjectOverText`, and the three variables that represent the three shapes on each slide are Set.

- Next, the title text is added. Here, a `Select Case` structure is used to add a dif-ferent title to each slide, and then the text is formatted.

- The picture is animated, and a shadow is added.

- The last chunk of code uses another `Select Case` to add the appropriate instructions for each slide, and then the instruction text is formatted.

Operating a Slide Show

With your presentation created and saved, slides added and set up, and shapes inserted and formatted, your file is just about ready to roll. All that remains is to add a few slide show settings and transition effects. This section shows you how to do that as well as how to run your slide show when it's complete.

Slide Show Transitions

Each Slide object has a `SlideShowTransition` property that determines how the slide advances during a slide show. This property is actually a `SlideShowTransitions` object, and you set up the transition effect by modifying this object's properties. Here's a list of the key properties:

`Slide.SlideShowTransition.AdvanceOnClick`—For the specified `Slide`, this property returns or sets whether or not the slide advances when it's clicked. Set this property to True to advance the slide by clicking it.

`Slide.SlideShowTransition.AdvanceOnTime`—For the specified `Slide`, this property returns or sets whether or not the slide advances after a period of time has elapsed (as set by the AdvanceTime property). Set this property to True to advance the slide after a period of time.

`Slide.SlideShowTransition.AdvanceTime`—This property returns or sets the amount of time, in seconds, after which the specified `Slide` will advance, assuming the AdvanceOnTime property is set to True.

`Slide.SlideShowTransition.EntryEffect`—A constant that determines the special effect used in the transition for the specified `Slide`. Look up this property in the VBA Help system to see the dozens of available constants.

`Slide.SlideShowTransition.Hidden`—This property returns or sets whether or not the specified `Slide` is hidden during the slide show. Use True to hide the slide or False to make the slide visible.

`Slide.SlideShowTransition.Speed`—This property returns or sets the speed of the transition for the specified `Slide`. Use one of the following constants:

- ppTransitionSpeedSlow
- ppTransitionSpeedMedium
- ppTransitionSpeedFast
- ppTransitionSpeedMixed

> **note**
>
> To allow a slide to advance based on time, you also need to set the `SlideShowSettings` object's AdvanceMode property to ppSlideShowUseSlideTimings. This object is a property of the Presentation object, and I'll discuss it in detail in the section "Slide Show Settings."

Slide Show Settings

The Presentation object has a `SlideShowSettings` property that controls various global settings for the slide show. This property is actually a `SlideShowSettings` object, and the settings are the properties of this object. Here's a rundown of the settings you'll utilize most often:

Presentation.SlideShowSettings.AdvanceMode—Returns or sets how the slides advance for the specified *Presentation*. Use ppSlideShowManualAdvance to advance slides manually (by clicking) or ppSlideShowUseSlideTimings to advance slides based on the AdvanceTime property for each slide. You can also use the ppSlideShowRehearseNewTimings constant to run the slide show in Rehearsal mode (which lets you set the timings by advancing the slides manually).

Presentation.SlideShowSettings.EndingSlide—Returns or sets the index number of the last slide that is displayed in the slide show for the specified *Presentation*.

Presentation.SlideShowSettings.LoopUntilStopped—Returns or sets whether or not the slide show for the specified *Presentation* plays continuously. Set this property to True to play the slide show in a continuous loop until the user presses Esc; set this property to False to play the slide show just once.

Presentation.SlideShowSettings.ShowType—Returns or sets the slide show type for the specified *Presentation*. Use ppShowTypeSpeaker (for the standard, full-screen slide show), ppShowTypeWindow (to run the slide show in a window), or ppShowTypeKiosk (to run the slide show in kiosk mode—full screen with a continuous loop).

Presentation.SlideShowSettings.ShowWithAnimation—Returns or sets whether or not the slide show for the specified *Presentation* uses the animation settings applied to each slide's shapes. Set this property to True to enable animation; use False to disable animation.

Presentation.SlideShowSettings.ShowWithNarration—Returns or sets whether or not the slide show for the specified *Presentation* uses narration. Set this property to True to enable narration; use False to disable narration.

Presentation.SlideShowSettings.StartingSlide—Returns or sets the index number of the first slide that is displayed in the slide show for the specified *Presentation*.

Running the Slide Show

At long last you're ready to display the presentation's slide show for all to see. To do so, simply invoke the Run method of the SlideShowSettings object:

Presentation.SlideShowSettings.Run

For example, Listing 9.6 shows the last of the Juggling application's procedures. In this case, the procedure presents a dialog box that asks the user whether he or she wants to run the slide show. If Yes is clicked, some transition effects are applied to the instruction slides, and then the Run method is invoked.

LISTING 9.6 This Procedure Asks the User if He or She Wants to Run the Presentation's Slide Show

```
Sub RunJugglingSlideShow
    If MsgBox("Start the slide show?", vbYesNo, "Juggling") _
            = vbYes Then
        With pres
            .Slides("Juggling1").SlideShowTransition.EntryEffect =
            ➥ppEffectBlindsHorizontal
            .Slides("Juggling2").SlideShowTransition.EntryEffect =
            ➥pEffectCheckerboardAcross
            .Slides("Juggling3").SlideShowTransition.EntryEffect =
            ➥ppEffectBoxIn
            .Slides("Juggling4").SlideShowTransition.EntryEffect =
            ➥ppEffectStripsLeftDown
            .SlideShowSettings.Run
        End With
    End If
End Sub
```

THE ABSOLUTE MINIMUM

This chapter showed you the ins and outs of PowerPoint VBA. You began with a look at a few properties of PowerPoint's Application object. From there, you went through a number of PowerPoint-specific objects, including the Presentation, Slide, and Shape objects. I then showed you how to work with slide shows in your VBA code. Throughout this chapter, I illustrated the concepts with a sample application that creates a PowerPoint presentation from scratch.

Here's a list of chapters where you'll find related information:

- For a general discussion of VBA objects, see Chapter 5, "Working with Objects."

- I show you how to work with For Each...Next, For..Next, and Select Case in Chapter 6, "Controlling Your VBA Code."

- You can also assign sound effects to slide animations and slide show transitions. I show you how it's done in Chapter 12, "Interacting with the User."

IN THIS CHAPTER

- Learning about database programming
- Getting your projects and system set up to program databases
- Opening data in a recordset
- Accessing recordset data
- Navigating, finding, editing, adding, and deleting records
- Retrieving data into an Excel worksheet

10

PROGRAMMING ACCESS DATABASES

In the past few chapters, you've learned about the objects, properties, and methods associated with Word, Excel, and PowerPoint. You've seen that it's possible to manipulate these objects to automate routine tasks and gain an unprecedented amount of control over these programs.

In this chapter, you'll see that using VBA with Access is quite a bit different because you won't learn anything about Access objects. Yes, Access does have an `Application` object, and there's a whole hierarchy of objects for things like forms and reports. However, it's a rare that a VBA programmer ever has to manipulate Access using these objects. Instead, what Access programmers really want to get their hands on is the *data* contained in Access tables and queries.

The secret to doing this is that database info is accessed using an entirely different object hierarchy altogether. It's called *ActiveX Data Objects (ADO)* and it's the link between your Access VBA programs and the databases, tables, and queries you want to work with. The amazing thing about all of this is that you can use ADO to work with Access databases from *other* Office applications. For example, you could use ADO programming to grab data from an Access table and insert it into an Excel range. This chapter takes you through the basics of using ADO to access and work with Access databases.

Getting Ready: Two Steps Before You Begin

When programming Word, Excel, and PowerPoint, you just create or open a module in the Visual Basic Editor and start typing away. Database programming is a bit different because there's a bit of prep work you need to do before you start "slinging code," as programming types like to say. The next two sections explain the details.

Step One: Create a Reference

This may sound strange, but the ability to program a database is *not* built into Access VBA by default! As I mentioned at the top of the chapter, Access VBA is set up to program forms and reports (among other things); it just can't work with the data that's in those forms and reports, not to mention the tables where the data actually resides. It's weird, I know, so why did Microsoft set things up this way? In simplest terms, there are actually several different ways to program data, and Microsoft quite rightly didn't want to foist a particular method on VBA programmers. (Dedicated database coders are *very* particular about how they access their data; not only that, but Microsoft has developed several new ways to program databases in recent years, so there are compatibility issues to worry about: a program written using a old method won't work with any of the new methods.)

So the first thing you need to do is tell Access which method of database programming you want to use. Technically, you're choosing the database *object model*. If you have no idea which one to choose, don't worry about it: As a beginning database programmer, your best bet by far is to choose the most recent object model, which is the Microsoft ActiveX Data Objects 2.7 Library, a mouthful that I'll usually just shorten to ADO in the rest of this chapter. Follow these steps:

1. In the Visual Basic Editor, highlight your project in the Project Explorer. (Access only allows one project—that is, one database—to be open at a time, so this step isn't technically necessary.)

2. Select Tools, References to display the References dialog box.

3. In the Available References list, activate the check box beside the Microsoft ActiveX Data Objects 2.7 Library item, as shown in Figure 10.1.

FIGURE 10.1

Use the References dialog box to activate the Microsoft ActiveX Data Objects 2.7 Library check box.

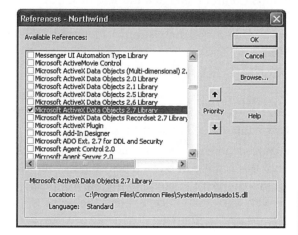

4. Click OK.

Note that you although you only have to do this once for a given Access database, you must repeat these steps for each subsequent Access database that you use.

Step Two: Create a Data Source

Another strange thing about database programming is that you always have to set up a *connection*, which is a kind of behind-the-scenes communications link that your code uses to request and change the data. There are two ways to set up a connection.

The first way is to declare a variable as a `Connection` type and then use the `CurrentProject` object's `Connection` property to return the connection:

```
Dim conn As Connection
Set conn = CurrentProject.Connection
```

> **note**
>
> The interesting thing about database programming is that you can do it from programs other than Access! For example, you could create a VBA program in Excel that works with data in a separate Access database. The secrets to this powerful idea are the Available References dialog box and the Microsoft ActiveX Data Objects 2.7 Library. By following the steps in this section in, say, Excel (for Step 1, you'd highlight the Excel VBA project you wanted to work with), you can use all of the database programming techniques that you'll learn in the rest of this chapter.

Alternatively, you need to create a *data source* that specifies the database, and then (as you'll see in the next section) you use your program code to connect to that data source. The good news is that you only have to do this once for each database. Here are the steps to follow:

1. Open the Windows Control Panel and launch the ODBC Data Sources icon. (In Windows XP, if you see just the Control Panel categories, first click Switch to Classic View. Double-click Administrative Tools and then double-click Data Sources (ODBC).)

2. In the System DSN tab, click Add. The Create New Data Source dialog box appears.

3. Highlight Microsoft Access Driver (*.mdb), and click Finish. The ODBC Microsoft Access Setup dialog box appears.

4. Use the Data Source Name text box to enter the name of the new data source. Note that this is the name you'll be using in your VBA code. For the code listings in this chapter, I'm going to use the sample Northwind.mdb database that ships with Microsoft Office, so enter the name Northwind.

5. Enter an optional Description.

6. Click Select, use the Select Database dialog box to highlight the Access database file you want to use (the Northwind.mdb file's default location is C:\Program Files\Microsoft Office\Office11\Samples\), and click OK. Figure 10.2 shows the completed dialog box.

7. Click OK to return to the ODBC Data Source Administrator.

8. Click OK.

FIGURE 10.2

Use the ODBC Microsoft Access Setup dialog box to define the data source.

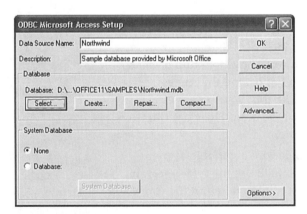

Working with Database Records: Opening a Recordset

With all those preliminaries out of the way, you can finally get down to the business of database programming. For the purposes of this chapter, database programming will consist of manipulating a *recordset*, which represents either the records in a table from an Access database or the records that result from a query. In ADO, you use the `Recordset` object to do all this.

The first thing your procedures will always do is open a recordset. You do that by setting up a connection to a data source, which then gives you access to whatever database was specified when you created the data source. From there, you just specify the table you want to work with, or you set up a query. As you'll see, ADO handily enables you to do all of this with a single statement.

Before all that, however, you must declare a variable as a `Recordset` type:

```
Dim rs As Recordset
```

With that done, you then `Set` the variable equal to a new `Recordset` object:

```
Set rs = CreateObject("ADODB.Recordset")
```

Since ADO isn't "built in" to Access (or any other program), its objects must be created explicitly by using VBA's `CreateObject` method.

Now you're ready to open the `Recordset` object by invoking its `Open` method:

```
Recordset.Open Source, Connection, CursorType, LockType, Options
```

`Recordset`	The `Recordset` object.
`Source`	The source of the recordset, which can be a table name or an SQL `SELECT` statement (which I'll explain a bit later).
`Connection`	The connection to use, which for our purposes is just the name of the data source that contains the data you want to work with.
`CursorType`	A constant that specifies how the recordset is opened:

`adOpenForwardOnly`	This is a read-only, forward-scrolling cursor. Use this option for faster performance if you're just making a single pass through the records. This is the default.
`adOpenDynamic`	This is a dynamic cursor that enables you to insert and update records and to see changes made by other users.
`adOpenKeyset`	This is a keyset cursor that enables you to insert and update records and to see all changes made by other users, except record inserts.

	`adOpenStatic`	This is a static copy of the records. You can insert and update records, but you can't see changes made by other users.
`LockType`		A constant that specifies the locking characteristics of the new recordset:
	`adLockReadOnly`	Prevents users from making changes to the records. This is the default.
	`adLockPessimistic`	In a multiuser environment, the current record is locked as soon as you make changes to it.
	`adLockOptimistic`	In a multiuser environment, the current recordset isn't locked until you run the `Update` method.
	`adLockOptimisticBatch`	Implements batch optimistic updating (batch mode). You use this when you want to change multiple records and then update all of them at once.
`Options`		A constant that specifies how the provider should interpret the `Source` value. See the VBA Help system for the various `adCmd` and `adAsync` constants that are available.

It's also worth noting that you can also open a recordset after first setting the following `Recordset` object properties:

`Recordset.Source`—A table name or SQL SELECT statement that specifies the source of the `Recordset` object.

`Recordset.ActiveConnection`—The connection to use for the `Recordset` object.

`Recordset.CursorType`—The cursor to use with the `Recordset` object.

`Recordset.LockType`—A constant that specifies the locking characteristics of the `Recordset` object.

After setting these properties, you then run the `Open` method without specifying any parameters (see Listing 10.2, later in this chapter) .

Opening a Recordset Using a Table

The easiest way to pen a `Recordset` object is to open a table that already exists within the data source. For example, the following statement opens the table named

Employees in the Northwind data source:

```
rs.Open "Employees", "Northwind"
```

Listing 10.1 shows a complete procedure that shows you how to declare, open, and close a `Recordset` object.

LISTING 10.1 Opening a `Recordset` Object Using a Table

```
Sub RecordsetOpenTable()
    Dim rs As Recordset
    '
    ' Create the Recordset object
    '
    Set rs = CreateObject("ADODB.Recordset")
    '
    ' Open it
    '
    rs.Open "Employees", "Northwind"
    '
    ' Close it
    '
    rs.Close
    Set rs = Nothing
End Sub
```

note

The code used in this chapter's examples can be found on my Web site at the following address:

http://www.mcfedries.com/ABGVBA/Chaptr10.xls

This example doesn't do much, although it shows you how to fully handle a `Recordset` object. The first few statements declare the `Recordset` object, create it, and then open it. In this case, the code opens the Exployees table using the Northwind data source. We're not ready to do anything with the recordset just yet, so the last two statements close the `Recordset` and Set the variable to the keyword `Nothing`, which is a useful housekeeping chore that saves memory.

Listing 10.2 shows the same code, only this time the `Recordset` object's `Source` and `ActiveConnection` properties are set before running the `Open` method.

LISTING 10.2 Opening a `Recordset` Object Using Properties

```
Sub RecordsetOpenProperties()
    Dim rs As Recordset
    '
    ' Create the Recordset object
    '
```

LISTING 10.2 (continued)

```
    Set rs = CreateObject("ADODB.Recordset")
    '
    ' Open it
    '
    With rs
        .Source = "Employees"
        .ActiveConnection = "Northwind"
        .Open
    End With
    '
    ' Close it
    '
    rs.Close
    Set rs = Nothing
End Sub
```

Opening a Recordset Using a SELECT String

Rather than opening an entire table, you may prefer to open only a subset of a table. The easiest way to do that is to create a Structured Query Language (SQL) statement. This is the language that Access uses when you create a query. SQL is a complex bit of business, but you need only concern yourself with a small portion of it called the SELECT statement. The SELECT statement is used to create a recordset based on the table, fields, criteria, and other clauses specified in the statement. Here's a simplified syntax of the SELECT statement:

```
SELECT [DISTINCT] field_names
    FROM table_name
    WHERE criteria
    ORDER BY field_names [DESC];
```

SELECT	The SELECT statement always begins with the SELECT keyword.
DISTINCT	This optional keyword specifies that you want only unique records (that is, no duplicates).
field_names	If you only want certain fields to appear in the recordset, enter their names here, separated by commas. If you want all the fields, use *, instead.
FROM table_name	This is the name of table that contains the data.

WHERE *criteria*	This filters the data to give you only those records that match the specified *criteria*.
ORDER BY *field_names* [DESC]	This sorts the results in ascending order based on the data in the fields specified by *field_names* (separated by commas, if you have more than one). Use the optional DESC keyword to sort the records in descending order.

For example, the following SELECT statement takes all of the fields from the Customers table, restricts the data to those records where the Country field contains "Sweden," and sorts the results using the data in the CompanyName field:

```
SELECT * FROM Customers WHERE
Country='Sweden' ORDER BY CompanyName;
```

As another example, the following SELECT statement takes just the ProductName and UnitPrice fields from the Products table and restricts the data to those records where the UnitPrice field is less than 20:

```
SELECT ProductName, UnitPrice FROM Products
WHERE UnitPrice < 20;
```

To use a SELECT statement in your VBA database code, either enter the SELECT string directly into the Recordset object's Open method as the *Source* value, or store it in a String variable and put the variable in the Open method, as shown in Listing 10.3.

> **tip**
>
> If you're new to SELECT statements, there's an easy way to avoid errors: use Access to create a temporary Select query in Access. When the resulting data is what you want, select the View, SQL View command to display the underlying SELECT statement. You can then copy this statement to your VBA code and delete the query. (One caution: change any double quotation marks (") to single quotes (') to avoid errors when using the SELECT statement within a VBA string variable.)

LISTING 10.3 Opening a Recordset Object Using a SELECT Statement

```
Sub RecordsetOpenSELECT()
    Dim rs As Recordset
    Dim strSELECT As String
    '
    ' Create the Recordset object
    '
    Set rs = CreateObject("ADODB.Recordset")
    '
    ' Open it
    '
```

LISTING 10.3 (continued)

```
    strSELECT = "SELECT * FROM Customers WHERE Country='Sweden'" & _
                "ORDER BY CompanyName;"
    rs.Open strSELECT, "Northwind", adOpenKeyset
    '
    ' Close it
    '
    rs.Close
    Set rs = Nothing
End Sub
```

Working with a Recordset

The examples you've seen so far haven't done very much with the Recordset objects they've opened. To do something useful with the records you need to wield the Recordset object's properties and methods. You learn the most useful of these properties and methods in the next few sections.

Getting at the Recordset Data

In most cases, the point of opening a recordset is to get your hands on the data that's in a certain record. More specifically, you'll most often want to get whatever data is in a certain *field* within a record. You do that by invoking the Recordset object's Fields property:

Recordset.Fields(*FieldName*)

Recordset	The Recordset object you want to work with.
FieldName	A string or String variable containing the name of the field that contains the data you want.

For example, if you're working with Northwind's Customers table, the following statement stores the data from the current record's ContactName field in a variable named currentContact:

```
currentContact = rs.Fields("ContactName")
```

Note, however, that Fields is the default property for a Recordset object, so you can save some typing by leaving out the .Fields part. In other words, the following two values are equivalent:

```
rs.Fields("ContactName")
rs("ContactName")
```

Listing 10.4 shows another example.

LISTING 10.4   Getting Recordset Data

```
Sub RecordsetData()
    Dim rs As Recordset
    Dim strSELECT As String
    '
    ' Create the Recordset object
    '
    Set rs = CreateObject("ADODB.Recordset")
    '
    ' Open it
    '
    strSELECT = "SELECT * FROM Customers WHERE Country='Canada'" & _
                "ORDER BY CompanyName;"
    rs.Open strSELECT, "Northwind", adOpenKeyset
    '
    ' Display the Contact Name and Company Name
    '
    MsgBox rs("ContactName") & ", " & rs("CompanyName")
    '
    ' Close it
    '
    rs.Close
    Set rs = Nothing
End Sub
```

caution

When using a SELECT statement with a WHERE clause, there's always the possibility that the resulting recordset may contain no records. In that case, if your code attempts to access the data in the "current" record, an error will result. To avoid this, open the recordset using either the adOpenKeyset or adOpenStatic cursor types, and then check the Recordset object's RecordCount property. If this is greater than 0, it means the recordset has at least one record, and so it's safe to proceed. Here's a snippet that modifies part of Listing 10.4 to check for at least one record before displaying the data:

```
rs.Open strSELECT, "Northwind", adOpenKeyset

If rs.RecordCount > 0 Then

    MsgBox rs("ContactName") & ", " & rs("CompanyName")

End If
```

In this procedure, a recordset is opened using a SELECT statement that restricts the customers to just those where the Country field equals "Canada." Then a MsgBox function (see Chapter 12, "Interacting with the User") displays the data from the ContactName and CompanyName fields.

Navigating Records

As I mentioned in the previous section, the Fields property returns the data from a field in the current record. When you first open a recordset, the current record is the first record. To get to another record, you need to navigate to it. There are a number of ways to do this, but the following four methods are the ones you'll probably use most often:

> **caution**
>
> Note that the MoveLast and MovePrevious methods don't work if you open the recordset using the adOpenForwardOnly cursor.

Recordset.MoveFirst—Moves to the first record in the specified Recordset object.

Recordset.MoveLast—Moves to the last record in the specified Recordset object.

Recordset.MoveNext—Moves to the next record in the specified Recordset object.

Recordset.MovePrevious—Moves to the previous record in the specified Recordset object.

With these methods you're changing a value that points to the current record. This is all straightforward except for two situations:

- You're on the first record and you run the MovePrevious method.
- You're on the last record and you run the MoveNext method.

VBA will let you do these things, but in a sense they enable you to move "outside" of the recordset. If you try to access the data, you'll get an error message that begins Either BOF or EOF is True…. Here, BOF means *beginning of file* and EOF means *end of file*. These are properties of the Recordset object:

Recordset.BOF—Returns True if the cursor is before the first record in the specified Recordset object.

Recordset.EOF—Returns True if the cursor is after the first record in the specified Recordset object.

To avoid the error, you should use test properties in your code. For example, the following snippet runs the MoveNext method and then checks the EOF property. If it's True, then the cursor is moved to the last record:

```
rs.MoveNext
If rs.EOF Then
    rs.MoveLast
End If
```

Another way to move is to use the Recordset object's Move method, which moves the cursor a set number of records from the current record:

Recordset.Move NumRecords, Start

Recordset	The Recordset object you want to work with.
NumRecords	The number of records you want to move. Use a positive number to move toward the end of the recordset; use a negative number to move toward the beginning of the recordset.
Start	Use this optional parameter to specify a starting record from which to perform the move.

The Start parameter should be the name of a Variant variable that contains a *bookmark*, which is a saved location in a recordset. You set and read bookmarks using the Recordset object's Bookmark property. Listing 10.5 provides an example.

LISTING 10.5   Navigating a Recordset Using a Bookmark

```
Sub RecordsetBookmarkNavigation()
    Dim rs As Recordset
    Dim strSELECT As String
    Dim savedRecord As Variant
    '
    ' Create the Recordset object
    '
    Set rs = CreateObject("ADODB.Recordset")
    '
    ' Open it
    '
    strSELECT = "SELECT * FROM Customers WHERE Country='USA'" & _
                "ORDER BY CompanyName;"
    rs.Open strSELECT, "Northwind", adOpenKeyset
    '
    ' Move, save the current record as a Bookmark, and display the data
    '
    rs.Move 3
    savedRecord = rs.Bookmark
    MsgBox rs("ContactName") & ", " & rs("CompanyName")
    '
    ' Move the current record
    '
    rs.Move -2
    MsgBox rs("ContactName") & ", " & rs("CompanyName")
    '
    ' Move relative to the Bookmark
```

LISTING 10.5 (continued)

```
    '
    rs.Move 5, savedRecord
    MsgBox rs("ContactName") & ", " & rs("CompanyName")
    '
    ' Move to the bookmark
    '
    rs.Bookmark = savedRecord
    MsgBox rs("ContactName") & ", " & rs("CompanyName")
    '
    ' Close it
    '
    rs.Close
    Set rs = Nothing
End Sub
```

After the recordset is opened, the Move method is used to move forward three records, and then the current record is saved to the savedRecord variable using the Bookmark property. The code moves back two records and then moves forward five records from the bookmark. Finally the cursor is returned to the saved record by setting it as the value of the Bookmark property. Note that the following two statements do the same thing:

```
rs.Bookmark = savedRecord
rs.Move 0, savedRecord
```

Finding a Record

Another way to navigate a recordset is to search for a specific record using one or more criteria. ADO gives you two methods to use—Find and Seek. However, you only need to learn how to use the Find method since it's simpler than Seek and works well on all but the largest recordsets.

Here's the syntax for the Find method:

`Recordset.Find Criteria, SkipRows, SearchDirection, Start`

Recordset	The Recordset object you want to work with.
Criteria	An expression that specifies the criteria you want to use to find the record.
SkipRows	An optional value that specifies the number of rows from the current record (or the record specified by the Start parameter) where the search should begin. The default value is 0.

SearchDirection	An optional constant that specifies which direction the search should take. Use `adSearchForward` (the default value) to search forward through the records; use `adSearchBackward` to search backward.
Start	An optional bookmark that specifies the starting record from which to perform the search.

When you run this method, one of two things will happen:

■ **A record is found that matches the criteria**—In this case, the cursor is moved to that record.

■ **No record is found that matches the criteria**—If the *SearchDirection* parameter is `adSearchForward`, the search stops at the end of the recordset (the `EOF` property returns True); if the *SearchDirection* parameter is `adSearchBackward`, the search stops at the beginning of the recordset (the `BOF` property returns True).

This tells you that you can determine whether or not the search was successful by testing the `EOF` or `BOF` property (depending on the search direction) after running the `Find` method. Listing 10.6 gives an example.

LISTING 10.6   Using the `Find` Method

```
Sub SearchRecordsWithFind()
    Dim rs As Recordset
    Dim strCriteria As String
    '
    ' Create the Recordset object
    '
    Set rs = CreateObject("ADODB.Recordset")
    '
    ' Open it
    '
    With rs
        .Source = "Employees"
        .ActiveConnection = "Northwind"
        .CursorType = adOpenKeyset
        .Open
    End With
    '
    ' Run the Find method
    '
    strCriteria = "City='London'"
    rs.Find strCriteria
```

LISTING 10.6 (continued)

```
    '
    ' Loop to find other records that meet the criteria
    '
    Do While Not rs. EOF
        '
        ' Display the data
        '
        MsgBox rs("FirstName") & " " & rs("LastName")
        '
        ' Search again, but skip a row
        '
        rs.Find strCriteria, 1
    Loop
    '
    ' Close the recordset
    '
    rs.Close
    Set rs = Nothing
End Sub
```

After opening the Employees table as the recordset, this code uses the strCriteria variable to hold the criteria string "City='London'". Then the Find method locates the first record that meets this criteria. A Do While...Loop is set up to loop as long as rs.EOF is False. Inside the loop, the employee's name is displayed and then the Find method is run again, although with the SkipRows parameter set to 1 to avoid finding the same record over and over again.

Editing a Record

Once you've navigated to or found the record you want, you may want to do more than just display the data or store the data in a variable or two. Instead, you may want to edit the data by making changes to one or more fields. Editing the current record is a two-step process:

1. Change the data in one more fields. Changing the data is straightforward because you treat each field just like a variable:
   ```
   rs("Title") = "Account Manager"
   rs("UnitPrice") = 19.95
   ```

2. Update the record to write the new data to the table. You do this by running the Recordset object's Update method.

Listing 10.7 puts these steps to work.

LISTING 10.7   Editing Recordset Data

```
Sub EditingARecord()
    Dim rs As Recordset
    Dim strCriteria As String
    '
    ' Create the Recordset object
    '
    Set rs = CreateObject("ADODB.Recordset")
    '
    ' Open it
    '
    With rs
        .Source = "Employees"
        .ActiveConnection = "Northwind"
        .CursorType = adOpenKeyset
        .LockType = adLockPessimistic
        .Open
    End With
    '
    ' Run the Find method
    '
    strCriteria = "Title='Sales Representative'"
    rs.Find strCriteria
    '
    ' Loop to find other records that meet the criteria
    '
    Do While Not rs.EOF
        '
        ' Display the data
        '
        rs("Title") = "Account Manager"
        rs.Update
        MsgBox rs("FirstName") &" " & rs("LastName") & ", " & rs("Title")
        '
        ' Search again, but skip a row
        '
        rs.Find strCriteria, 1
    Loop
    '
    ' Close the recordset
    '
    rs.Close
    Set rs = Nothing
End Sub
```

After opening the Employees table, the `Find` method is used to locate the first record where the `Title` field equals "Sales Representative." A `Do While...Loop` checks the `EOF` property. Inside the loop, the `Title` field is changed to "Account Manager" and the `Update` method finalizes the changes for the current record. The `Find` method is run again to continue the process.

Adding a New Record

If you have new information to insert into a table, ADO enables you to add a new record and populate its fields with the new data. This is accomplished with the Recordset object's `AddNew` method.

There are two ways to use `AddNew`. In the simplest case, you follow a three-step procedure:

1. Run the `AddNew` method.

2. Add the data to the new record's fields.

3. Call the `Update` method to write the new record and data to the table.

> **caution**
>
> To successfully add a new record to a table, you need to open the recordset with the `LockType` parameter or property set to either `adLockOptimistic` or `adLockPessimistic`.

Listing 10.8 takes you through an example.

LISTING 10.8 Adding a New Record

```
Sub AddingARecord()
    Dim rs As Recordset
    '
    ' Create the Recordset object
    '
    Set rs = CreateObject("ADODB.Recordset")
    '
    ' Open it
    '
    With rs
        .Source = "Customers"
        .ActiveConnection = "Northwind"
        .CursorType = adOpenKeyset
        .LockType = adLockOptimistic
        .Open
    End With
    '
```

LISTING 10.8   (continued)

```
' Create the new record
'
rs.AddNew
'
' Enter the data for the new record
'
rs("CustomerID") = "AYRSH"
rs("CompanyName") = "Ayrshire Haggis"
rs("ContactName") = "Angus Dunlop"
rs("ContactTitle") = "Owner"
rs("Address") = "123 Cathcart St."
rs("City") = "Ayr"
rs("Region") = "Ayrshire"
rs("PostalCode") = "KA18 4PN"
rs("Country") = "Scotland"
rs("Phone") = "01290 555555"
rs("Fax") = "01290 666666"
'
' Write the new record to the table
'
rs.Update
'
' Close the recordset
'
rs.Close
Set rs = Nothing
End Sub
```

This code opens the Customers table (notice that LockType is set to adLockOptimistic). Then the AddNew method is run and the various fields in the new record are populated with data. Finally, the Update method writes the new record to the table.

The second way to use the AddNew method combines the first two steps into a single statement:

Recordset.AddNew FieldList, Values

Recordset	The Recordset object you want to work with.
FieldList	A field name or an array of field names.
Values	A single value or an array of values for the fields in the new record.

Here's a statement that creates a new record and populates a single field:

```
rs.AddNew "CustomerID", "AYRSH"
```

Here's another that uses the `Array` function to populate an entire record in a single statement:

```
rs.AddNew Array("CustomerID", "CompanyName", "ContactName", _
                "ContactTitle", "Address", "City", "Region", _
                "PostalCode", "Country", "Phone", "Fax"), _
          Array("AYRSH", "Ayrshire Haggis", "Angus Dunlop", _
                "Owner", "123 Cathcart St.", "Ayr", "Ayrshire", _
                "KA18 4PN", "Scotland", "01290 555555", "01290 666666")
```

Deleting a Record

If a record is obsolete or simply no longer needed for some reason, you should delete it from the table to reduce clutter and keep the table up-to-date. This is handled easily by the `Recordset` object's `Delete` method, which marks the current record for deletion. You then run the `Update` method to confirm the deletion.

Listing 10.9 puts the `Delete` method through its paces.

tip

If you run the `Delete` method and then decide against the deletion, you can back out of it by running the `CancelUpdate` method before running the `Update` method.

LISTING 10.9 Deleting a Record

```
Sub DeletingARecord()
    Dim rs As Recordset
    Dim strCriteria As String
    '
    ' Create the Recordset object
    '
    Set rs = CreateObject("ADODB.Recordset")
    '
    ' Open it
    '
    With rs
        .Source = "Customers"
        .ActiveConnection = "Northwind"
```

LISTING 10.9   (continued)

```
        .CursorType = adOpenKeyset
        .LockType = adLockOptimistic
        .Open
    End With
    '
    ' Run the Find method
    '
    strCriteria = "CustomerID='AYRSH'"
    rs.Find strCriteria
    '
    ' Loop to find other records that meet the criteria
    '
    If Not rs.EOF Then
        rs.Delete
        rs.Update
        MsgBox "The customer with " & strCriteria & " has been deleted."
    Else
        MsgBox "The customer with " & strCriteria & " was not found!"
    End If
    '
    ' Close the recordset
    '
    rs.Close
    Set rs = Nothing
End Sub
```

After opening the recordset (again, notice that you need to set LockType to either adLockOptimistic or adLockPessimistic), the Find method is used to locate the record to be deleted. If the record is found (that is, the recordset's EOF property is False), the code runs the Delete method followed by the Update method. A message tells the user that the record has been deleted.

Retrieving Data into Excel

As I mentioned near the beginning of the chapter, you normally use ADO from a program other than Access (or in Access when the database you want to work with isn't the current database). Most people work with table data from within Excel since the row-and-column layout of a worksheet fits well with the record-and-field layout of a table.

To get data from a table into an Excel worksheet, you have three choices:

- Retrieving an individual field value.
- Retrieving one or more entire rows.
- Retrieving an entire recordset.

Retrieving an Individual Field Value

For individual field values, move to the record you want to work with and then assign the value of the field to the worksheet cell. For example, the following statement returns the value of the current record's `Country` field and stores it in cell A1 of the active worksheet:

```
ActiveSheet.[A1] = rs("Country")
```

Retrieving One or More Entire Rows

To get full records, use the `Recordset` object's `GetRows` method:

```
Recordset.GetRows Rows, Start, Fields
```

`Recordset`	The `Recordset` object you want to work with.
`Rows`	The number of records you want to retrieve, starting from the current record. If you want to retrieve the rest of the records (that is, all the records from the current record to the end of the recordset), use the constant value `adGetRowsRest`.
`Start`	Use this optional parameter to specify a bookmark as the starting point from which to retrieve the records.
`Fields`	Use this optional parameter to specify the fields that are retrieved. Use a single field name or an array of field names.

The `GetRows` method returns the records in a two-dimensional array, where the first subscript is a number that represents the field (the first field is 0) and the second subscript represents the record number (where the first record is 0). Listing 10.10 shows an example.

LISTING 10.10 Retrieving Entire Records Into Excel

```
Sub RetrievingEntireRecords()
    Dim rs As Recordset
    Dim strCriteria As String
    Dim recordArray As Variant
    '
```

LISTING 10.10   (continued)

```
' Create the Recordset object
'
Set rs = CreateObject("ADODB.Recordset")
'
' Open it
'
With rs
    .Source = "Customers"
    .ActiveConnection = "Northwind"
    .CursorType = adOpenKeyset
    .Open
End With
'
' Head for Database Records worksheet
'
Worksheets("Database Records").Activate
With Worksheets("Database Records").[a1]

    ' Clear the sheet
    '
    .CurrentRegion.Clear
    '
    ' Read the data using GetRows
    '
    recordArray = rs.GetRows(50)
    '
    ' Run through the array and write the data to the worksheet
    '
    For i = 0 To UBound(recordArray, 2)
        For j = 0 To UBound(recordArray, 1)
            .Offset(i + 1, j) = recordArray(j, i)
        Next j
    Next i
    '
    ' Enter the field names in the first row and format the cells
    '
    For j = 0 To rs.Fields.Count - 1
        .Offset(0, j) = rs.Fields(j).Name
        .Offset(0, j).Font.Bold = True
        .Offset(0, j).EntireColumn.AutoFit
    Next j
```

LISTING 10.10 (continued)

```
End With
'
' Close the recordset
'
rs.Close
Set rs = Nothing
End Sub
```

After opening the Customers table, this procedure performs a few Excel VBA chores, including activating the "Database Records" worksheet and clearing the sheet to remove any existing data. Then GetRows is used to retrieve the first 50 rows of the table. A For...Next loop runs through the two-dimensional array writing the data in the worksheet's rows and columns. Then another For...Next loop writes the column names on the top row and formats the cells for easier reading.

Retrieving an Entire Recordset

If you need to retrieve an entire recordset into a worksheet, one way to do it is to run GetRows(adGetRowsRest) from the first record and then use the technique in Listing 10.10 to write the data to the worksheet. However, Excel offers you an easier method—the Range object's CopyFromRecordset method:

Range.CopyFromRecordset(*Data, MaxRows, MaxColumns*)

Range	A *Range* object that specifies the upper-left corner of the destination range.
Data	The recordset containing the data you want to retrieve.
MaxRows	The maximum number of records to retrieve. If you omit this optional parameter, Excel copies every record.
MaxColumns	The maximum number of fields to retrieve. If you omit this optional parameter, Excel copies every field.

Here are a few notes to bear in mind when working with CopyFromRecordset:

- Excel begins the copying from the current record. If you want to retrieve every record, make sure you run the MoveFirst method to move to the first record.

- When the CopyFromRecordset method is done, the Recordset object's EOF property is True.

- CopyFromRecordset will fail if the Recordset object has a field that contains binary data (that is, if it's an OLE object field) .

Listing 10.11 shows the RetrieveCategories procedure that uses the CopyFromRecordset method.

LISTING 10.11 Retrieving an Entire Recordset

```
Sub RetrieveCategories()
    Dim rs As Recordset
    Dim fld As Field
    Dim strSELECT As String, i As Integer
    '
    ' Create the Recordset object
    '
    Set rs = CreateObject("ADODB.Recordset")
    '
    ' Open it
    '
    With rs
        .Source = "Categories"
        .ActiveConnection = "Northwind"
        .CursorType = adOpenKeyset
        .Open
    End With
    '
    ' The strSELECT variable will hold the SQL SELECT statement
    ' that filters the Recordset to remove binary fields
    '
    strSELECT = "SELECT "
    '
    ' Run through the recordset fields
    '
    For Each fld In rs.Fields
        '
        ' Check for binary fields
        '
        If fld.Type <> adBinary And fld.Type <> adLongVarBinary Then
            '
            ' If it's not an OLE Object field,
            ' add it to the SELECT statement
            '
            strSELECT = strSELECT & fld.Name & ","
        End If
    Next fld
```

LISTING 10.11 (continued)

```vba
'
' Remove the trailing comma
'
strSELECT = Left(strSELECT, Len(strSELECT) - 1)
'
' Add the FROM clause
'
strSELECT = strSELECT & " FROM Categories"
'
' Open the filtered recordset
'
With rs
    .Close
    .Source = strSELECT
    .ActiveConnection = "Northwind"
    .CursorType = adOpenKeyset
    .Open
End With
'
' Activate the Database Records worksheet
'
Worksheets("Database Records").Activate
With Worksheets("Database Records").[a1]
    '
    ' Clear the sheet
    '
    .CurrentRegion.Clear
    '
    ' Get the entire recordset
    '
    .Offset(1).CopyFromRecordset rs
    '
    ' Enter the field names and format the cells
    '
    For i = 0 To rs.Fields.Count - 1
        .Offset(0, i) = rs.Fields(i).Name
        .Offset(0, i).Font.Bold = True
        .Offset(0, i).EntireColumn.AutoFit
    Next i
End With
'
```

LISTING 10.11 (continued)

```
' Close and release the objects
'
    rs.Close
    Set rs = Nothing
    Set fld = Nothing
End Sub
```

The RetrieveCategories procedure opens the Categories table as the Recordset object. You want to make sure that you don't try to copy any OLE Object fields, so the procedure constructs a SQL SELECT statement that excludes any fields that contain binary data (OLE objects). The strSELECT variable holds the SELECT statement, so it's initialized to "SELECT ". Then a For...Next loop runs through each field in rs and looks for OLE Object fields (where the Type property is adBinary or adLongVarBinary). If a field isn't an OLE Object type, its name (and a comma separator) is appended to the SELECT statement.

Next, the trailing comma is removed and the FROM clause is concatenated to the SELECT statement. A new recordset is opened based on strSELECT, and then the CopyFromRecordset method retrieves the records.

THE ABSOLUTE MINIMUM

This chapter showed you how to use the ActiveX Data Objects model to work with Access databases from other applications. You first learned how to set up the appropriate references and data sources. Remember: You need to set up the reference in *each* project where you want to use ADO programming techniques; you need only set up the data source for an Access database once.

You also learned various methods for opening recordsets and getting recordset data. You then learned how to navigate a recordset, either by moving the cursor or by finding records. From there you learned how to edit records, add new records, and delete records. You completed the chapter by learning how to retrieve data into Excel.

Here are a couple of related chapters to check out:

- For information on working with Excel's objects, see Chapter 8, "Programming Excel."

- I used the MsgBox function a few times in this chapter. See Chapter 12, "Interacting with the User," for the details on this function.

IN THIS CHAPTER

- Specifying, copying, moving, and deleting email folders

- Determining the sender's name and address, the subject and body, and other email message data

- Displaying, closing, moving, and deleting email messages

- Sending new messages as well as replying to and forwarding received messages

- Adding, saving, and removing email attachments

- Working with Outlook's email capabilities from other applications

11

PROGRAMMING OUTLOOK EMAIL

Not many people know it, but Microsoft Outlook also incorporates VBA, so you can create Outlook-based VBA macros and applications. Outlook itself is a big program, so you can imagine that the Outlook object model is huge, with dozens of objects and untold numbers of properties, methods, and events. The proverbial space limitations prevent me from examining this model in detail, so this chapter just takes you through those objects related to Outlook's email features.

Although Outlook has an `Application` object at the top of its hierarchy, your Outlook programming will rarely need to use it. Instead, your programs will always begin with the `NameSpace` object. The oddly named object acts as a kind of top-level object for a *data source*, which, as its name implies, is a kind of container for data. The `NameSpace` object enables you to log in to the source, access the data, and then log out. In Outlook's case, the only supported data source is something called *MAPI*— Mail Application Programming Interface—which represents the data in an Outlook personal folders store (a `.pst` file).

After you've started Outlook, you've already logged in, so your code can simply refer to the current session as the namespace. To do that, you use the default Outlook object, which is called `ThisOutlookSession`. Use this object's `Session` property to get the `NameSpace` object:

```
Dim ns As NameSpace
Set ns = ThisOutlookSession.Session
```

Working with Outlook Folders

The `NameSpace` object stores all the Outlook folders, which means you can use it to return a reference to a folder and then work with that folder. Note that in the Outlook object model, folders are `MAPIFolder` objects.

Referencing Default Folders

One way to return a `MAPIFolder` object is to use the `GetDefaultFolder` method, which returns the default folder for a given type in the current profile. Here's the syntax:

NameSpace.GetDefaultFolder(*FolderType*)

NameSpace	The `NameSpace` object.
FolderType	A constant that specifies the type of folder. You can use any of the following defined constants: `olFolderCalendar`, `olFolderContacts`, `olFolderDeletedItems`, `olFolderInbox`, `olFolderJournal`, `olFolderNotes`, `olFolderOutbox`, `olFolderSentMail`, and `olFolderTasks`.

For example, if you want to work with the Inbox folder, your procedure would start with the following statements:

```
Dim ns As NameSpace
Dim ib As MAPIFolder
Set ns = ThisOutlookSession.Session
Set ib = ns.GetDefaultFolder(olFolderInbox)
```

Using the `Folders` Property

Alternatively, you can use the `NameSpace` object's `Folders` property to return a `Folders` object that represents all of the `MAPIFolder` objects in the PST file. To reference a specific folder, use `Folders(Index)`, where `Index` is one of the following:

- An integer value with the first folder being 1, the second folder being 2, and so on.

- The name of the folder in quotation marks.

The `NameSpace` object has only one folder—known as the *root*—which is usually called "Personal Folders." Therefore, the following statements are equivalent (assume `ns` is a `NameSpace` object):

```
ns.Folders(1)
ns.Folders("Personal Folders")
```

All the other mail folders are subfolders of this root. To get at them, you tack on another `Folders` property in the same way. For example, the first subfolder in the root is usually Deleted Items, so the following are equivalent:

```
ns.Folders(1).Folders(1)
ns.Folders("Personal
Folders").Folders("Deleted Items")
```

To help give you a feel for how these folders work, Listing 11.1 shows a procedure that runs through the first- and second-level folders in the namespace. Before you run this code, however, display the Visual Basic Editor's Immediate window by activating the View, Immediate Window command. (Check out Chapter 15, "Debugging VBA Procedures," for more information.)

note

For the Outlook procedures in this chapter, I've put everything into a text file named `Chaptr11.txt`, which you'll find on my Web site:

`http://www.mcfedries.com/ABGVBA/Chapter11.txt`

To use the code, create a module in Outlook's Visual Basic Editor, copy the code from `Chapter11.txt`, and then paste it into the module.

LISTING 11.1   A Procedure That Lists the First- and Second-Level Folders in the Outlook Namespace

```
Sub ListFolders()
    Dim ns As NameSpace
    Dim folder As MAPIFolder
    Dim subfolder As MAPIFolder
    '
```

LISTING 11.1 (continued)

```
' Set up the namespace
'
Set ns = ThisOutlookSession.Session
'
' Run through the first-level folders
'
For Each folder In ns.Folders
    Debug.Print folder.Name
    '
    ' Run through the second-level folders, if any
    '
    If folder.Folders.Count > 1 Then
        For Each subfolder In folder.Folders
            Debug.Print "    " & subfolder.Name
        Next 'subfolder
    End If
Next 'folder
Set ns = Nothing
End Sub
```

After establishing the namespace session, the `For Each...Next` loop runs through the folders. The `Debug.Print` command is used to display the name of each folder (as given by the `Name` property) in the Immediate window, as shown in Figure 11.1. If the folder has subfolders, another `For Each...Next` loop runs through the subfolders in the same manner.

Prompting the User for a Folder

Another way to get a folder is to use the `NameSpace` object's `PickFolder` method:

NameSpace.PickFolder

   NameSpace The `NameSpace` object.

This method displays the Select Folder dialog box so that the user can choose a folder. The return value depends on the button the user clicks:

■ If the user clicks OK, the return value is a `MAPIFolder` object corresponding to the folder highlighted by the user.

■ If the user clicks Cancel, the return value is Nothing.

Listing 11.2 shows an example that invokes `PickFolder` and then tests the result.

FIGURE 11.1

When you run the `ListFolders` procedure, the names of the email folders and subfolders are printed in the Immediate window.

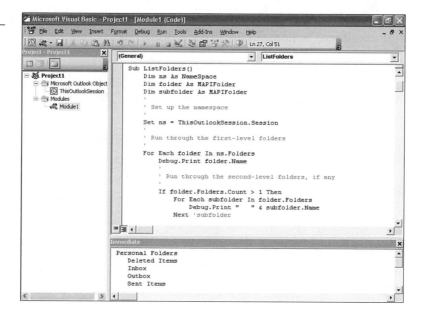

LISTING 11.2   A Procedure to Test the `PickFolder` Method

```
Sub PickFolderTest()
    Dim ns As NameSpace
    Dim folder As MAPIFolder
    '
    ' Set up the namespace
    '
    Set ns = ThisOutlookSession.Session
    '
    ' Display the Select Folder dialog box
    '
    Set folder = ns.PickFolder
    '
    ' Test the return value
    '
    If Not folder Is Nothing Then
        MsgBox "You picked " & folder.Name
    End If
End Sub
```

Notice that the code uses the following test for the dialog box result:

```
If Not folder Is Nothing Then
```

If this returns True (that is, if the value of the folder variable is not equal to Nothing), then the name of the folder is displayed.

Some `MAPIFolder` Methods

Although you probably won't use them very often, the `MAPIFolder` object does come with a few methods:

`MAPIFolder.CopyTo`—Copies the specified `MAPIFolder` to another folder:

```
MAPIFolder.CopyTo(DestinationFolder)
```

MAPIFolder	The `MAPIFolder` object you want to copy.
DestinationFolder	The `MAPIFolder` object to which you want the folder copied.

`MAPIFolder.Delete`—Deletes the specified `MAPIFolder`.

`MAPIFolder.MoveTo`—Moves the specified `MAPIFolder` to another folder:

```
MAPIFolder.MoveTo(DestinationFolder)
```

MAPIFolder	The `MAPIFolder` object you want to move.
DestinationFolder	The `MAPIFolder` object to which you want the folder moved.

Working with Email Messages

After you've got your `NameSpace` session and have referenced the `MAPIFolder` object you want to work with, you'll probably want to do something with the messages in that folder: display them, move them, respond to them, and so on. To access the messages, you use the `MAPIFolder` object's `Items` collection, which contains all the messages in the folder. Each of these messages is a `MailItem` object, and it's to this object that you'll turn your attention for most of the rest of this chapter.

`MailItem` Object Properties

The `MailItem` object boasts dozens of properties that cover everything from the message recipients to the assigned sensitivity. Here's a list of the most useful `MailItem` properties:

`MailItem.BCC`—Returns the display names (separated by semicolons) of the addresses listed as blind courtesy copy recipients for the specified `MailItem`.

`MailItem.Body`—Returns or sets the body text for the specified `MailItem`.

MailItem.BodyFormat—Returns or sets the format of the body text for the specified *MailItem*. Possible values are the following constants: olFormatHTML, olFormatPlain, olFormatRichText, and olFormatUnspecified.

MailItem.CC—Returns the display names (separated by semicolons) of the addresses listed as courtesy copy recipients for the specified *MailItem*.

MailItem.FlagDueBy—Returns or sets the due date for a flagged *MailItem*. Note that the FlagStatus property (described below) must be set to olFlagMarked.

MailItem.FlagRequest—Returns or sets a string that specifies the action to take for a flagged *MailItem*. Note that the FlagStatus property must be set to olFlagMarked.

MailItem.FlagStatus—Returns or sets the flag status for the specified *MailItem*. To set a flag, use olFlagMarked; to set a flag's status to "complete," use olFlagComplete; to remove a flag, use olNoFlag.

MailItem.HTMLBody—Returns or sets the HTML body text for the specified *MailItem*.

MailItem.Importance—Returns or sets the importance level for the specified *MailItem*. This property can be one of the following constants—olImportanceHigh, olImportanceLow, or olImportanceNormal.

MailItem.ReadReceiptRequested—Returns True if the sender has requested a read receipt for the specified *MailItem*; returns False otherwise.

MailItem.ReceivedTime—Returns or sets the date and time when the specified *MailItem* was received.

MailItem.Recipients—Returns a Recipients object—the collection of recipients—for the specified *MailItem*. See "Specifying the Message Recipients," later in this chapter.

MailItem.SenderName—Returns the display name of the sender of the specified *MailItem*.

MailItem.SenderEmailAddress—Returns the email address of the sender of the specified *MailItem*.

MailItem.Sensitivity—Returns or sets the sensitivity level of the specified *MailItem*. This property can be one of the following constants—olConfidential, olNormal, olPersonal, or olPrivate.

MailItem.SentOn—Returns the date and time when the specified *MailItem* was sent.

MailItem.Size—Returns the size of the specified *MailItem* in bytes.

MailItem.Subject—Returns or sets the subject line of the specified *MailItem*.

MailItem.To—Returns the display names (separated by semicolons) of the addresses listed in the To line of the specified *MailItem*. To learn how to add recipients, see "Specifying the Message Recipients," later in this chapter.

MailItem.UnRead—Returns True if the specified *MailItem* has not been read; returns False otherwise. You can also set this property.

`MailItem` Object Methods

With the methods available to the `MailItem` object, you can send messages, as well as reply to and forward messages. See "Sending a Message," later in this chapter, to learn how to use these methods that send messages. Otherwise, you can also open messages, move them to another folder, delete them, and more. Here's a summary of some of these more useful `MailItem` object methods:

`MailItem.Close`—Closes the window in which the specified `MailItem` object is displayed (see the `Display` method, later in this list). This method uses the following syntax:

`MailItem.Close(SaveMode)`

MailItem	The `MailItem` object you want to close.	
SaveMode	A constant that determines how the window is closed:	
	`olDiscard`	Closes the window without saving changes.
	`olPromptForSave`	Prompts the user to save changes.
	`olSave`	Saves changes automatically.

`MailItem.Copy`—Creates a copy of the specified `MailItem` object. This method returns a `MailItem` object that represents the copy.

`MailItem.Delete`—Deletes the specified `MailItem` object (that is, sends the message to the Deleted Items folder).

`MailItem.Display`—Displays the specified `MailItem` object in a new window using the following syntax:

`MailItem.Display(Modal)`

MailItem	The `MailItem` object you want to work with.
Modal	(optional) Use True to display the message in a *modal* window, which means the user can't switch back to Outlook until he or she closes the window; use False for a nonmodal window (this is the default).

`MailItem.Move`—Moves the specified `MailItem` object to a different folder using the following syntax:

`MailItem.Move(DestinationFolder)`

MailItem	The `MailItem` object you want to work with.
DestinationFolder	The `MAPIFolder` object to which you want to move the message.

`MailItem.PrintOut`—Prints the specified `MailItem` object.

MailItem.Save—Saves the specified *MailItem* object.

Listing 11.3 shows a procedure that runs through the messages in the Inbox folder.

LISTING 11.3   A Procedure That Processes Inbox Messages

```
Sub ProcessInboxMessages()
    Dim ns As NameSpace
    Dim ib As MAPIFolder
    Dim msg As MailItem
    '
    ' Set up the namespace
    '
    Set ns = ThisOutlookSession.Session
    '
    ' Get the default Inbox folder
    '
    Set ib = ns.GetDefaultFolder(olFolderInbox)
    '
    ' Run through each item in the Inbox
    '
    For Each msg In ib.Items
        '
        ' Flag important messages
        '
        If msg.Importance = olImportanceHigh Then
            msg.FlagStatus = olFlagMarked
            msg.FlagRequest = "Handle this, will ya!"
            msg.FlagDueBy = Date + 7
            msg.Importance = olImportanceNormal
            msg.Save
        End If
        '
        ' Look for expired flags
        '
        If msg.FlagDueBy < Date Then
            msg.Display
            MsgBox "The displayed message has an expired flag!"
        End If
        '
        ' Move sensitive messages to "Confidential" folder
        '
        If msg.Sensitivity = olConfidential Then
```

LISTING 11.3   (continued)

```
            msg.Move ns.Folders(1).Folders("Confidential")
        End If
    Next 'msg
End Sub
```

This procedure loops through the messages in the Inbox folder. It checks for three things:

- If a message was sent with "high" importance, it's marked with a flag, and the due date is set to a week from now.

- If a message has an expired flag, the message is displayed.

- If a message was sent with "confidential" sensitivity, it's moved to a folder named "Confidential." (If you plan on trying out this code, make sure this folder exists.)

Sending a Message

Besides simply reading messages, Outlook VBA also enables you to send messages. As you'll see over the next few sections, Outlook VBA gives you a number of ways to go about this.

Creating a New Message

To send a new message (that is, one that isn't a reply or forward), you first need to create a new `MailItem` object. You do this by invoking the `Application` object's `CreateItem` method and specifying the `olMailItem` constant as the type of item you want to create.

For example, the following statements declare a `MailItem` object and then create it:

```
Dim mi as MailItem
Set mi = Application.CreateItem(olMailItem)
```

Creating a Reply or Forward

Alternatively, you can create a `MailItem` object by replying to or forwarding an existing message. You have three choices:

`MailItem.Forward`—Forwards the specified `MailItem` object. This method returns a new `MailItem` object that represents the message to be forwarded.

`MailItem.Reply`—Replies to the sender of the specified `MailItem` object. This method returns a new `MailItem` object that represents the reply to be sent.

MailItem.ReplyAll—Replies to the sender and to all the other recipients of the specified *MailItem* object. This method returns a new *MailItem* object that represents the reply to be sent.

Here's a code snippet that sets up a reply to the first message in the Inbox folder:

```
Dim ns As NameSpace
Dim ib As MAPIFolder
Dim msg As MailItem
Dim msgReply As MailItem
'
' Set up the namespace
'
Set ns = ThisOutlookSession.Session
'
' Get the default Inbox folder
'
Set ib = ns.GetDefaultFolder(olFolderInbox)
'
' Get the first message
'
Set msg = ib.Items(1)
'
' Create the Reply
'
Set msgReply = msg. Reply
```

Specifying the Message Recipients

Now that your MailItem object has been created, you may also need to add one or more recipients. The collection of recipients for a MailItem object is contained in the Recipients object. To add a recipient, you use the Recipients object's Add method:

MailItem.Recipients.Add(*Name*)

MailItem	The MailItem object to which you want to add the recipient.
Name	The recipient's email address. If the recipient is in the Contacts list, you can just use his or her display name.

You can run the Add method as many times as you like for the same MailItem. Outlook separates each new recipient with a semicolon (;).

Each recipient in a message is a `Recipient` object and has the following properties (among others) :

`Recipient.Address`—Returns or sets the email address of the specified `Recipient`.

`Recipient.Name`—Returns or set the display name of the specified `Recipient`.

`Recipient`.Type—Determines the address line to which the specified `Recipient` will be added (To, Cc, or Bcc). Use `olTo` for the To line, `olCC` for the Cc line, or `olBCC` for the Bcc line. For example, assuming that `msg` is an object variable that represents a MailItem, the following statements add two recipients—one on the To line and one on the Cc line:

```
msg.Recipients.Add("Millicent Peeved").Type = olTo
msg.Recipients.Add("bob@weave.com").Type = olCC
```

Sending the Message

With the recipients determined, you can also tweak other `MailItem` properties such as `Subject`, `Body`, and `Importance` (see "`MailItem` Object Properties," earlier in this chapter). With that done, you can then send the message by running the `Send` method

`MailItem`.Send

> `MailItem`   The `MailItem` object you want to send.

Listing 11.4 shows a procedure that creates a new `MailItem` object, sets up the recipient, subject, and body, and then sends the message.

note

If you add a recipient and then later decide to remove that person, use the `Recipient`.Delete method, which deletes the specified `Recipient`.

LISTING 11.4   A Procedure That Sends an Email Message

```
Sub SendAMessage()
    Dim ns As NameSpace
    Dim msg As MailItem
    '
    ' Set up the namespace
    '
    Set ns = ThisOutlookSession.Session
    '
    ' Create the new MailItem
    '
    Set msg = Application.CreateItem(olMailItem)
```

LISTING 11.4   (continued)

```
'
' Specify the recipient, subject, and body
' and then send the message
'
With msg
    '
    ' Adjust the following address!
    '
    .Recipients.Add "blah@yadda.com"
    .Subject = "Just Testing"
    .Body = "This is only a test"
    .Send
End With
End Sub
```

Working with Attachments

If you want to work with files attached to a message, use the `MailItem` object's `Attachments` property. This returns the collection of `Attachment` objects for the message. For each `Attachment` object, you can manipulate the following properties and methods:

Attachment.DisplayName—Returns the name below the icon for the specified *Attachment*.

Attachment.Filename—Returns the filename of the specified *Attachment*.

Attachment.Delete—Deletes the specified *Attachment*.

Attachment.SaveAs—Saves the specified *Attachment* to disk:

Attachment.SaveAs(Path)

Attachment	The `Attachment` object you want to save.
Path	The path and filename to which you want to save the file.

Listing 11.5 shows a procedure that creates a forwarded message and removes all the attachments before sending it.

LISTING 11.5   A Procedure That Creates a Forwarded Message and Deletes Any Existing Attachments Before Sending the Message

```
Sub ForwardAndDeleteAttachments()
    Dim ns As NameSpace
    Dim ib As MAPIFolder
```

Listing 11.5   (continued)

```
Dim msg As MailItem
Dim att As Attachment
'
' Set up the namespace and Inbox
'
Set ns = ThisOutlookSession.Session
Set ib = ns.GetDefaultFolder(olFolderInbox)
'
' Create the forwarded MailItem
'
Set msg = ib.Items(ib.Items.Count).Forward
With msg
    '
    ' Delete all the attachments
    '
    For Each att in .Attachments
        att.Delete
    Next 'att
    '
    ' Send it (change the address!)
    '
    .Recipients.Add "blah@yadda.com"
    .Send
End With
End Sub
```

To add an attachment to an outgoing message, use the `Attachments` object's `Add` method:

`MailItem.Attachments.Add(Source, Type, Position, DisplayName)`

MailItem	The `MailItem` object to which you want to add the attachments.
Source	The path and filename for the attachment.
Type	(optional) A constant that specifies what kind of attachment you want to send:

`olByValue`	Sends the attachment as is (this is the default).
`olByReference`	Sends the attachment as a link to the original file.
`olEmbeddedItem`	Sends the attachment as a link to an Outlook item.

Position	(optional) The position of the attachment within the message body. Use 1 to place the attachment at the beginning of the message; use any value *n* to position the attachment before the *n*th character in the message.
DisplayName	(optional) The name that appears below the attachment icon if *Type* is olByValue.

You can run the Add method as many times as you like for the same MailItem.

Programming Outlook from Other Applications

If you want to interact with Outlook from another application, there are a few things you need to do differently. I'll use this section to explain what you need to do.

Setting Up a Reference to Outlook

In the other application's Visual Basic Editor, follow these steps to set up a reference to Outlook:

1. In the Project Explorer, highlight the project you'll be using for the Outlook programming.
2. Select Tools, References to display the References dialog box.
3. In the Available References list, activate the check box beside the Microsoft Outlook 11.0 Object Library item, as shown in Figure 11.2.

FIGURE 11.2

Use the References dialog box to activate the Microsoft Outlook 11.0 Object Library check box.

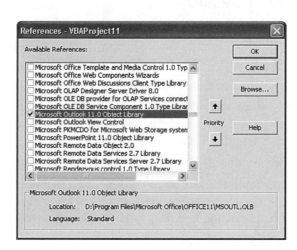

4. Click OK.

Remember that this reference only works for the project you selected. If you want to program Outlook from another project (either in the same application or in a different application), you have to repeat these steps.

Getting the `NameSpace` Object

When you work with Outlook from another application, you need to start right at the top of the object hierarchy, at the `Application` object. You use this object to return information about the current Outlook session and to gain access to the rest of the Outlook hierarchy. To establish a connection with this object, you use the `CreateObject` function. For example, the following statements establish a connection to Outlook:

```
Dim ol As Outlook.Application
Set ol = CreateObject("Outlook.Application")
```

Now you need to get a `NameSpace` object so you can log on and off, return information about the current user, and more. To return a `NameSpace` object, you use the `GetNameSpace` method with the "MAPI" argument:

```
Dim ol As Outlook.Application
Dim ns As NameSpace
Set ol = CreateObject("Outlook.Application")
Set ns = ol.GetNameSpace("MAPI")
```

Logging On to an Outlook Session

After you have the `NameSpace` object, you can log on to establish a MAPI session by invoking the `Logon` method:

```
NameSpace.Logon(Profile, Password, ShowDialog, NewSession)
```

NameSpace	The `NameSpace` object.
Profile	(optional) The name of the Outlook profile to use in the MAPI session. If you omit this value, VBA logs on to the default profile.
Password	(optional) The password used with the profile.
ShowDialog	(optional) A Boolean value that determines whether or not Outlook displays the Logon dialog box. Use False to bypass the dialog box (this is the default); use True to display the dialog box.
NewSession	(optional) A Boolean value that determines whether or not Outlook creates a new MAPI session. Set this argument to True to start a new session (this is the default); use False to log on to the current session.

In most cases, you'll use the `Logon` method without any arguments (assuming that the current `NameSpace` is represented by a variable named `ns`):

`ns.Logon`

If you have multiple profiles set up, however, then you need to specify which one you want to use. For example, the following statement logs on to an Outlook session using the "Personal E-Mail" profile:

`ns.Logon "Personal E-Mail"`

Logging Off an Outlook Session

When you've completed your labors in an Outlook session, you can log off by running the `NameSpace` object's `Logoff` method:

NameSpace`.Logoff`

note

To add, edit, or delete profiles, open the Windows Control Panel and launch the Mail icon.

> *NameSpace*   The `NameSpace` object.

Listing 11.6 shows a procedure that logs on to a MAPI session, runs through the items in the default Inbox folder, and records the `SenderName`, `SenderEmailAddress`, `Subject`, `Size`, `ReceivedTime`, and the first 100 characters of the `Body` onto a worksheet. To try this code, open `Chaptr11.xls` from the CD.

LISTING 11.6   A Procedure That Reads Inbox Data into a Worksheet

```
Sub ReadInboxData()
    Dim ol As Outlook.Application
    Dim ns As NameSpace
    Dim folder As MAPIFolder
    Dim ws As Worksheet
    Dim i As Integer
    '
    ' Establish a connection and log on
    '
    Set ol = CreateObject("Outlook.Application")
    Set ns = ol.GetNamespace("MAPI")
    ns.Logon
    '
    ' Get the default Inbox folder
    '
```

LISTING 11.6 (continued)

```vba
    Set folder = ns.GetDefaultFolder(olFolderInbox)
    '
    ' Set the Receive Mail worksheet
    '
    Set ws = Worksheets("Receive Mail")
    '
    ' Run through each item in the Inbox
    '
    For i = 1 To folder.Items.Count
        With folder.Items(i)
            '
            ' Record the sender, subject, size,
            ' received time, and some of the body
            '
            ws.[A1].Offset(i, 0) = .SenderName
            ws.[A1].Offset(i, 1) = .SenderEmailAddress
            ws.[A1].Offset(i, 2) = .Subject
            ws.[A1].Offset(i, 3) = .Size
            ws.[A1].Offset(i, 4) = .ReceivedTime
            ws.[A1].Offset(i, 5) = Left(.Body, 100)
        End With
    Next 'i
    '
    ' Log off the session
    '
    ns.Logoff
    Set ol = Nothing
End Sub
```

You'll find Listing 11.6 in the file named Chapter11.xls on my Web site:

http://www.mcfedries.com/ABGVBA/ Chapter11.xls

THE ABSOLUTE MINIMUM

This chapter showed you how to use Outlook's built-in VBA capabilities to program the Outlook object model. You began by understanding how the object hierarchy in Outlook is different than the object hierarchies in the other applications you've programmed. (For example, you start not with the Application object but with the NameSpace object.) From there, you learned quite a few techniques for working with folders, including how to specify folders and how to copy, move, and delete folders. In the rest of the chapter you learned about email messages, particularly how to extract data such as the sender's name and address, the subject line, and the body of the message. You also learned how to send messages (new messages as well as replies and forwards) and work with attachments. I finished by showing you how to access Outlook remotely from other applications.

For related information, check out the following chapters:

- Excel's VBA techniques were the subject of Chapter 8, "Programming Excel."

- For another example of working with data remotely, see Chapter 10, "Programming Access Databases."

- To learn more about the useful Immediate window, see Chapter 15, "Debugging VBA Procedures."

PART III

GETTING THE MOST OUT OF VBA

12

INTERACTING WITH THE USER

Most of your VBA programs will be for your own use only, although once you get proficient at coding, you may find yourself cobbling together macros and functions for other people, as well. Either way, it's important to remember that a well-designed program keeps the user (whoever he or she may be) involved by displaying messages at appropriate times and by asking for input. The advantage to using these and other forms of interaction is that the user feels that he or she is a part of the process and has some control over what the program does or doesn't do—which means that the user won't lose interest in the program and will be less likely to make careless mistakes. This chapter takes you through various methods of giving and receiving user feedback.

Programming Sounds

You'll see later in this chapter that there are a number of ways to present information to the user visually. Also, Chapter 13, "Creating Custom VBA Dialog Boxes," shows you how to create dialog boxes and input forms to gather information from the user. However, these visual cues might get lost in the shuffle if the user has a number of windows and programs open at once. In this case, you might need to supplement visual displays with accompanying sounds that will help focus the user's attention. This section looks at various methods you can employ to work with sounds in your VBA procedures.

Beeping the Speaker

VBA's most rudimentary form of communication is the simple, attention-getting beep. It's VBA's way of saying "Ahem!" or "Excuse me!" and it's handled, appropriately enough, by the `Beep` statement.

Although a single beep is usually sufficient, you can use a `For...Next` loop to sound multiple beeps, as shown in Listing 12.1. (To see the `InsertHyperlinks` procedure that is called from Listing 12.1, see Listing 12.2.)

caution

Avoid overusing the `Beep` statement. You need to get the user's attention, but constant beeping only defeats that purpose; most users get annoyed at any program that barks at them incessantly. Good uses for the `Beep` statement are signaling errors and signaling the end of long operations.

LISTING 12.1 A Procedure That Runs Another Procedure and Then Beeps the Speaker Three Times

```
Sub InsertHeadingHyperlinks()
    Dim i As Integer
    '
    ' Run the InsertHyperlink procedure
    '
    InsertHyperlinks "Main Heading"
    '
    ' Signal the end of the procedure with 3 beeps
    '
    For i = 1 To 3
        Beep
    Next 'i
End Sub
```

note

I use Word as the underlying application for most of the procedures in this chapter. To get the code for these procedures, see my Web site:

http://www.mcfedries.com/ ABGVBA/Chapter12.doc

Programming PowerPoint Sound Effects

The Beep statement is useful, but it's primitive. If you're working with PowerPoint and you have the necessary hardware, you can get your presentations to play much more sophisticated sounds.

PowerPoint has a SoundEffect property that lets you assign and play sounds in a presentation. This property is part of the hierarchy of two PowerPoint objects:

▪ AnimationSettings—The sound effect is applied to the animation associated with an object (such as a picture) on a slide.

▪ SlideShowTransition—The sound effect is applied to a slide's transition.

The SoundEffect property returns or sets a SoundEffect object that represents the sound to be played during the animation or transition. To specify a sound, use the ImportFromFile method:

Object.SoundEffect.ImportFromFile(*FileName*)

Object	The object to which you want to apply the sound.
FileName	The name and path of the sound file.

For example, the following statements import the tada.wav file as the sound effect for the slide named Start (check your computer for the correct location of the tada.wav file):

```
Set currSlide = ActivePresentation.Slides("Start")
currSlide.SlideShowTransition.SoundEffect.ImportFromFile _
    FileName:="C:\Windows\Media\tada.wav"
```

The SlideShowTransition object also has a LoopSoundUntilNext property. This property returns or sets whether or not the sound effect for the specified slide loops continuously until the next sound starts. Use True to loop the sound or False to play the sound just once.

Displaying Information to the User

Displaying information is one of the best (and easiest) ways to keep your users involved. For example, if an operation will take a long time, make sure the user has some visual clue about the progress of the operation. Similarly, if a user makes an error (for example, he enters the wrong argument in a user-defined function), he should be gently admonished so that he'll be less likely to repeat the error. This section presents several methods of displaying information to the users of your VBA applications.

Displaying a Message in the Status Bar

Most applications have a status bar at the bottom of the screen that's used for displaying messages and indicating the progress of the current operation. In Office 2003, Word, Excel, and Access let you display your own messages in the status bar. The next couple of sections show you how it's done.

Status Bar Messages in Word and Excel

For Word and Excel, you can use the Application object's StatusBar property to display text messages in the status bar at the bottom of the screen. This gives you an easy way to keep the user informed about what a procedure is doing or how much is left to process.

Listing 12.2 demonstrates the StatusBar property using the InsertHyperlinks procedure that was called in Listing 12.1.

LISTING 12.2   A Procedure That Inserts Hyperlinks for a Specified Style of Heading

```
Sub InsertHyperlinks(heading As String)
    Dim b As Bookmark
    Dim p As Paragraph
    Dim lastParagraph As Paragraph
    Dim anchorText As Range
    Dim strBookmark As String
    Dim totalParagraphs As Integer
    Dim i As Integer
    Dim j As Integer
    i = 0
    j = 0
    With ActiveDocument
        '
        ' Delete the existing "Anchor" bookmarks
        '
        For Each b In .Bookmarks
            If InStr(b.Name, "Anchor") Then b.Delete
        Next 'b
        '
        ' Run through the paragraphs
        '
        totalParagraphs = .Paragraphs.Count
        For Each p In .Paragraphs
```

LISTING 12.2   (continued)

```
    '
    ' Display the progress in the status bar
    '
    j = j + 1
    Application.StatusBar = "Checking paragraph " _
        & j & " of " & totalParagraphs
    '
    ' Look for the specified style
    '
    If p.Style = heading Then
        '
        ' Create a bookmark
        '
        i = i + 1
        .Bookmarks.Add "Anchor" & i, p.Range
        '
        ' Add a hyperlink for the heading
        '
        Set lastParagraph = .Paragraphs(.Paragraphs.Count)
        Set anchorText = .Range(p.Range.Start, p.Range.End - 1)
        lastParagraph.Range.InsertParagraphAfter
        lastParagraph.Range.Hyperlinks.Add _
            Anchor:=lastParagraph.Range, _
            Address:="", _
            SubAddress:="Anchor" & i, _
            ScreenTip:=anchorText, _
            TextToDisplay:=anchorText

    End If
    '
    ' Delay briefly so the status bar text is visible
    '
    startTime = Timer
    Do While Timer - startTime < 0.45
        DoEvents
    Loop
Next 'p
Application.StatusBar = ""
    End With
End Sub
```

This procedure runs through every paragraph in the active document and looks for those paragraphs that use whatever style is specified as the heading argument. When it finds such a paragraph, a hyperlink to that paragraph is inserted at the bottom of the document.

To keep the user informed of the progress of the operation, the status bar is updated with each pass, as shown in the following snippet:

```
totalParagraphs = .Paragraphs.Count
For Each p In .Paragraphs
    '
    ' Display the progress in the status bar
    '
    j = j + 1
    Application.StatusBar = "Checking paragraph " _
        & j & " of " & totalParagraphs
```

The variable `totalParagraphs` stores the total number of paragraphs, and the variable `j` counts the paragraphs. The `StatusBar` property is then used to display a message such as the following:

```
Checking paragraph 1 of 208
```

This loop executes quickly in a small document, so I've included a loop that delays the main loop for about half a second so that you can see the changes in the status bar. You generally wouldn't include such a delay in your code.

When the loop is done, the procedure sets the `StatusBar` property to the null string ("") to clear the status bar.

note

I don't discuss programming hyperlinks in this book, but the text in the example file (`Chapter12.doc`) contains a tutorial on creating and working with hyperlinks via VBA.

Programming the Status Bar in Access

Access uses the status bar to display messages and to display progress meters that let you know the progress of a long operation (such as importing records). You can use the `SysCmd` function to provide the same feedback to the users of your Access applications. Here's the syntax:

```
SysCmd(Action, Text, Value)
```

Action	A constant that specifies what Access does to the status bar:
	`acSysCmdInitMeter` Initializes the progress meter.
	`acSysCmdUpdateMeter` Updates the progress meter.

acSysCmdRemoveMeter	Removes the progress meter.
acSysCmdSetStatus	Displays *Text* in the status bar.
acSysCmdClearStatus	Clears the status bar.

Text   The text to be displayed in the status bar. You must specify this argument when *Action* is acSysCmdInitMeter or acSysCmdSetStatus.

Value   Controls the display of the progress meter. You must specify this argument when *Action* is acSysCmdInitMeter or acSysCmdUpdateMeter.

note

The Access code listings for this chapter can be found on my Web site in the file named Chaptr12.txt:

http://www.mcfedries.com/ABGVBA/ Chapter12.txt

If you just want to display text in the status bar, use acSysCmdSetStatus for the *Action* argument and specify the status bar text with the *Text* argument. Listing 12.3 shows a procedure that opens a form and then loops, depending on the number of controls in the form. While in the loop, the status bar message is updated to indicate the progress of the loop. To slow things down a bit, a Do While loop delays for half a second on each pass through the main loop.

LISTING 12.3   A Procedure That Displays Text in the Access Status Bar

```
Sub StatusBarText()
    Dim frm As Form
    Dim strStatus As String
    Dim ctrlCount As Integer
    Dim i As Integer
    Dim start As Long
    '
    ' Open the Orders form
    '
    DoCmd.OpenForm "Startup", acDesign
    Set frm = Forms("Startup")
    '
    ' Get the control count
    '
```

LISTING 12.3 (continued)

```
    ctrlCount = frm.Controls.Count
    '
    ' Loop ctrlCount times
    '
    For i = 1 To ctrlCount
        '
        ' Update the status bar text
        '
        strStatus = "Control " & i & " of " & ctrlCount
        SysCmd acSysCmdSetStatus, strStatus
        '
        ' Delay for half a second
        '
        start = Timer
        Do While Timer < (start + 0.5)
            DoEvents
        Loop
    Next i
    '
    ' Clear the status bar
    '
    SysCmd acSysCmdClearStatus
End Sub
```

Using a progress meter involves three steps:

1. Run SysCmd with acSysCmdInitMeter to initialize the progress bar. Here, you use the *Text* argument to specify text that will appear in front of the progress meter, and you use the *Value* argument to set the maximum value of the meter.

2. During the operation whose progress you want to show, run the SysCmd function at regular intervals. In this case, the *Action* argument is acSysCmdUpdateMeter and you use the *Value* argument to specify the current value of the meter. For example, if your maximum progress meter value is 100 and you update the meter to 50, the meter will appear half filled in.

3. When the operation is complete, run SysCmd once again using acSysCmdRemoveMeter as the *Action* argument to clear the status bar.

Listing 12.4 shows a slightly different example that uses a progress meter instead of text to indicate the loop's progress.

LISTING 12.4   A Procedure That Displays a Progress Meter in the Access Status Bar

```
Sub StatusBarProgressMeter()
    Dim frm As Form
    Dim ctrlCount As Integer
    Dim i As Integer
    Dim start As Long
    '
    ' Open the Orders form
    '
    DoCmd.OpenForm "Startup", acDesign
    Set frm = Forms!Startup
    '
    ' Get the control count
    '
    ctrlCount = frm.Controls.Count
    '
    ' Initialize the progress meter
    '
    SysCmd acSysCmdInitMeter, "Control Loop:", ctrlCount
    '
    ' Loop ctrlCount times
    '
    For i = 1 To ctrlCount
        '
        ' Update the progress meter
        '
        SysCmd acSysCmdUpdateMeter, i
        '
        ' Delay for half a second
        '
        start = Timer
        Do While Timer < (start + 0.5)
            DoEvents
        Loop
    Next i
    '
    ' Clear the status bar
    '
    SysCmd acSysCmdRemoveMeter
End Sub
```

Displaying a Message Using `MsgBox`

The problem with using the `StatusBar` property to display messages is that it's often a bit too subtle. Unless the user knows to look in the status bar, she might miss your messages altogether. When the user really needs to see a message, you can use the `MsgBox` function:

```
MsgBox(Prompt, Buttons, Title, HelpFile,
Context)
```

Prompt	The message you want to display in the dialog box. (You can enter a string up to 1,024 characters long.)
Buttons	(optional) A number or constant that specifies, among other things, the command buttons that appear in the dialog box. (See the next section.) The default value is 0.
Title	(optional) The text that appears in the dialog box title bar. If you omit the title, VBA uses the name of the underlying application (for example, Microsoft Excel).
HelpFile	(optional) The text that specifies the Help file that contains the custom help topic. (I don't discuss custom help topics in this book.) If you enter *HelpFile*, you also have to include *Context*. If you include *HelpFile*, a Help button appears in the dialog box.
Context	(optional) A number that identifies the help topic in *HelpFile*.

note

The `MsgBox` function, like all VBA functions, needs parentheses around its arguments only when you use the function's return value. See the section later in this chapter called "Getting Return Values from the Message Dialog Box" to learn about the return values produced by the `MsgBox` function.

tip

For long prompts, VBA wraps the text inside the dialog box. If you would prefer to create your own line breaks, use either VBA's `Chr(13)` function or VBA's `vbCr` constant to insert a carriage-return character between each line:

```
MsgBox "First line" & Chr(13) &
"Second line"
MsgBox "First line" & vbCr &
"Second line"
```

For example, the following statement displays the message dialog box shown in Figure 12.1:

```
MsgBox "You must enter a number between 1 and 100!",,"Warning"
```

FIGURE 12.1

A simple message dialog box produced by the MsgBox function.

Setting the Style of the Message

The default message dialog box displays only an OK button. You can include other buttons and icons in the dialog box by using different values for the *Buttons* parameter. Table 12.1 lists the available options.

TABLE 12.1   The MsgBox buttons Parameter Options

Constant	Value	Description
Buttons		
vbOKOnly	0	Displays only an OK button. (This is the default.)
vbOKCancel	1	Displays the OK and Cancel buttons.
vbAbortRetryIgnore	2	Displays the Abort, Retry, and Ignore buttons.
vbYesNoCancel	3	Displays the Yes, No, and Cancel buttons.
vbYesNo	4	Displays the Yes and No buttons.
vbRetryCancel	5	Displays the Retry and Cancel buttons.
Icons		
vbCritical	16	Displays the Critical Message icon.
vbQuestion	32	Displays the Warning Query icon.
vbExclamation	48	Displays the Warning Message icon.
vbInformation	64	Displays the Information Message icon.
Default Button		
vbDefaultButton1	0	The first button is the default (that is, the button selected when the user presses Enter).
vbDefaultButton2	256	The second button is the default.
vbDefaultButton3	512	The third button is the default.

TABLE 12.1 (continued)

Constant	Value	Description
Modality		
vbApplicationModal	0	The user must respond to the message box before continuing work in the current application.
vbSystemModal	4096	All applications are suspended until the user responds to the message box.

You derive the *Buttons* argument in one of two ways:

- By adding up the values for each option
- By using the VBA constants separated by plus signs (+)

For example, Listing 12.5 shows a procedure named ButtonTest, and Figure 12.2 shows the resulting dialog box. Here, three variables—msgPrompt, msgButtons, and msgTitle—store the values for the MsgBox function's *Prompt*, *Buttons*, and *Title* arguments, respectively. In particular, the following statement derives the Buttons argument:

msgButtons = vbYesNo + vbQuestion + vbDefaultButton2

You also could derive the Buttons argument by adding up the values that these constants represent (4, 32, and 256, respectively), but the procedure becomes less readable that way.

LISTING 12.5 A Procedure that Creates a Message Dialog Box

```
Sub ButtonTest()

    Dim msgPrompt As String, msgTitle As String
    Dim msgButtons As Integer, msgResult As Integer

    msgPrompt = "Are you sure you want to insert " & Chr(13) & _
                "the heading hyperlinks?"
    msgButtons = vbYesNo + vbQuestion + vbDefaultButton2
    msgTitle = "Insert Heading Hyperlinks"

    msgResult = MsgBox(msgPrompt, msgButtons, msgTitle)

End Sub
```

FIGURE 12.2

The dialog box that's displayed when you run the code in Listing 12.5.

Getting Return Values from the Message Dialog Box

A message dialog box that displays only an OK button is straightforward. The user either clicks OK or presses Enter to remove the dialog from the screen. The multibutton styles are a little different, however; the user has a choice of buttons to select, and your procedure should have a way to find out which button the user chose.

You do this by storing the MsgBox function's return value in a variable. Table 12.2 lists the seven possible return values.

TABLE 12.2 The MsgBox Function's Return Values

Constant	Value	Button Selected
vbOK	1	OK
vbCancel	2	Cancel
vbAbort	3	Abort
vbRetry	4	Retry
vbIgnore	5	Ignore
vbYes	6	Yes
vbNo	7	No

To process the return value, you can use an If...Then...Else or Select Case structure to test for the appropriate values. For example, the ButtonTest procedure shown earlier used a variable called msgResult to store the return value of the MsgBox function. Listing 12.6 shows a revised version of ButtonTest that uses a Select Case statement to test for the three possible return values.

LISTING 12.6 This Example Uses Select Case to Test the Return Value of the MsgBox Function

```
Sub ButtonTest2()

    Dim msgPrompt As String, msgTitle As String
    Dim msgButtons As Integer, msgResult As Integer
```

LISTING 12.6   (continued)

```
msgPrompt = "Do you want to insert the Main Heading hyperlinks?" & _
            vbCr & vbCr & _
            "Yes = Insert links for Main Heading style" & vbCr & _
            "No = Insert links for Listing style" & vbCr & _
            "Cancel = No links inserted"
msgButtons = vbYesNoCancel + vbQuestion + vbDefaultButton1
msgTitle = "Insert Hyperlinks"

msgResult = MsgBox(msgPrompt, msgButtons, msgTitle)

Select Case msgResult
    Case vbYes
        InsertHyperlinks "Main Heading"
    Case vbNo
        InsertHyperlinks "Listing"
    Case vbCancel
        Exit Sub
End Select

End Sub
```

The result is stored in the `msgResult` variable and then a Select Case structure handles the three possibilities:

- **The user clicks Yes**—In this case, `msgResult` is `vbYes`, so the code runs the `InsertHyperlinks` procedure and passes "Main Heading" as the parameter.

- **The user clicks No**—In this case, `msgResult` is `vbNo`. This time, the code runs the `InsertHyperlinks` procedure using "Listing" as the parameter.

- **The user clicks Cancel**—In this case, the code runs `Exit Sub` to cancel the procedure. (This is a bit redundant since the procedure would exit anyway after the `Select Case` was done. However, this is a good trick to remember in cases where the procedure would run other code if you didn't exit the procedure explicitly using `Exit Sub`.)

Getting Input from the User

As you've seen, the `MsgBox` function lets your procedures interact with the user and get some feedback. Unfortunately, this method limits you to simple command-button responses. For more varied user input, you need to use more sophisticated techniques. The rest of this chapter shows you two such methods: prompting the user for input and accessing an application's built-in dialog boxes.

Prompting the User for Input

The `InputBox` function displays a dialog box with a message that prompts the user to enter data, and it provides a text box for the data itself. Here's the syntax for this function:

`InputBox(Prompt, Title, Default, Xpos, Ypos, HelpFile, Context)`

Prompt	The message you want to display in the dialog box (1,024-character maximum).
Title	(optional) The text that appears in the dialog box title bar. The default value is the null string (nothing).
Default	(optional) The default value displayed in the text box. If you omit *Default*, the text box is displayed empty.
Xpos	(optional) The horizontal position of the dialog box from the left edge of the screen. The value is measured in points (there are 72 points in an inch). If you omit *Xpos*, the dialog box is centered horizontally.
Ypos	(optional) The vertical position, in points, from the top of the screen. If you omit *Ypos*, the dialog is centered vertically in the current window.
HelpFile	(optional) The text specifying the Help file that contains the custom help topic. (Again, I don't cover Help files in this book.) If you enter *HelpFile*, you also have to include *Context*. If you include *HelpFile*, a Help button appears in the dialog box.
Context	(optional) A number that identifies the help topic in *HelpFile*.

For example, Listing 12.7 shows a procedure called `GetInterestRate` that uses the `InputBox` method to prompt the user for an interest rate value. Figure 12.3 shows the dialog box that appears.

LISTING 12.7   A Procedure That Prompts the User for an Interest Rate Value

```
Function GetInterestRate()

    Dim done As Boolean
    '
    ' Initialize the loop variable
    '
    done = False

    While Not done
```

LISTING 12.7   (continued)

```
    '
    ' Get the interest rate
    '
    GetInterestRate = InputBox( _
            Prompt:="Enter an interest rate between 0 and 1:", _
            Title:="Enter Interest Rate")
    '
    ' First, check to see if the user cancelled
    '
    If GetInterestRate = "" Then
        GetInterestRate = 0
        Exit Function
    Else
        '
        ' Now make sure the entered rate is betwen 0 and 1
        '
        If GetInterestRate >= 0 And GetInterestRate <= 1 Then
            done = True
        End If
    End If
Wend

End Function
```

FIGURE 12.3

A dialog box generated by the InputBox function in Listing 12.7.

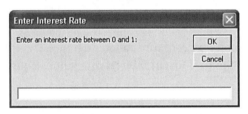

The InputBox method returns one of the following values:

- The value entered into the text box if the user clicked OK
- An empty string if the user clicked Cancel

In Listing 12.7, the result of the InputBox method is stored in the GetInterestRate variable. The procedure first checks to see if InputBox returned the empty string (""). If so, the Exit Function statement bails out of the procedure. Otherwise, an If...Then statement checks to make sure the number is between 0 and 1. If it is, the done variable is set to True so that the While...Wend loop will exit; if the number isn't between 0 and 1, the procedure loops and the dialog box is redisplayed.

It's also worth noting here that Excel has its own version of `InputBox` that's an `Application` object method. It has the same syntax as the VBA `InputBox` function, except that it tacks on an extra argument—*Type*:

```
Application.InputBox(Prompt, Title, Default, Xpos, Ypos, HelpFile,
➥Context, Type)
```

Here, *Type* is an optional number that specifies the data type of the return value, as follows:

Type	Data Type
0	Formula
1	Number
2	Text (the default)
4	Boolean (True or False)
8	Reference (a Range object)
16	Error value
32	An array of values

Accessing an Application's Built-In Dialog Boxes

Many VBA methods are known as *dialog box equivalents* because they let you select the same options that are available in an application's built-in dialog boxes. Using dialog box equivalents works fine if your procedure knows which options to select, but there are times when you might want the user to specify some of the dialog box options.

For example, if your procedure will print a document (using the `PrintOut` method), you might need to know how many copies the user wants or how many pages to print. You could use the `InputBox` method to get this data, but it's usually easier to just display the Print dialog box.

The built-in dialog boxes are `Dialog` objects, and `Dialogs` is the collection of all the built-in dialog boxes. Note that these objects are implemented only in Word and Excel.

note

To see a complete list of constants for Word and Excel's built-in dialog boxes, first open the Object Browser by selecting **View, Object Browser**. In the list of libraries, select the application (such as Excel or Word), and highlight <globals> in the Classes list. In the Member list, look for the *xxDialog* constants, where *xx* varies between applications: wdDialog for Word and xlDialog for Excel.

To reference a particular dialog box, use one of the predefined application constants. Table 12.3 lists a few of the more common ones from Word and Excel.

TABLE 12.3 Some of Word and Excel's Built-in Dialog Box Constants

Word Constant	Excel Constant	Dialog Box
wdDialogFormatFont	xlDialogFont	Font
wdDialogFileNew	xlDialogNew	New
wdDialogFileOpen	xlDialogOpen	Open
wdDialogFilePageSetup	xlDialogPageSetup	Page Setup
wdDialogEditPasteSpecial	xlDialogPasteSpecial	Paste Special
wdDialogFilePrint	xlDialogPrint	Print
wdDialogFilePrintSetup	xlDialogPrinterSetup	Printer Setup
wdDialogFileSaveAs	xlDialogSaveAs	Save As
wdDialogInsertObject	xlDialogObject	Object
wdDialogFormatStyle	xlDialogStyle	Style
wdDialogTableSort	xlDialogSort	Sort

To display any of these dialog boxes, use the Dialog object's Show method. For example, the following statement displays Excel's Print dialog box:

```
Application.Dialogs(xlDialogPrint).Show
```

If the user clicks Cancel to exit the dialog box, the Show method returns False. This means that you can use Show inside an If statement to determine what the user did:

```
If Not Application.Dialogs(xlDialogPrint).Show Then
    MsgBox "File was not printed"
End If
```

Note, too, that the Show method can take arguments. For example, Word's Show method uses the following syntax:

```
Dialog.Show(Timeout)
```

Dialog   The Dialog object you want to show.

Timeout The time, in thousandths of a second, after which the dialog box is dismissed. (Changes made by the user are accepted.)

For example, the following statement shows the Font dialog box, and then dismisses it after approximately 10 seconds:

```
Application.Dialogs(wdDialogFormatFont).Show 10000
```

Here's the syntax for Excel's Show method:

```
Dialog.Show(Arg1, Arg2....)
```

Dialog	The Dialog object you want to show.
Arg1, Arg2,...	These arguments represent specific controls in the dialog box, and they enable you to set the value of the controls in advance.

For example, here's the syntax for Excel's Font dialog box:

```
Application.Dialogs(xlDialogFont).Show name_text, size_num
```

Here, *name_text* and *size_num* represent the Face and Size controls, respectively, in the Font dialog box. The following statement shows Excel's Font dialog box, and it sets the Face list to Garamond and the Size list to 16:

```
Application.Dialogs(xlDialogFont).Show "Garamond", 16
```

To do the same thing in Word, you use the predefined argument names as though they were properties of the specified Dialog object. For example, you use Font to return or set the Font control value in the Font dialog box:

```
With Dialogs(wdDialogFormatFont)
    .Font = "Garamond"
    .Show
End With
```

note

To see a complete list of the control arguments used by Word and Excel, see the following Microsoft Web sites:

Word:

```
http://msdn.microsoft.com/library/default.asp?url=/library/en-us/
vbawd10/html/wohowDialogArguments.asp
```

Excel:

```
http://msdn.microsoft.com/library/default.asp?url=/library/en-us/
vbawd10/html/wohowDialogArguments.asp
```

Word's Dialog object is much more flexible and powerful than Excel's in that it supports extra properties and methods. For example, the DefaultTab property enables you to specify which dialog box tab has the focus when you display a dialog box. Here's an example that displays the Save tab in the Options dialog box:

```
With Application.Dialogs(wdDialogToolsOptions)
    .DefaultTab = wdDialogToolsOptionsTabSave
    .Show
End With
```

Word's Dialog object also has a Display method that uses a syntax similar to that of the Show method:

```
Dialog.Display(Timeout)
```

> Dialog   The Dialog object you want to show.
>
> Timeout   The time, in thousandths of a second, after which the dialog box is dismissed.

The difference is that if you specify a *Timeout* value, when the dialog box is dismissed after the specified time, Word does *not* accept the user's changes.

Another Dialog object method is Execute, which runs the dialog box without showing it to the user. Listing 12.8 shows an example.

LISTING 12.8 A Function Procedure That Uses Word's Word Count Dialog Box to Get the Total Number of Words in the Active Document

```
Function CountDocumentWords() As Long
    With Dialogs(wdDialogToolsWordCount)
        .Execute
        CountDocumentWords = .Words
    End With
End Function


Sub DisplayWordCount()
    MsgBox "This document contains " & CountDocumentWords & " words."
End Sub
```

This procedure uses Execute to run the Word Count dialog box, and then uses the Words argument to return the number of words in the document.

The Absolute Minimum

This chapter introduced you to a few methods for interacting with the users of your VBA applications (including yourself). You began with a look at sounds, including the simple Beep function and PowerPoint's more sophisticated SoundEffects object. From there, you progressed to displaying information to the user. You learned how to display messages in the status bar and how to display a message dialog box with the MsgBox function. You closed this chapter with two techniques for getting input from the user: the InputBox function and the application's built-in dialog boxes.

Here's a list of chapters where you'll find related information on user interaction:

- To get maximum control over your code's user interaction, you'll need to build your own custom dialog boxes and user forms. To find out how, see Chapter 13, "Creating Custom VBA Dialog Boxes."

- To make it easier for users to interact with your procedures, you can assign your procedures to menus and toolbars. I show you how this is done in Chapter 14, "Creating Custom Menus and Toolbars."

- A proper application interface shields the user from program errors. I show you a few techniques for doing this in Chapter 15, "Debugging VBA Procedures."

IN THIS CHAPTER

- Adding a user form (custom dialog box) to your project

- Changing the look and behavior of the form

- Inserting, selecting, and manipulating form controls

- Understanding and working with the various form controls, from command buttons to check boxes

- Displaying and closing forms and getting the form results

13

CREATING CUSTOM VBA DIALOG BOXES

VBA procedures are only as useful as they are convenient. There isn't much point in creating a procedure that saves you (or your users) a few keystrokes if you (or they) have to expend a lot of time and energy hunting down a routine. Shortcut keys are true time-savers, but some applications (such as Excel) have only a limited supply to dole out (and our brains can memorize only so many Ctrl+*key* combinations).

Instead, you need to give some thought to the type of user interface you want to create for your VBA application. The interface includes not only the design of the documents, but also three other factors that let the user interact with the model: dialog boxes, menus, and toolbars. Although you certainly can give the user access to the application's built-in dialogs, menus, and toolbars, you'll find that you often need to create your own interface elements from scratch. This chapter starts you off by showing you how to use VBA's Microsoft Forms feature to create custom dialog boxes and input forms. Chapter 14, "Creating Custom Menus and Toolbars," shows you how to set up custom menus and toolbars.

The InputBox function you learned about in Chapter 12, "Interacting with the User," works fine if you need just a single item of information, but what if you need four or five? Or, what if you want the user to choose from a list of items? In some cases, you can use the application's built-in dialog boxes (which I also discussed in Chapter 12), but these might not have the exact controls you need, or they might have controls to which you don't want the user to have access.

The solution is to build your own dialog boxes. You can add as many controls as you need (including list boxes, option buttons, and check boxes), and your procedures will have complete access to all the results. Best of all, the Visual Basic Editor makes constructing even the most sophisticated dialog boxes as easy as clicking and dragging the mouse pointer. The next few sections show you how to create dialog boxes and integrate them into your applications.

> **note**
>
> In VBA, dialog boxes are called *user forms* or just *forms*, for short. (A VBA form is a close cousin to the form objects that are used for data entry in Microsoft Access.) Since the term "form" is used in the Visual Basic Editor, I'll use that term throughout the rest of this chapter. Just remember, however, that a form is nothing but a dialog box that you create yourself.

Adding a Form to Your Project

Forms are separate objects that you add to your VBA projects. To do this, open the Visual Basic Editor and either select Insert, UserForm or drop down the Insert toolbar button (the second from the left) and select UserForm. As you can see in Figure 13.1, VBA performs the following tasks in response to this command:

- ■ It adds a Forms branch to the project tree in the Project Explorer.
- ■ It creates a new UserForm object and adds it to the Forms branch.

■ It displays the form in the work area.

■ It displays the Toolbox.

FIGURE 13.1

Selecting Insert, UserForm adds a new form to the project.

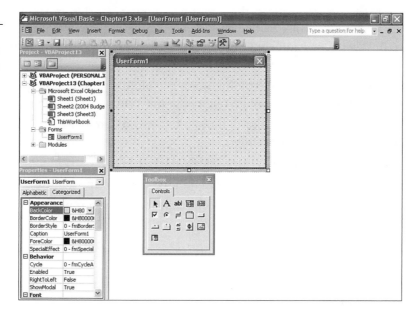

Changing the Form's Design-Time Properties

Forms (and all the control objects you can add to a form) have an extensive list of properties that you can manipulate by entering or selecting values in the Properties window. (Recall that you display the Properties window by activating View, Properties Window or by pressing F4.)

For a form, there are more than three dozen properties arranged into seven categories (in the Properties window, activate the Categories tab to see the properties arranged by category, as shown in Figure 13.1), as described in the next few sections.

> **note**
>
> Besides modifying form properties at design time, you can also modify many of the properties at runtime by including the appropriate statements in your VBA procedures. I talk about this in greater detail later in this chapter (see the section "Using a Form in a Procedure").

The Appearance Category

The properties in the Appearance category control the look of the form:

BackColor—Sets the color of the form's background. For this and all the color properties, you select a color by first clicking the drop-down arrow to display a color menu. In this menu, you can either choose a predefined color from the System tab or a built-in color from the Palette tab.

BorderColor—Sets the color of the form's border. Note that for this property to have any effect, you have to assign a border to the form using the BorderStyle property.

BorderStyle—Choose fmBorderStylSingle to apply a border around the form. Use fmBorderStyleNone for no border.

Caption—Specifies the text that's displayed in the form's title bar.

ForeColor—Sets the default color of text used in the form's controls.

SpecialEffect—Controls how the form appears relative to the form window (for example, raised or sunken) .

The Behavior Category

The properties in the Behavior category control aspects of how the user interacts with the form:

Cycle—Determines what happens when the user presses Tab while the focus is on the last control in the form. If this property is set to fmCycleAllForms and the form has multiple pages (see "Tab Strips and MultiPage Controls," later in this chapter), focus is set to the first control on the next page. If this property is set to fmCycleCurrentForm, focus is set to the first control on the current page.

Enabled—Set this property to True to enable the form or False to disable it (this prevents the user from manipulating the form or any of its controls).

RightToLeft—When True, this property changes the tab order of the form so that pressing Tab moves the highlight among the controls from right to left (instead of the usual left to right).

ShowModal—Set this property to True to display the form as modal, which means the user won't be able to interact with the underlying application until he or she closes the form.

The Font Category

The Font property determines the default font used throughout the form. When you activate this property, click the ellipsis (...) button to display the Font dialog box, from which you can select the font, style, size, and effects.

The Misc Category

As its name implies, the Misc category contains a collection of properties that don't fit anywhere else, although almost all of these properties are obscure and can be safely ignored. The one exception in the `Name` property, which you use to give a name to your form. (You'll use this name to refer to the form in your VBA code, so use only alphanumeric characters in the name.)

> **tip**
>
> Although you might be tempted to stick with the default form name supplied by VBA (such as UserForm1), your code will be easier to read if you give the form a more descriptive name. Indeed, this advice applies not only to forms, but to *all* controls.

The Picture Category

In the Picture category, use the `Picture` property to set a background image for the form. (Again, click the ellipsis button to select a picture file from a dialog box.) The other properties determine how the picture is displayed:

`PictureAlignment`—Specifies where on the form the picture is displayed.

`PictureSizeMode`—Specifies how the picture is displayed relative to the form:

`fmPictureSizeModeClip`—Crops any part of the picture that's larger than the form.

`fmPictureSizeModeStretch`—Stretches the picture so that it fits the entire form

`fmPictureSizeModeZoom`—Enlarges the picture until it hits the vertical or horizontal edge of the form.

`PictureTiling`—For small images, set this property to True to fill the background with multiple copies of the image.

The Position Category

The properties in the Position category specify the dimensions of the form (height and width) and the position of the form within the application window. For the latter, you can either use the `StartUpPosition` property to center the form relative to the application window (`CenterOwner`) or to the screen (`CenterScreen`), or you can choose Manual and specify the `Left` and `Top` properties. (The latter two properties set the form's position in points from the application window's left and top edges, respectively.)

The Scrolling Category

The properties in the Scrolling category determine whether the form displays scroll bars and, if it does, what format the scroll bars have:

`KeepScrollBarsVisible`—Determines which of the form's scroll bars remain visible even if they aren't needed.

`ScrollBars`—Determines which scrollbars are displayed on the form.

`ScrollHeight`—Specifies the total height of the form's scrollable region. For example, if the form's `Height` property is set to 200 and you set the `ScrollHeight` property to 400, you double the total vertical area available in the form.

`ScrollLeft`—If `ScrollWidth` is greater than the width of the form, use the `ScrollLeft` property to set the initial position of the horizontal scroll bar's scroll box. For example, if the `ScrollWidth` is 200, setting `ScrollLeft` to 100 starts the horizontal scroll bar at the halfway position.

`ScrollTop`—If `ScrollHeight` is greater than the height of the form, use the `ScrollTop` property to set the initial position of the vertical scroll bar's scroll box.

`ScrollWidth`—Specifies the total width of the form's scrollable region.

Working with Controls

Now that your form is set up with the design-time properties you need, you can get down to the brass tacks of form design. In other words, you can start adding controls to the form, adjusting those controls to get the layout you want, and setting the design-time properties of each control. I discuss the unique characteristics of each type of control later in this chapter (see the section "Types of Form Controls"). For now, though, I'll run through a few techniques that you can apply to any control.

Inserting Controls on a Form

The new form object is an empty shell that doesn't become a useful member of society until you populate it with controls. As with the form-building tools in Word and Access, the idea is that you use this shell to "draw" the controls you need. Later, you can either link the controls directly to other objects (such as Excel worksheet cells) or create procedures to handle the selections.

The Toolbox contains buttons for all the controls you can add to a form. Here are the basic steps to follow to add any control to the form:

1. Click the button you want to use.

2. Move the mouse pointer into the form and position it where you want the top-left corner of the control to appear.

3. Click and drag the mouse pointer. VBA displays a gray border indicating the outline of the control.

4. When the control is the size and shape you want, release the mouse button. VBA creates the control and gives it a default name (such as CheckBox*n,* where *n* signifies that this is the *n*th check box you've created on this form).

Selecting Controls

Before you can work with a control, you must select it. For a single control, you select it by clicking it. If you prefer to work with multiple controls, the Visual Basic Editor gives you a number of techniques:

- Hold down the Ctrl key and click each control.

- You also can "lasso" multiple controls by clicking and dragging the mouse. Move the mouse pointer to an empty part of the form, hold down the left button, and then click and drag. The VBE displays a box with a dashed outline, and any control that falls within this box (in whole or in part) will be selected.

- To select every control, make sure the form is active and then select Edit, Select All. (For faster service, you can also either press Ctrl+A or right-click an empty part of the form and choose Select All from the shortcut menu.)

To exclude a control from the selection, hold down the Ctrl key and click inside the control.

After you've selected multiple controls, you can set properties for all the controls at once. Note, however, that the Properties window will show only those properties that are common to all of the controls. (See "Common Control Properties" later in this chapter.) Not only that, but if you size, move, copy, or delete one of the selected controls (as described in the next few sections), your action will apply to all of the controls.

Each control is surrounded by an invisible rectangular *frame.* When you select a control, the VBE displays a gray outline that represents the control's frame and this outline is studded with white *selection handles* at the frame's corners and midpoints, as shown in Figure 13.2.

FIGURE 13.2

A selected control displays a frame and various selection handles.

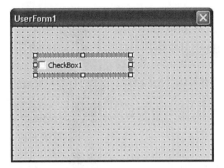

Sizing Controls

You can resize any control to change its shape or dimensions. The following procedure outlines the steps to work through:

1. Select the object you want to size.

2. Position the mouse pointer over the selection handle you want to move. The pointer changes to a two-headed arrow. To change the size horizontally or vertically, use the appropriate handle on the middle of a side. To change the size in both directions at once, use the appropriate corner handle.

3. Click and drag the handle to the position you want.

4. Release the mouse button. The VBE redraws the object and adjusts the frame size.

note

To size the form itself, click an empty part of the form and then click and drag the selection handles that appear around the form.

Moving Controls

You can move any control to a different part of the form by following these steps:

1. Select the control you want to move.

2. Position the mouse pointer inside the control. (You can also position the pointer over the control's frame, although you need to make sure the pointer isn't over a selection handle. In this case, the pointer changes to a four-headed arrow.)

3. Click and drag the control to the position you want. As you drag the object, a dashed outline shows you the new position.

4. Release the mouse button. The VBE redraws the control in the new position.

Copying Controls

If you've formatted a control and then decide that you need a similar control, don't bother building the new control from scratch. Instead, follow the steps outlined next to make as many copies of the existing control as you need:

1. Select the control you want to copy.

2. Hold down the Ctrl key, position the mouse pointer inside the control, and press the left mouse button. The pointer changes to an arrow with a plus sign.

3. Click and drag the pointer to the position you want. As you drag the mouse, a dashed outline shows you the position of the copied control.

4. Release the mouse button. The VBE copies the control to the new position.

tip

You also can right-click the control and select Copy from the control's shortcut menu. To paste the control, right-click an empty part of the form, and then click Paste. Alternatively, use Ctrl+C to copy a selected control and Ctrl+V to paste it.

You also can use the Clipboard to copy controls. In this case, you click the control; select Edit, Copy; and then select Edit, Paste. The Visual Basic Editor will add a copy of the control to the form that you can then move to the appropriate position.

Deleting Controls

To delete a control, select it and then select Edit, Delete. The Visual Basic Editor deletes the control.

Grouping Controls

The Visual Basic Editor lets you create control *groups*. A group is a collection of controls you can format, size, and move—similar to the way you format, size, and move a single control. To group two or more controls, select them and use any of the following techniques

tip

To delete a control quickly, select it and press the Delete key. Alternatively, you can right-click the control and select Delete from the short-cut menu.

■ Select the Format, Group command.

■ Right-click inside any one of the selected controls and select Group from the shortcut menu.

■ Click the UserForm toolbar's Group button.

The Visual Basic Editor treats a group as a single control with its own frame. To select an entire group, you just need to select one control from the group.

To ungroup controls, select the group and use one of these methods:

- Select Format, Ungroup.
- Right-click inside any one of the selected controls and select Ungroup from the shortcut menu.
- Click the UserForm toolbar's Ungroup button.

note

The UserForm toolbar contains many useful one-click shortcuts for working with forms. To display this toolbar, either select View, Toolbars, UserForm or right-click the Standard toolbar and select UserForm from the shortcut menu.

Setting Control Properties

Form controls are objects with their own sets of properties. A check box, for example, is a CheckBox object, and it has properties that control the name of the check box, whether it is initially checked, what its accelerator key is, and more.

You can manipulate control properties during program execution (in other words, at runtime) either before you display the form or while the form is displayed. (For example, you might want to disable a control in response to a user's action.) However, you can also set some control properties in the Visual Basic Editor (in other words, at design time) by using the Properties window. To display a particular control's properties in the Properties window, you have two choices:

- Click the control in the form.
- Select the control from the drop-down list near the top of the Properties window.

Common Control Properties

Later in this chapter I'll run through each of the default controls and explain their unique features. However, a few properties are common to many of the controls. Most of these properties perform the same function as those I outlined for a form earlier in this chapter. These properties include the following: BackColor, ForeColor, SpecialEffect, Enabled, Font, Picture, PicturePosition, Height, Width, Left, and Top. (Note that the latter two are relative to the left and top edges of the form.)

Here's a list of a few other properties that are common to some or all of the default controls:

Accelerator—This property determines the control's accelerator key. (In other words, the user will be able to select this control by holding down Alt and pressing the specified key.) The letter you enter into this property will appear underlined in the control's caption.

AutoSize—If this property is set to True, the control resizes automatically to fit its text (as given by the Caption property).

BackStyle—Determines whether the control's background is opaque (use fmBackStyleOpaque) or transparent (use fmBackStyleTransparent).

ControlSource—In the Visual Basic Editor for Excel, this property specifies which cell will be used to hold the control's data. You can enter either a cell reference or a range name.

Caption—Sets the control's text.

ControlTipText—Sets the "control tip" that pops up when the user lets the mouse pointer linger over the control for a second or two.

Locked—Set this property to True to prevent the user from editing the current value of the control.

TabIndex—Determines where the control appears in the tab order (in other words, the order in which VBA navigates through the controls when the user presses the Tab key). See the next section, "Setting the Tab Order."

TabStop—Determines whether the user can navigate to the control by pressing Tab. If this property is set to False, the user won't be able to select the control using the Tab key.

Visible—Determines whether the user can see the control (True) or not (False) .

> **tip**
>
> Some controls (such as list boxes and text boxes) don't have a Caption property. However, you can still assign an accelerator key to these controls by using a Label control. I'll show you how this is done when I discuss labels in the section "Types of Form Controls."

> **caution**
>
> The value of a cell linked to a control changes whenever the value of the control changes, even when the user clicks Cancel to exit the form. It's usually better (and safer) to assign the value of a control to a variable and then, if appropriate, place the value in the cell under program control.

Setting the Tab Order

As you know, you can navigate a form by pressing the Tab key. The order in which the controls are selected is called the *tab order*. VBA sets the tab order according to the order you create the controls on the form. You'll often find that this order isn't what you want to end up with, so the Visual Basic Editor lets you control the tab order yourself. The following procedure shows you how it's done:

1. Select View, Tab Order. (You can also right-click an empty part of the form and select Tab Order from the shortcut menu.) The Visual Basic Editor displays the Tab Order dialog box, shown in Figure 13.3.

2. In the Tab Order list, highlight the control you want to work with.

3. Click Move Up to move the item up in the tab order, or click Move Down to move the control down.

4. Repeat steps 2 and 3 for other controls you want to move.

5. Click OK.

Handling Form Events

An *event-driven* language is one in which code can respond to specific events, such as a user clicking a command button or selecting an item from a list. The procedure can then take appropriate action, whether it's validating the user's input or asking for confirmation of the requested action. A form responds to more than 20 separate events, including activating and deactivating the form, displaying the form, clicking the form, and resizing the form.

For each event associated with an object, VBA has set up mini procedures called *event handlers*. These procedures are really just Sub and End Sub statements. You process the event by filling in your own VBA code between these statements. Here are the steps to follow:

1. Click the object for which you want to define an event handler.

2. Either select View, Edit Code or double-click the object. (You can also right-click the object and select Edit Code from the shortcut menu.) VBA displays the code module for the object, as shown in Figure 13.4.

FIGURE 13.4

For each event, VBA defines a mini procedure. You define the procedure by entering code into this stub.

3. Use the procedure drop-down list (the one on the right) to select the event you want to work with.

4. Enter the rest of the procedure code between the Sub and End Sub statements.

Types of Form Controls

The default Toolbox offers 14 different controls for your custom forms. The next few sections introduce you to each type of control and show you the various options and properties associated with each object.

Command Buttons

Most forms include command buttons to let the user accept the form data (an OK button), cancel the form (a Cancel button), or carry out some other command at a click of the mouse.

To create a command button, use the CommandButton tool in the Toolbox. A command button is a CommandButton object that includes many of the common control properties mentioned earlier, as well as the following design-time properties (among others):

Cancel—If this property is set to True, the button is selected when the user presses Esc.

Caption—Returns or sets the text that appears on the button face.

Default—If this property is set to True, the button is selected when the user presses Enter. Also, the button is displayed with a thin black border.

Labels

You use labels to add text to the form. To create labels, use the Label button in the Toolbox to draw the label object, and then edit the Caption property. Although labels are mostly used to display text, you can also use them to name controls that don't have their own captions—such as text boxes, list boxes, scroll bars, and spinners.

It's even possible to define an accelerator key for the label and have that key select another control. For example, suppose you want to use a label to describe a text box, but you also want to define an accelerator key that the user can press to select the text box. The trick is that you must first create a label and set its Accelerator property. You then create the text box immediately after. Because the text box follows the label in the tab order, the label's accelerator key will select the text box.

> **tip**
>
> To assign a label and accelerator key to an existing control, add the label and then adjust the tab order so that the label comes immediately before the control in the tab order.

Text Boxes

Text boxes are versatile controls that let the user enter text, numbers, and, in Excel, cell references and formulas. To create a text box, use the TextBox button in the Toolbox. Here are a few useful properties of the TextBox object:

EnterFieldBehavior—Determines what happens when the user tabs into the text box. If you select 0 (fmEnterFieldBehaviorSelectAll), the text within the field is selected. If you select 1 (fmEnterFieldBehaviorRecallSelect), only the text that the user selected the last time he was in the field will be selected.

EnterKeyBehavior—When set to True, this property lets the user start a new line within the text box by pressing Enter. (Note that this is applicable only if you set MultiLine to True, as described in a moment.) When this property is False, pressing Enter moves the user to the next field.

MaxLength—This property determines the maximum number of characters that the user can enter.

MultiLine—Set this property to True to let the user enter multiple lines of text.

PasswordChar—If this property is set to True, the text box displays the user's entry as asterisks (which is useful if you're using the text box to get a password or other sensitive data).

Text—Returns or sets the text inside the text box.

WordWrap—When this property is True, the text box wraps to a new line when the user's typing reaches the right edge of the text box.

Frames

You use frames to create groups of two or more controls. There are three situations in which frames come in handy:

- **To organize a set of controls into a logical grouping**—Let's say your form contains controls for setting program options and obtaining user information. You could help the user make sense of the form by creating two frames—one to hold all the controls for the program options, and one to hold the controls for the user information.

- **To move a set of controls as a unit**—When you draw controls inside a frame, these controls are considered to be part of the frame object. Therefore, when you move the frame, the controls move right along with it. This can make it easier to rearrange multiple controls on a form.

- **To organize option buttons**—If you enter multiple option buttons inside a frame (see the next section), VBA treats them as a group and therefore allows the user to activate only one of the options.

To create a frame, click the Frame button in the Toolbox and then click and drag a box inside the form. Note that you use the `Frame` object's `Caption` property to change the caption that appears at the top of the box.

Option Buttons

Option buttons are controls that usually appear in groups of two or more; the user can select only one of the options. To create an option button, use the OptionButton tool. You can determine whether an option button starts off activated or deactivated by setting the `Value` property: If it's True, the option is activated; if it's False, the option is deactivated.

For option buttons to work effectively, you need to group them so that the user can select only one of the options at a time. VBA gives you three ways to do this:

- Create a frame and then draw the option buttons inside the frame.

- Use the same `GroupName` property for the options you want to group.

- If you don't draw the option buttons inside a frame or use the `GroupName` property, VBA treats all the option buttons in a form as one group.

tip

If you already have one or more "unframed" option buttons on your form, you can still insert them into a frame. Just select the buttons, cut them to the Clipboard, select the frame, and paste. VBA will add the buttons to the frame.

Check Boxes

Check boxes let you include options that the user can toggle on or off. To create a check box, click the CheckBox button in the Toolbox.

As with option buttons, you can control whether a check box is initially activated (checked). Set its `Value` property to True to activate the check box, or to False to deactivate it.

Toggle Buttons

A toggle button is a cross between a check box and a command button: Click it once, and the button stays pressed; click it again, and the button returns to its normal state. You create toggle buttons by using the ToggleButton tool in the Toolbox.

You control whether a toggle button is initially activated (pressed) by setting its `Value` property to True to "press" the button or to False to "unpress" the button.

List Boxes

VBA offers two different list objects you can use to present the user with a list of choices: a `ListBox` and a `ComboBox`.

The `ListBox` Object

The `ListBox` object is a simple list of items from which the user selects an item or items. Use the ListBox button to create a list box. Here are some `ListBox` object properties to note:

`ColumnCount`—The number of columns in the list box.

`ColumnHeads`—If this property is True, the list columns are displayed with headings.

`MultiSelect`—If this property is True, the user may select multiple items in the list.

`RowSource`—Determines the items that appear in the list. In Excel, enter a range or a range name.

`Text`—Sets or returns the selected item.

The `ComboBox` Object

The `ComboBox` object is a control that combines a text box with a list box. The user clicks the drop-down arrow to display the list box and then selects an item from the list or enters an item in the text box. Use the ComboBox button to create this control.

Because the `ComboBox` is actually two separate controls, the available properties are an amalgam of those discussed earlier for a text box and a list box. You can also work with the following properties that are unique to a `ComboBox` object:

`ListRows`—Determines the number of items that appear when the user drops the list down.

`MatchRequired`—If this property is True, the user can only enter values from the list. If it's False, the user can enter new values.

`Style`—Determines the type of ComboBox. Use 0 (`fmStyleDropDownCombo`) for a list that includes a text box; use 2 (`fmStyleDropDownList`) for a list only.

List Box Techniques

How do you specify the contents of a list if the `RowSource` property isn't applicable (that is, if you're not working in Excel or if the data you want in the list isn't part of an Excel range)? In this case, you must build the list at runtime. You can use the `AddItem` method, described later in this section, or you can set the `List` property. For the latter, you must specify an array of values. For example, the following statements use a form's `Initialize` event to populate a list box with the days of the week:

```
Private Sub UserForm_Initialize()
    ListBox1.List() = Array("Monday", "Tuesday", "Wednesday",
➡"Thursday", "Friday", "Saturday", "Sunday")
End Sub
```

List boxes also have a few useful methods for controlling from your VBA code the items that appear in a list box:

`AddItem`—Adds an item to the specified list box. Here's the syntax:

`object.AddItem(text,index)`

object	The name of the `ListBox` object to which you want to add the item.
text	The item's text.
index	The new item's position in the list. If you omit this argument, VBA adds the item to the end of the list.

`Clear`—Removes all the items from the specified list box.

`RemoveItem`—Removes an item from the specified list box using the following syntax:

`object.RemoveItem(index)`

object	The `ListBox` object from which you want to remove the item.
index	The index number of the item you want to remove.

Scrollbars

Scrollbars are normally used to navigate windows, but by themselves, you can use them to enter values between a predefined maximum and minimum. Use the ScrollBar button to create either a vertical or horizontal scrollbar. Here's a rundown of the ScrollBar object properties you'll use most often in your VBA code:

LargeChange—Returns or sets the amount that the scrollbar value changes when the user clicks between the scroll box and one of the scroll arrows.

Max—Returns or sets the maximum value of the scrollbar.

Min—Returns or sets the minimum value of the scrollbar.

SmallChange—Returns or sets the amount that the scrollbar value changes when the user clicks one of the scroll arrows.

Value—Returns or sets the current value of the scrollbar.

Spin Buttons

A spin button is similar to a scrollbar in that the user can click the button's arrows to increment or decrement a value. To create a spin button, use the SpinButton tool in the Toolbox. The properties for a SpinButton object are the same as those for a ScrollBar (except that there is no LargeChange property).

Most spin buttons have a text box control beside them to give the user the choice of entering the number directly or selecting the number by using the spin button arrows. You have to use VBA code to make sure that the values in the text box and the spinner stay in sync. (In other words, if you increment the spinner, the value shown in the text box increments as well, and vice versa.)

To do this, you have to add event handler code for both controls. For example, suppose you have a text box named TextBox1 and a spin button named SpinButton1. Listing 13.1 shows the basic event handler code that will keep the values of these two controls synchronized.

note

I use Excel as the underlying application for the procedures in this chapter. To get the code for these procedures, see my Web site:

http://www.mcfedries.com/ABGVBA/Chapter13.xls

For Listing 13.1, see the code for the form named TestForm.

LISTING 13.1 Event Handler Code that Keeps a Text Box and a Spin Button in Sync

```
Private Sub TextBox1_Change()
    SpinButton1.Value = TextBox1.Value
End Sub

Private Sub SpinButton1_Change()
    TextBox1.Value = SpinButton1.Value
End Sub
```

Tab Strips and MultiPage Controls

I mentioned earlier that you can use frames to group related controls visually and help the user make sense of the form. However, there are two situations in which a frame falls down on the job.

The first situation is when you need the form to show multiple sets of the same (or similar) data. For example, suppose you have a form that shows values for sales and expense categories. You might want the form to be capable of showing separate data for various company divisions. One solution would be to create separate frames for each division and populate each frame with the same controls, but this is clearly inefficient. A second solution would be to use a list or a set of option buttons. This will work, but it might not be obvious to the user how he is supposed to display different sets of data, and these extra controls just serve to clutter the frame. A better solution is to create a tabbed form where each tab represents a different set of data.

The second situation is when you have a lot of controls. In this case, even the judicious use of frames won't be enough to keep your form from becoming difficult to navigate and understand. In situations where you have a large number of controls, you're better off creating a tabbed form that spreads the controls over several tabs.

In both of these situations, the tabbed form solution acts much like the tabbed dialog boxes you work with in Windows, Office, and other modern programs. To create tabs in your forms, VBA offers two controls: TabStrip and MultiPage.

The TabStrip Control

The TabStrip is an ideal way to give the user an intuitive method of displaying multiple sets of data. The basic idea behind the TabStrip control is that as the user navigates from tab to tab, the visible controls remain the same, and only the data displayed inside each control changes. The advantage here is that you need to create only a single set of controls on the form, and you use code to adjust the contents of these controls.

You create a `TabStrip` by clicking the `TabStrip` button in the Toolbox and then clicking and dragging the mouse until the strip is the size and shape you want. Here are a few points to keep in mind:

- The best way to set up a `TabStrip` is to add it as the first control on the form and then add the other controls inside the `TabStrip`.

- If you already have controls defined on the form, draw the `TabStrip` over the controls and then use the Send to Back command (described earlier) to send the `TabStrip` to the bottom of the Z-order.

- You can also display a series of buttons instead of tabs. To use this format, select the `TabStrip` and change the `Style` property to `fmTabStyleButtons` (or 1).

Figure 13.5 shows a form that contains a `TabStrip` control and an Excel worksheet that shows budget data for three different divisions. The goal here is to use the `TabStrip` to display budget data for each division as the user selects the tabs.

FIGURE 13.5

Using the form's TabStrip to display budget data from the three divisions in the Excel worksheet.

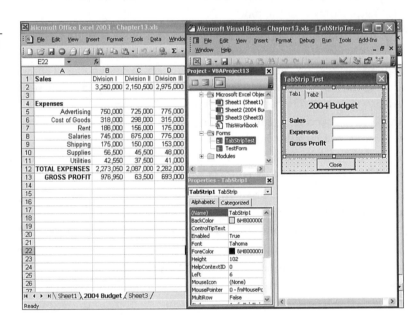

The first order of business is to use code to change the tab captions, add a third tab, and enter the initial data. Listing 13.2 shows an `Initialize` event procedure that does just that.

LISTING 13.2   An `Initialize` Event Procedure that Sets Up a TabStrip

```vba
Private Sub UserForm_Initialize()
    '
    ' Rename the existing tabs
    '
    With TabStrip1
        .Tabs(0).Caption = "Division I"
        .Tabs(1).Caption = "Division II"
        '
        ' Add a new tab
        '
        .Tabs.Add "Division III"
    End With
    '
    ' Enter the intial data for Division I
    '
    With Worksheets("2004 Budget")
        txtSales = .[B2]
        txtExpenses = .[B12]
        txtGrossProfit = .[B13]
    End With
End Sub
```

The code first uses the `Tabs` collection to change the captions of the two existing tabs. The `Tabs` collection represents all the tabs in a `TabStrip`, and you refer to individual tabs using an index number (where the first tab is 0, the second is 1, and so on). Then the `Tabs` collection's `Add` method is used to add a third tab titled Division III to the `TabStrip`. Finally, the three text boxes within the `TabStrip` (named `txtSales`, `txtExpenses`, and `txtGrossProfit`) are set to their respective values for Division I in the 2004 Budget worksheet.

Now you must set up a handler for when the user clicks a tab. This fires a `Change` event for the `TabStrip`, so you use this event handler to adjust the values of the text boxes, as shown in Listing 13.3.

LISTING 13.3   A `Change` Event Procedure that Modifies the Controls Within a Tab Strip Whenever the User Selects a Different Tab

```vba
Private Sub TabStrip1_Change()
        With Worksheets("2004 Budget")
            Select Case TabStrip1.Value
                Case 0
```

LISTING 13.3 (continued)

```
                        '
                        ' Enter the data for Division I
                        '
                        txtSales = .[B2]
                        txtExpenses = .[B12]
                        txtGrossProfit = .[B13]
                        Case 1
                        '
                        ' Enter the data for Division II
                        '
                        txtSales = .[C2]
                        txtExpenses = .[C12]
                        txtGrossProfit = .[C13]
                        Case 2
                        '
                        ' Enter the data for Division III
                        '
                        txtSales = .[D2]
                        txtExpenses = .[D12]
                        txtGrossProfit = .[D13]
                End Select
        End With
End Sub
```

Here, a Select Case checks the Value property of the TabStrip (where the first tab has the value 0, the second tab has the value 1, and so on). Figure 13.6 shows the form in action. (See "Displaying the Form" later in this chapter to learn how to run a form.)

The MultiPage Control

The MultiPage control is similar to a TabStrip in that it displays a series of tabs along the top of the form. The major difference, however, is that each tab represents a separate form (called a *page*). Therefore, you use a MultiPage control whenever you want to display a different set of controls each time the user clicks a tab.

You add a MultiPage control to your form by clicking the MultiPage button in the Toolbox and then clicking and dragging the mouse until the control is the size and shape you want.

It's important to remember that each page in the control is a separate object (a Page object). So each time you select a page, the values that appear in the Properties window apply only to the selected page. For example, the Caption property determines the text that appears in the page's tab. Also, you set up a page by selecting it and then drawing controls inside the page. (If you have controls on the form already, you can put them inside a page by cutting them to the Clipboard, selecting the page, and pasting the controls.)

FIGURE 13.6

Clicking each tab displays the data for the appropriate division.

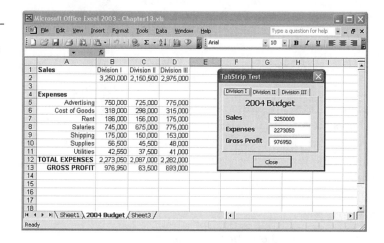

Working with a MultiPage control in code is very similar to working with a TabStrip:

■ The Pages collection represents all the pages inside a MultiPage control. You refer to individual pages using their index numbers.

■ Use the Pages.Add method to add more pages to the control.

■ When the user selects a different tab, the MultiPage control's Change event fires.

Using a Form in a Procedure

After you've created your form, the next step is to incorporate your handiwork into some VBA code. This involves three separate techniques:

■ Displaying the form

■ Handling events while the form is displayed

■ Processing the form results

Displaying the Form

Each UserForm object has a Show method that you use to display the form to the user. For example, to display a form named UserForm1, you would use the following statement:

```
UserForm1.Show
```

Alternatively, you may want to load the form into memory but keep it hidden from the user. For example, you may need to perform some behind-the-scenes manipulation of the form before showing it to the user. You can do this by executing the Load statement:

Load *Form*

> *Form*   The name of the form you want to load.

This statement brings the form object into memory and fires the form's Initialize event. From there, you can display the form to the user at any time by running the form's Show method as discussed above.

Unloading the Form

Once the user has filled out the form, you'll probably want her to click a command button to put whatever values she entered into effect. Alternatively, she could click some sort of Cancel button to dismiss the form without affecting anything.

However, just clicking a command button doesn't get rid of the form—even if you've set up a command button with the Default or Cancel property set to True. Instead, you have to add the following statement to the event handler for the command button:

Unload Me

The Unload command tells VBA to dismiss the form. Note that the Me keyword refers to the form in which the event handler resides. For example, the following event handler processes a click on a command button named cmdCancel:

```
Private Sub cmdCancel_Click()
    Dim result as Integer
    result = MsgBox("Are you sure you want to Cancel?", _
                    vbYesNo + vbQuestion)
    If result = vbYes Then Unload Me
End Sub
```

You should note, however, that simply unloading a form doesn't remove the form object from memory. To ensure proper cleanup (technically, to ensure that the form object class fires its internal Terminate event), Set the form object to Nothing. For example, the following two lines Show the `TabStripTest` form and then Set it to `Nothing` to ensure termination:

```
TabStripTest.Show
Set TabStripTest = Nothing
```

Processing the Form Results

When the user clicks OK or Cancel (or any other control that includes the `Unload Me` statement in its Click event handler), you usually need to examine the form results and process them in some way.

Obviously, how you proceed depends on whether the user has clicked OK or Cancel because this almost always determines whether the other form selections should be accepted or ignored.

■ If OK is clicked, the Click event handler for that button can process the results. In other words, it can read the `Value` property for each control (for example, by storing them in variables for later use in the program).

■ If Cancel is clicked, the code can move on without processing the results. (As shown earlier, you can include code to ask the user if he's sure he wants to cancel.)

Table 13.1 lists all the controls that have a `Value` property and provides a description of what kind of data gets returned.

TABLE 13.1   Value Properties for Some Form Controls

Object	What It Returns
CheckBox	True if the check box is activated; False if it's deactivated; Null otherwise.
ComboBox	The position of the selected item in the list (where 1 is the first item).
ListBox	The position of the selected item in the list (where 1 is the first item).
MultiPage	An integer that represents the active page (where 0 is the first page).
OptionButton	True if the option is activated; False if it's deactivated; Null otherwise.
ScrollBar	A number between the scrollbar's minimum and maximum values.
SpinButton	A number between the spinner's minimum and maximum values.
TabStrip	An integer that represents the active tab (where 0 is the first tab).
TextBox	The value entered in the box.
ToggleButton	True if the button is pressed; False otherwise.

For example, Figure 13.7 shows the Convert Case form created in the Visual Basic Editor. The idea behind this form is to convert the selected cells to proper case, uppercase, or lowercase, depending on the option chosen.

FIGURE 13.7

A custom form that lets the user change the case of the selected worksheet cells.

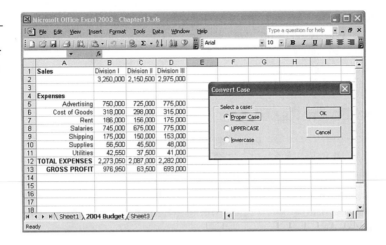

To load this form, I created a macro named ConvertCase that contains the two statements shown earlier:

```
ConvertCase.Show
Set ConvertCase = Nothing
```

Here, ConvertCase is the name of the form shown in Figure 13.7. The three option buttons are named optProper, optUpper, and optLower; the OK button is named cmdOK. Listing 13.4 shows the event handler that runs when the user clicks OK.

LISTING 13.4 A Procedure that Processes the Convert Case Custom Form

```
Private Sub cmdOK_Click()
    Dim c As Range
    For Each c In Selection
        If optProper.Value = True Then
            c.Value = StrConv(c, vbProperCase)
        ElseIf optUpper.Value = True Then
            c.Value = StrConv(c, vbUpperCase)
        ElseIf optLower.Value = True Then
            c.Value = StrConv(c, vbLowerCase)
        End If
    Next 'c
    Unload Me
End Sub
```

The procedure runs through the selected cells, checking to see which option button was chosen, and then converts the text by using VBA's StrConv function:

StrConv(*String, Conversion*)

String	The string you want to convert.
Conversion	A constant that specifies the case you want:

Conversion	Resulting Case
vbProperCase	Proper Case
vbUpperCase	UPPERCASE
vbLowerCase	lowercase

THE ABSOLUTE MINIMUM

This chapter showed you how to work with VBA's Microsoft Forms feature to create custom dialog boxes. After a brief introduction to user forms, you learned you how to add a form to your project and how to set a number of form design-time properties. From there, you turned your attention to controls, and you learned numerous techniques for working with the various Toolbox objects, including inserting, selecting, sizing, moving, copying, and deleting controls. After a brief discussion of form event handlers, I took you on a tour of the various control types that are available in the Toolbox. You finished by learning how to handle forms inside your VBA procedures. Here are some places to go for related material:

- Handling form results often means using loops and control structures (such as If...Then...Else and Select Case). I explain these VBA statements in Chapter 6, "Controlling Your VBA Code."

- The MsgBox and InputBox functions provide simple form capabilities in a single statement. I show you how to use these functions in Chapter 12, "Interacting with the User." This chapter also shows you how to access the built-in dialog boxes available in VBA applications.

- You complete your look at VBA user-interface design in Chapter 14, "Creating Custom Menus and Toolbars."

14

CREATING CUSTOM MENUS AND TOOLBARS

In Chapter 1, "Recording Your First Macro," and Chapter 2, "Creating Your Own Macros," I showed you a number of methods for running your VBA macros. However, all these methods assume that you know which task each macro performs. If you're constructing procedures for others to wield, they might not be so familiar with what each macro name represents. Not only that, but you might not want novice users scrolling through a long list of procedures in the Macro dialog box or, even worse, having to access the Visual Basic Editor.

To help you avoid these problems, this chapter presents some techniques for making your macros more accessible. To wit, I'll show you how to give your users the ability to use familiar tools—namely, menus and toolbars—to run your macros. You'll learn not only how to modify menus and toolbars by hand using the built-in application tools, but also how to build custom menus and toolbars using VBA code.

Assigning Macros to Menu Commands

We tend to take it for granted now, but one of Windows's biggest advantages is what technical types call its "consistent user interface." This just means that most Windows programs operate in more or less the same way. For example, pull-down menus are now such a common feature of the PC landscape that we hardly notice them; we just assume that anybody with even a modicum of Windows experience knows how to work with them. That's a huge plus for your own VBA interface design chores because it means you have a built-in mechanism for delivering access to your procedures—a mechanism, moreover, that requires no support or training on your part. In other words, you can add your macros as commands on the application's existing menu system, and therefore put your VBA procedures within easy reach. You can even create your own menus so as not to clutter the application's built-in menus. This section shows you how to create custom menus and commands and associate macros with them.

First, a Game Plan

Before you dive into the menu customization techniques outlined in the next few sections, you need to take a step back and plan what you want to do. For starters, bear in mind that these techniques require access to the user's computer, so they only apply to the following situations:

- You're a corporate developer and your VBA code is designed for a limited number of employees. (After all, you wouldn't want to tweak the menu systems of a thousand machines!)

- You're a consultant putting together a system for a client.

- You want easier access to the macros and procedures you've developed for your own use.

In each case, I'm assuming you can sit down in front of the computer, load the underlying application, and make the appropriate menu customizations.

On the other hand, there will be plenty of situations where you can't access the user's computer directly; for example, if you distribute your VBA code electronically or via some other means where you have no direct contact with the user. Similarly, you might be building VBA procedures for use on hundreds or thousands of computers, and it's impractical to customize each system by hand. For these and similar cases, you need to use code to customize your menus. I'll tell you how to do this later in this chapter (see "Menus, Toolbars, and VBA").

The next thing you have to consider is the layout of your custom menus. You can use three levels of customization:

- **Menus**—This level involves creating an entirely new menu that appears in the application's menu bar. Use this level when you have many different procedures and you don't want to cram them all into the application's built-in menus.

- **Submenus**—This level involves adding one or more submenus to the application's built-in menu system. (A submenu is a menu that appears when you select a menu command.) Use this level if you have several related procedures that you want to group together.

- **Menu commands**—This level involves tacking a new command or two onto one or more of the application's built-in menus. Use this level when you have just a few procedures.

Creating a New Menu

If you'll be adding a lot of new commands to the application's menu system, you might not want to bog down the existing menus with too many items. To keep things clean, you can create a custom menu just for your procedures. Here are the steps to follow:

1. Either select Tools, Customize or right-click the menu bar and select Customize from the shortcut menu. The application displays the Customize dialog box.

2. Activate the Commands tab.

3. In the Categories list, highlight New Menu, as shown in Figure 14.1.

FIGURE 14.1

Use the Commands tab in the Customize dialog box to create new menus in the application.

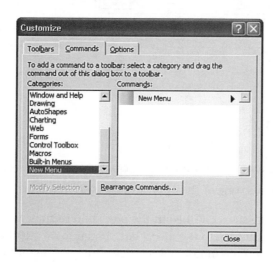

4. In the Commands list, drag the New Menu item up to the menu bar. You'll see a vertical bar that marks the spot where the new menu will appear. When the bar is positioned where you want your menu, drop the New Menu item.

5. Either click Modify Selection or right-click the new menu, and then use the Name box in the shortcut menu to name your new menu, as shown in Figure 14.2. Place an ampersand (&) before whichever letter you want to use as an accelerator key. (Remember: the accelerator key enables the user to drop down the menu by holding down Alt and pressing the key. Make sure the key you choose doesn't conflict with an accelerator key used by any other menu.)

FIGURE 14.2

Use this shortcut menu to rename the new menu bar item.

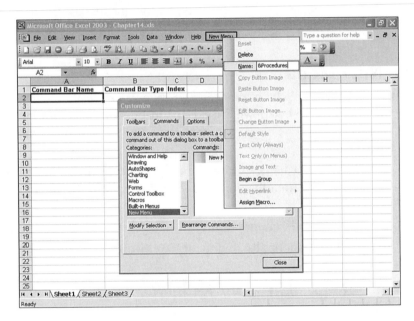

6. Press Enter.

Creating a New Submenu

To work with submenus, you have two choices:

- Add the submenu to the new menu you created in the last section.
- Add the submenu to one of the application's built-in menus.

Either way, you follow the steps outlined in the preceding section. However, instead of dragging the New Menu item to the menu bar, drag it to an existing menu. When the menu pulls down, drag the mouse pointer down into the menu to the position where you want the submenu to appear. When you drop the item, a new submenu is created.

To rename the submenu item, either right-click the item or highlight the item and click Modify Selection. Then use the Name text box to enter the new name (including an accelerator key) .

Adding Menu Commands and Assigning Macros

You're now ready to create the custom menu commands for your macros. Remember that you can create these commands in any of the following locations:

- On a custom menu that you've created
- On a custom submenu that you've created
- On one of the application's built-in menus

Here are the steps you need to work through:

1. Follow the steps outlined earlier to display the Commands tab in the Customize dialog box.

2. In the Categories list, highlight the Macros item.

3. In the Commands list, drag the Custom Menu Item to a custom menu, a custom submenu, or a built-in menu.

4. When the menu opens, drag the item down into the menu and then drop the item at the position where you want the command to appear.

5. Right-click the new command, or click Modify Selection, and then use the Name box in the shortcut menu to name your new menu. As before, place an ampersand (&) prior to whichever letter you want to use as an accelerator key. (To ensure that the Modify Selection menu remains onscreen, don't press Enter when you're done.)

6. In the Modify Selection menu, click Assign Macro. The Assign Macro dialog box appears, as shown in Figure 14.3.

FIGURE 14.3

Use this dialog box to choose the macro you want to assign to the new menu item.

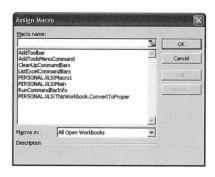

7. Use the Macro name list to highlight the macro you want to assign to the new menu command, and then click OK.

Deleting Menus and Menu Commands

If you don't need a custom menu, submenu, or command any longer, you can use a couple of methods to delete these items. First, display the Customize dialog box and then try either of the following techniques:

- Use the mouse to drag the item off the menu or menu bar and drop it outside the application's menu system.

- Right-click the item and then click Delete in the shortcut menu.

note

Although my focus in this chapter is only on creating menu items to run macros and procedures, you can use the Customize dialog box to remake any of the application's menus in your own image. Just follow the basic instructions in the last couple of sections to create submenus and menu commands. Instead of macros, however, you use the other items in the Categories list to create commands for application features that don't have existing commands.

Creating Custom Toolbars for Your Macros

Menu commands are fine, but there's nothing like a toolbar's one-click access for making your macros easy to run. This section shows you how to create custom toolbars, populate them with buttons, and assign macros to these buttons.

Creating a New Toolbar

Theoretically, you *could* add new buttons to the application's built-in toolbars, but you run the risk of overcrowding them and possibly confusing your users. Instead, you can create a toolbar from scratch and add custom buttons to it. Here are the steps to follow to create a new toolbar:

1. Either select Tools, Customize or right-click a toolbar and select Customize from the shortcut menu. The application displays the Customize dialog box.

2. Activate the Toolbars tab.

3. Click the New button. The New Toolbar dialog box appears, as shown in Figure 14.4.

4. Use the Toolbar name text box to enter the name you want to use for the toolbar and then click OK. The application displays a new, empty toolbar.

Adding a Toolbar Button and Assigning a Macro

Once you have your new toolbar, you can start adding buttons to it for your macros. Follow these steps:

1. In the Customize dialog box, select the Commands tab.

2. In the Categories list, highlight the Macros item.

3. In the Commands list, drag the Custom Button item and drop it on your new toolbar.

4. Either right-click the button or click Modify Selection and then use the Name box on the shortcut menu to name your new button. This is the text that will appear when the user hovers the mouse pointer over the button for a second or two.

5. To change the button face, click Change Button Image and then choose an image from the menu that appears. Alternatively, you can click Edit Button Image and use the Button Editor to create a custom image.

6. In the Modify Selection list, click Assign Macro to display the Assign Macro dialog box.

7. Use the Macro name list to highlight the macro you want to assign to the new menu command and then click OK.

Menus, Toolbars, and VBA

As I mentioned earlier, there might be times when it's inconvenient, impractical, or downright impossible to make design-time modifications to a user's menus or toolbars. What do you do in these situations if you want to give the user pull-down menu or toolbar access to your VBA procedures?

If you're building an Excel project, there *is* a way to distribute custom toolbars with your project:

1. Activate the workbook to which you want to attach the custom toolbar.
2. Select Tools, Customize and choose the Toolbars tab in the Customize dialog box.
3. Highlight your custom toolbar and then click Attach. Excel displays the Attach Toolbars dialog box.
4. Highlight the custom toolbar and then click Copy.
5. Click OK.

What do you do in other applications or if you don't want to attach a toolbar in Excel? Easy: Get your project to build its own menus, submenus, commands, and toolbars at runtime. For example, the document that contains your VBA project has an Open event that you can use to construct the necessary menu structure each time the user runs the application, as well as a Close event to remove the custom items when the project shuts down.

The secret of controlling menus and toolbars programmatically is VBA's CommandBars object. This Microsoft Office object is a collection that represents all the command bars in the current application, where a "command bar" can be any of the following: a menu bar, a shortcut menu, or a toolbar.

You can use the properties and methods of the CommandBars collection to make modifications to the application's menus and toolbars within procedures. This includes not only simulating the basic design-time techniques of adding menus, commands, and toolbars, but also some techniques that are only available at runtime, such as renaming, disabling, and enabling menus and commands. The rest of this chapter takes you on a brief tour of some of these techniques.

Understanding Command Bars

To work with command bars effectively, you'll likely need to change the way you think about menu bars, shortcut menus, and toolbars. In other words, instead of thinking of these as distinct objects, you need to start thinking of them as variations on the same theme. What theme? Well, for lack of anything better, how about the palette-of-controls-that-you-click-on-to-perform-an-action theme? Think about it. Whether it's a menu bar, a shortcut menu, or a toolbar, you interact with the object in the same way: You click a control (a menu bar item, a menu command, a toolbar button, and so on) and something happens (a menu pulls down, a command is executed, a submenu appears, a pop-up box appears, and so on).

This, in a nutshell, is why Microsoft decided to gather menu bars, shortcut menus, and toolbars under the umbrella of the `CommandBars` object. Each of these items is now a `CommandBar` object and the only difference between them is that they have a different `Type` property.

In a similar vein, the objects that can appear on a command bar—menu commands, toolbar buttons, pop-up boxes, drop-down menus, and so on—are called *controls*, and they're all variations of the `CommandBarControl` object.

Specifying a Command Bar

You use the `CommandBars` object to specify individual members—that is, `CommandBar` objects—of the collection. You can specify either an index number or the name of the command bar. For example, both of the following statements refer to the menu bar that appears when the focus is on an Excel worksheet:

```
CommandBars(1)
CommandBars("Worksheet Menu Bar")
```

Unlike most collections, the index numbers used in the `CommandBars` object aren't all that useful. For example, Excel's `Worksheets` collection contains all the worksheets in a workbook, and the index numbers correspond to the order the sheets appear in the workbook. In the `CommandBars` collection, however, the index numbers for the built-in menus and toolbars have been assigned by the application's design team, so they have no intrinsic meaning. This means that you'll usually have to refer to individual `CommandBar` objects by their names:

- **Custom CommandBar objects**—Any menus or toolbars that you create at runtime can also be named within the code. Therefore, your procedures will always know the names of these objects.

- **Built-in toolbars**—The names of the application's built-in toolbars are easy enough to figure out: The name of the toolbar is just the text that appears in the toolbar's title bar (when the toolbar is floating, that is).

- **Built-in menu bars and shortcut menus**—The application supplies a name for each built-in menu bar and shortcut menu, but there's no easy method for determining the names of these objects.

Not knowing the names of the built-in menu bars and shortcut menus is a problem, to be sure. To help you solve that problem, Listing 14.1 presents an Excel procedure that runs through the entire `CommandBars` collection and displays the name, type, and index number for each command bar.

LISTING 14.1 A Procedure That Runs Through Excel's `CommandBars` Collection and Writes the Name, Type, and Index Number of Each Command Bar

```
Sub ListExcelCommandBars()
    Dim i As Integer
    Dim cb As CommandBar
    Dim cbType As String
    i = 0
    For Each cb In CommandBars
        Select Case cb.Type
            Case msoBarTypeNormal      '0
                cbType = "Toolbar"
            Case msoBarTypeMenuBar      '1
                cbType = "Menu Bar"
            Case msoBarTypePopup        '2
                cbType = "Shortcut Menu"
        End Select
        With Worksheets("Sheet1").[a2]
            .Offset(i, 0) = cb.Name
            .Offset(i, 1) = cbType
            .Offset(i, 2) = cb.Index
        End With
        i = i + 1
    Next
    Set cb = Nothing
End Sub
```

If you'd like to list the command bars in Word, substitute the `With...End With` statement in Listing 14.1 with the following:

```
With ActiveDocument.Paragraphs(2).Range
    With .ParagraphFormat.TabStops
        .Add Position:=InchesToPoints(2)
        .Add Position:=InchesToPoints(3.5)
    End With
    .InsertAfter cb.Name & vbTab
    .InsertAfter cbType & vbTab
    .InsertAfter cb.Index
    .InsertParagraphAfter
End With
```

note

Listing 14.1 and most of the other code in this chapter is available on my Web site:

http://www.mcfedries.com/ABGVBA/ Chapter14.xls

For the modification to Listing 14.1 that works in Word, see the following file:

http://www.mcfedries.com/ABGVBA/ Chapter14.doc

Creating a New Command Bar

Whether you want to create a new toolbar, shortcut menu, or menu bar, the procedure is exactly the same. In other words, you invoke the Add method of the CommandBars object and use it to specify the type of command bar you want. Here's the syntax:

CommandBars.Add(*Name, Position, MenuBar, Temporary*)

Name	(optional) The name you want to use for the new command bar. Although this argument is optional, it's always a good idea to include it so that you can be sure of the command bar's name. Otherwise, the application assigns a generic name such as "Custom1."
Position	(optional) Determines where the command bar appears within the application's window:

Position	Description
msoBarTop	Command bar is docked at the top of the window.
msoBarBottom	Command bar is docked at the bottom of the window.
msoBarLeft	Command bar is docked on the left side of the window.
msoBarRight	Command bar is docked on the right side of the window.
msoBarFloating	Command bar is undocked (this is the default).
msoBarPopup	Command bar is a shortcut menu.
msoBarMenuBar	(Macintosh only) Command bar replaces the system menu bar.

MenuBar	(optional) A Boolean value that determines whether or not the new command bar replaces the active menu bar. Use True to replace the menu bar; use False to leave the active menu bar in place (this is the default).
Temporary	(optional) A Boolean value that determines when the command bar is deleted. Use True to have the command bar deleted when the application is closed; use False to keep the command bar (this is the default) .

For example, Listing 14.2 shows a procedure that uses the Add method to create a new temporary toolbar named My Toolbar. Before doing so, the procedure runs through the CommandBars collection to make sure there is no existing command bar with the same name. (The application generates an error if you attempt to create a new command bar with the name of an existing command bar.)

LISTING 14.2   A Procedure That Creates a New Toolbar After First Checking to See if a Command Bar with the Same Name Already Exists

```
Sub AddToolbar()
    Dim cb As CommandBar
    Dim cbExists As Boolean

    cbExists = False
    For Each cb In CommandBars
        If cb.Name = "My Toolbar" Then
            cbExists = True
            Exit For
        End If
    Next cb
    If cbExists Then
        MsgBox "A command bar named ""My Toolbar"" already exists!"
    Else
        Set cb = CommandBars.Add( _
            Name:="My Toolbar", _
            Position:=msoBarFloating, _
            Temporary:=True)
    End If
    Set cb = Nothing
End Sub
```

Command Bar Properties

Whether you're dealing with one of the application's built-in command bars or a custom command bar that you've created via code, you can exploit a number of CommandBar object properties in your VBA procedures. Here's a look a few useful ones:

CommandBar.BuiltIn—Returns True if the specified *CommandBar* is native to the application; returns False for custom command bars.

CommandBar.Controls—Returns a CommandBarControls object that represents the collection of all the controls contained in the specified *CommandBar*.

CommandBar.Enabled—When this property is True, the user can work with the specified *CommandBar*. The command bar is disabled when this property is set to False.

CommandBar.Height—Returns or sets the height, in pixels, for the specified *CommandBar*. This property only has an effect on a non-empty command bar. Also, note that setting this property results in an error in two situations:

- If the command bar is docked (in other words, the command bar's Position property isn't set to msoBarFloating; see the Position property, discussed later).

- If the command bar is protected against resizing (in other words, the command bar's Protection property is set to msoNoResize; see the Protection property, discussed later).

Here's a procedure fragment that checks a command bar's Position and Protection properties before changing the height:

```
With CommandBars("My Toolbar")
    If .Position = msoBarFloating And _
        Not .Protection = msoBarNoResize Then
         .Height = 100
    End If
End With
```

CommandBar.Index—Returns the index number in the CommandBars collection for the specified *CommandBar*.

CommandBar.Left—If the command bar is floating, this property returns or sets the distance, in pixels, of the left edge of the specified *CommandBar* from the left edge of the screen (not the application window). If the command bar is docked, this property returns the distance from the left edge of the docking area.

CommandBar.Name—Returns or sets the name of the specified *CommandBar*.

CommandBar.Position—Returns or sets the position of the specified *CommandBar*. This property uses the same constants that I outlined earlier for the Position argument in the CommandBars object's Add method.

CommandBar.Protection—Returns or sets the protection options for the specified *CommandBar*. You use these options to prevent (or allow) user customization of the object. When setting this property, use any one of the following constants (or you can apply multiple levels of protection by using the sum of two or more constants):

Protection	Value	Resulting Protection
msoBarNoProtection	0	None.
msoBarNoCustomize	1	Prevents the user from adding, modifying, or deleting controls.
msoBarNoResize	2	Prevents the user from resizing the command bar.
msoBarNoMove	4	Prevents the user from moving the command bar.
msoBarNoChangeVisible	8	Prevents the user from hiding or unhiding the command bar.
msoBarNoChangeDock	16	Prevents the user from docking or undocking the command bar.
msoBarNoVerticalDock	32	Prevents the user from docking the command bar on the left or right side of the window.
msoBarNoHorizontalDock	64	Prevents the user from docking the command bar on the top or bottom of the window.

`CommandBar.Top`—If the command bar is floating, this property returns or sets the distance in pixels of the top edge of the specified `CommandBar` from the top edge of the screen (*not* the application window). If the command bar is docked, this property returns the distance from the top edge of the docking area.

`CommandBar.Type`—Returns the object type for the specified `CommandBar`, as follows:

Type	Type of Command Bar
msoBarTypeNormal	Toolbar
msoBarTypeMenuBar	Menu bar
msoBarTypePopup	Shortcut menu

`CommandBar.Visible`—Returns or sets whether or not the specified `CommandBar` is visible. Use True to display the command bar; use False to hide the command bar. Note that VBA sets this property to False by default when you create a custom command bar.

`CommandBar.Width`—Returns or sets the width, in pixels, for the specified `CommandBar`. This property only has an effect on a non-empty command bar and, as with `Height`, this property results in an error if the command bar is docked or if the command bar is protected against resizing.

Deleting a Custom Command Bar

Unless you specify otherwise, the command bars you create become permanent parts of the application. This might be a desirable situation in certain circumstances. For example, if your VBA project contains utilities that are useful for any document in the application, it makes sense to give you or a user full-time access to the procedures.

On the other hand, your procedures might be applicable only while the VBA project is running. In this case, there are a number of reasons why you should delete the command bars when your project shuts down:

- To avoid confusing the user with extra command bars.

- To prevent damage to the user's other files that might be caused by running one of your procedures on a document that wasn't designed for your project.

- To save memory and resources.

I mentioned earlier that you can create your command bars with the Add method's *Temporary* argument set to True. This tells the application to delete the command bar upon exiting. For immediate deleting, however, use the CommandBar object's Delete method:

CommandBar.Delete

Here, *CommandBar* is the custom CommandBar object that you want to delete. Note that you can't delete built-in command bars.

Resetting a Built-In Command Bar

If you make changes to one of the application's built-in command bars, you can restore the command bar to its default state by using the Reset method:

CommandBar.Reset

CommandBar is the built-in CommandBar object you want to reset. For example, Listing 14.3 shows the CleanUpCommandBars procedure that loops through the CommandBars collection and performs one of two tasks: If the command bar is built-in, it's restored to its default state; if the command bar is a custom object, it's deleted.

LISTING 14.3   A Procedure That Runs Through the CommandBars Collection, Resets the Built-in Command Bars, and Deletes the Custom Command Bars

```
Sub CleanUpCommandBars()
    Dim cb As CommandBar
    For Each cb In CommandBars
```

LISTING 14.3 (continued)

```
            If cb.BuiltIn Then
                cb.Reset
            Else
                cb.Delete
            End If
        Next cb
        Set cb = Nothing
End Sub
```

Working with Command Bar Controls

At this point, your custom command bars aren't particularly useful because they can't do much of anything. In other words, they don't contain any controls that the user can click or otherwise execute. This section solves that problem by giving you the lowdown on VBA's command bar controls and by showing you how to add and modify custom command bar controls.

VBA divides command bar controls into three categories:

CommandBarButton—This is an object that the user clicks to execute a command or run a procedure. Menu commands and toolbar buttons are examples of CommandBarButton objects.

CommandBarPopup—This is an object that the user clicks to display a menu of items. Examples of CommandBarPopup objects are menu bar commands and menu commands that display submenus.

CommandBarComboBox—This object takes one of three forms: a text box into which the user enters text (for example, the Name text box in the Modify Selection menu shown in Figure 14.2); a drop-down list from which the user selects an item; or a combo box that combines a text box and a drop-down list (for example, the Font and Font Size controls on the Formatting toolbar in Word and Excel) .

Specifying a Control

As you learned earlier, each CommandBar object has a Controls property that returns the collection of all the controls on the command bar. You use this collection to specify individual controls using their index number, where Controls(1) is the first control on the command bar, `Controls(2)` is the second control, and so on. In each case, a `CommandBarControl` object is returned.

Another way to specify a control is to use the `CommandBar` object's `FindControl` method:

`CommandBar.FindControl(`*`Type, Id, Tag, Visible, Recursive`*`)`

CommandBar	The `CommandBar` object in which you want to search.
Type	(optional) A constant that specifies the type of `CommandBarControl` object you want to find. For custom controls, use one of the following constants that correspond to the control types discussed above: `msoControlButton`, `msoControlPopup`, `msoControlEdit`, `msoControlDropdown`, or `msoControlComboBox`. For built-in controls, Office also defines quite a number of other constants. To see these constants, look up the `Type` property of the `CommandBarControl` object in the Office VBA Help system.
Id	(optional) This is a unique identifier that the application supplies for each control. This identifier is returned by the `CommandBarControl` object's `Id` property.
Tag	(optional) Specifies the `Tag` property of the control you want to find.
Visible	(optional) Use True to search only for controls that are visible; use False to search for hidden controls as well (this is the default).
Recursive	(optional) Use True to search not only the command bar, but all of its submenus and pop-up menus; use False to search only the command bar (this is the default) .

If `FindControl` is successful, it returns a `CommandBarControl` object for the first control that matches your search criteria. If the search fails, `FindControl` returns the value Nothing.

The `FindControl` method is most often used with the *Id* parameter. For example, the identifier for Excel's Tools menu is 30007. So, as shown in the following statements, you can specify the Tools menu object by running `FindControl` with *Id* set to 30007:

```
Dim menuTools As CommandBarControl
Set menuTools = Application.CommandBars.FindControl(Id:=30007)
```

How do you know which identifier to use? That's tricky, but I have a solution. See "The Command Bar Info Utility," later in this chapter.

Adding a Control to a Command Bar

When customizing command bars, you have a number of different routes to take:

- You can modify a built-in command bar by adding built-in controls.
- You can modify a built-in command bar by adding custom controls that execute your VBA procedures.
- You can modify a custom command bar by adding built-in controls.
- You can modify a custom command bar by adding custom controls.

Whichever route you take, you insert a control into a command bar by using the `Controls` object's `Add` method:

`CommandBar.Controls.Add(Type, Id, Parameter, Before, Temporary)`

CommandBar	The `CommandBar` object into which you want to insert the control.
Type	(optional) A constant that determines the type of custom control to add (the default is `msoControlButton`):

Type	Control Object
`msoControlButton`	`CommandBarButton`
`msoControlPopup`	`CommandBarPopup`
`msoControlEdit`	`CommandBarComboBox`
`msoControlDropdown`	`CommandBarComboBox`
`msoControlComboBox`	`CommandBarComboBox`

Id	(optional) An integer that specifies the built-in control you want to add.
Parameter	(optional) You use this argument to send a parameter to a built-in control. (The application uses this parameter to modify how it runs the command associated with the control.) For custom controls, you can use this argument to send information to the procedure associated with the control.
Before	(optional) The index number of the control before which the new control will be added. If you omit this argument, VBA adds the control to the end of the command bar.
Temporary	(optional) A Boolean value that determines when the control is deleted. Use True to have the control deleted when the application is closed; use False to keep the control (this is the default) .

For example, the following statement adds a `CommandBarButton` object to the end of the toolbar named My Toolbar:

```
CommandBars("My Toolbar").Controls.Add Type:=msoControlButton
```

The Command Bar Info Utility

One of the problems you face when working with command bars and controls is that you're often flying blind. For example, you saw earlier that there's no easy way to tell the name of a menu bar or shortcut menu. Similarly, you can't add a built-in control to a command bar unless you know its `Id` property, but VBA gives you no easy way to determine this property.

To help you out, I put together a small utility that solves this dilemma. I created a form named `CommandBarInfo` (see Chapter 14.xls on my Web site) that, when run, displays the dialog box shown in Figure 14.5. The idea is that you use the Name list to select the name of a command bar and then use the Caption list to choose a control. The labels beneath this list tell you the control's `Id`, `Type`, and `Index` properties. If the control is a menu bar, the Command Caption list will contain the menu commands. Again, the `Id`, `Type`, and `Index` properties are shown for the selected command.

FIGURE 14.5

Use the Command Bar Info utility to find out the `Id` property of a built-in control.

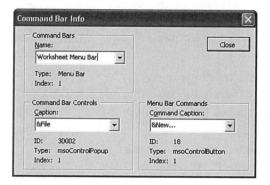

Control Properties

To make your custom controls do something useful, you have to set a few properties. For example, you'll want to specify the procedure to run when the user clicks the control, and you'll probably want to define a ToolTip for your toolbar-based controls. Here's a quick rundown of these and other control properties:

`Control.BeginGroup`—Returns True if the specified `Control` is at the beginning of a group of controls on a command bar. If True, the underlying application displays a separator bar before the `Control`.

`Control.BuiltIn`—Returns True if the specified `Control` is native to the application; returns False for custom controls.

`Control.Caption`—Returns or sets the caption for specified `Control`. If the control is a menu bar command or a menu command, the `Caption` property determines the command text, so you should include an ampersand before the letter you want to use as an accelerator key, like so:

```
Set newMenu = CommandBars(1).Controls.Add(Type:=msoControlPopup)
newMenu.Caption = "&My Menu"
```

`Control.Controls`—If the specified `Control` is a `CommandBarPopup` object, this property returns the collection of all the controls on the pop-up. For example, you can use this property to return all the menu items in a pull-down menu.

`Control.Enabled`—When this property is True, the user can work with the specified `Control`. The control is disabled when this property is set to False.

`Control.FaceId`—If the specified `Control` is a `CommandBarButton` object, this property returns or sets the ID number of the icon on the button's face. Note that this number is the same as the control's `Id` property in most cases.

`Control.Id`—As you've seen, this property returns a unique ID for the specified built-in `Control`. Note that all custom controls return 1 for the `Id` property.

`Control.Index`—Returns the index number in the Controls collection for the specified `Control`.

`Control.List(Index)`—If the specified `Control` is a `CommandBarComboBox` object, this property returns or sets the value of the list item given by `Index` (where 0 is the first item).

`Control.ListCount`—If the specified `Control` is a `CommandBarComboBox` object, this property returns the number of items in the list.

`Control.ListIndex`—If the specified `Control` is a `CommandBarComboBox` object, this property returns or sets the selected item in the list.

`Control.OnAction`—Returns or sets the name of the VBA procedure that will execute when the user clicks the specified `Control`. Listing 14.4 shows a procedure that adds a new command to the Tools menu.

LISTING 14.4 A Procedure That Modifies the Tools Menu by Adding a Command to Execute the `RunCommandBarInfo` Procedure

```
Sub AddToolsMenuCommand()
    Dim cb As CommandBar
    Dim menuTools As CommandBarControl
    Dim ctrl As CommandBarControl
    Dim ctrlExists As Boolean

    ctrlExists = False
    '
    ' Get the Tools menu (ID=30007)
    '
    Set menuTools = Application.CommandBars.FindControl(Id:=30007)
    '
    ' Make sure the command doesn't exist
    '
    For Each ctrl In menuTools.Controls
        If ctrl.Caption = "Command &Bar Info" Then
            ctrlExists = True
            Exit For
        End If
    Next ctrl
    '
    ' If the command doesn't exist, add it
    '
    If Not ctrlExists Then
        Set ctrl = menuTools.Controls.Add(Type:=msoControlButton)
        With ctrl
            .Caption = "Command &Bar Info"
            .OnAction = "RunCommandBarInfo"
        End With
    End If
    Set cb = Nothing
End Sub


' This procedure runs the CommandBarInfo utility.
'
Sub RunCommandBarInfo()
    CommandBarInfo.Show
End Sub
```

The procedure first checks to see if the command already exists. It does this by using the `FindControl` method to find the Tools menu (which the Command Bar Info utility tells us has ID 30007) and then using a `For Each...Next` loop to check the Caption of each item on the menu. If the command doesn't exist, the `Add` method tacks it onto the end of the menu, the `Caption` property is set to `Command &Bar Info`, and the `OnAction` property is set to `RunCommandBarInfo`. The latter procedure appears at the end of the listing, and it just runs the `Show` method to display the `CommandBarInfo` form.

`Control.ShortcutText`—If the specified `Control` is a `CommandBarButton` object that appears on a menu, this property returns or sets the shortcut key text that appears to the right of the control.

`Control.Style`—If the specified `Control` is a `CommandBarButton` object, this property returns or sets how the application displays the button:

Style	How the Button Is Displayed
msoButtonAutomatic	Using the application's default display.
msoButtonIcon	With an icon only.
msoButtonCaption	With a caption only.
msoButtonIconAndCaption	With an icon and a caption to the right of the icon.
msoButtonIconAndCaptionBelow	With an icon and a caption below the icon.
msoButtonIconAndWrapCaption	With an icon and a caption wrapped onto multiple lines to the right of the icon.
msoButtonIconAndWrapCaptionBelow	With an icon and a caption wrapped onto multiple lines below the icon.
msoButtonWrapCaption	With a caption only, wrapped onto multiple lines.

`Control.Text`—If the specified `Control` is a `CommandBarComboBox` object, this property returns or sets the text that appears in the text box part of the control.

`Control.ToolTipText`—Returns or sets the ToolTip text for specified `Control`.

`Control.Type`—Returns the object type for the specified `Control`. To see a complete list of control types, open the code window for the `CommandBarInfo` form and examine the `ControlType` function.

`Control.Visible`—Returns or sets whether or not the specified `Control` is visible. Use True to display the control; use False to hide the control.

Control Methods

To complete our examination of controls, this section looks at a few methods associated with controls. With these methods you can copy and move a control, execute the action that underlies a control, set the focus on a control, delete a control, and more. Here's the rundown:

`Control.AddItem`—If the specified `Control` is a `CommandBarComboBox` object, this method adds an item to the control's list using the following syntax:

`Control.AddItem(Text, Index)`

`Control`	The control to which you want to add the list item.
`Text`	A string that specifies the item to be added to the list.
`Index`	(optional) The position of the new item in the list. If you omit this argument, VBA adds the item to the end of the list.

`Control.Clear`—If the specified `Control` is a `CommandBarComboBox` object, this method clears the contents of the list. Note that you can't apply this method to a built-in control.

`Control.Copy`—Makes a copy of the specified `Control` using the following syntax:

`Control.Copy(Bar, Before)`

`Control`	The control you want to copy.
`Bar`	(optional) The `CommandBar` object to which you want to copy the control. If you omit this argument, VBA makes a copy of this control on the command bar that contains `Control`.
`Before`	(optional) The index number of the control before which the copied control will be inserted. If you omit this argument, VBA adds the control to the end of the command bar.

`Control.Delete`—Deletes the specified `Control` using the following syntax:

`Control.Delete(Temporary)`

`Control`	The control you want to delete.
`Temporary`	(optional) A Boolean value that determines the permanence of the deletion. If you use True, VBA deletes the control, but then restores the control the next time the application is started. If you use False, VBA deletes the control permanently (this is the default).

`Control.Execute`—Runs the built-in command or VBA procedure associated with the specified `Control`.

`Control.Move`—Moves the specified `Control` using the following syntax:

Control.Move(Bar, Before)

`Control`	The control you want to move.
`Bar`	(optional) The `CommandBar` object to which you want to move the control. If you omit this argument, VBA moves the control to the end of the command bar that contains `Control`.
`Before`	(optional) The index number of the control before which the moved control will be inserted. If you omit this argument, VBA adds the control to the end of the command bar.

`Control.RemoveItem`—If the specified `Control` is a `CommandBarComboBox` object, this method removes an item from the list using the following syntax:

Control.RemoveItem(*Index*)

`Control`	The control from which you want to remove the item.
`Index`	The number of the item that you want to remove.

`Control.Reset`—Restores the specified `Control` to its default state.

`Control.SetFocus`—Sets the focus on the specified `Control`.

THE ABSOLUTE MINIMUM

This chapter rounded out your VBA user interface education by showing you how to set up menus and toolbars to run your procedures. In the first part of this chapter, you learned how to use the built-in tools of the Office applications to create new menus and toolbars and to assign procedures to menu commands and toolbar buttons. From there, I showed you how to wield the `CommandBars` object model to create custom command bars and controls and to modify the application's built-in command bars and controls.

Here's a list of chapters where you'll find related information:

- I go through some basic user interface features—such as the `MsgBox` and `InputBox` functions—in Chapter 12, "Interacting with the User."

- The Command Bar Info utility is a custom user form, and the underlying code manipulates various objects in this form. To learn user forms and their objects, see Chapter 13, "Creating Custom VBA Dialog Boxes."

15

DEBUGGING VBA PROCEDURES

It's usually easy to get short Sub and Function procedures up and running. However, as your code grows larger and more complex, errors inevitably creep in. Many of these errors—programmers call them *bugs*—will be simple syntax problems you can fix easily, but others will be more subtle and harder to find. For the latter—whether the errors are incorrect values being returned by functions or problems with the overall logic of a procedure—you'll need to be able to look "inside" your code to scope out what's wrong. The good news is that VBA gives you several reasonably sophisticated *debugging* tools that can remove some of the burden of program problem solving. This chapter looks at these tools and shows you how to use them to help recover from most programming errors.

Trapping Program Errors

Your VBA procedures are, in final analysis, really quite dumb. After all, they can only do what you, the programmer, tell them to do. For example, if you tell a program to copy a file to a nonexistent disk, the dim brute just doesn't have the smarts to pull back from the abyss.

Later in this chapter you'll learn quite a few techniques that will prove invaluable for stomping on program bugs, so hopefully you'll be able to ship problem-free applications. However, a good and careful programmer *always* assumes that something, somewhere, at some time can and will go wrong (think of this as a kind of "Murphy's Law of Coding"). Given this heightened (enlightened?) state of paranoia, you must code your projects to allow for potential errors, no matter how obscure. A properly designed program doesn't leave you or another user out in the cold if an error rears its ugly head. Instead, you need to install code that *traps* these errors and either fixes the problem (if possible), alerts the user to the error so that he or she can fix it (such as by inserting a disk in a floppy drive), or reports a meaningful explanation of what went wrong so that the user can give you feedback. To that end, this section takes you through VBA's error-trapping techniques.

A Basic Error-Trapping Strategy

For many programmers, adding error-trapping code to a procedure can usually be found near the bottom of their to-do lists (probably just before adding comments to a procedure!). That's because error-trapping code isn't even remotely glamorous, and the optimistic (some would say foolhardy) programmer assumes it will never be needed.

note

There's a popular and appealing tale of how the word *bug* came about. Apparently, an early computer pioneer named Grace Hopper was working on a machine called the Mark II in 1947. While investigating a glitch, she found a moth among the vacuum tubes, so from then on glitches were called bugs. Appealing, yes, but true? Not quite. In fact, engineers had already been referring to mechanical defects as "bugs" for at least 60 years before Ms. Hopper's discovery. As proof, the *Oxford English Dictionary* offers the following quotation from an 1889 edition of the *Pall Mall Gazette*:

"Mr. Edison, I was informed, had been up the two previous nights discovering 'a bug' in his phonograph—an expression for solving a difficulty, and implying that some imaginary insect has secreted itself inside and is causing all the trouble."

That's a shame, because setting up a bare-bones error trap takes very little time. Even a more sophisticated trap can be reused in other procedures, so you really only have a one-time expenditure of energy. To help you get started down this crucial

path toward good program hygiene, this section presents a basic strategy for writing
and implementing error-trapping code. This strategy will unfold in four parts:

- Setting the error trap
- Coding the error handler
- Resuming program execution
- Disabling the error trap

Setting the Trap

In the simplest error-trapping case, VBA offers what I call the "never mind" statement:

```
On Error Resume Next
```

When inserted within a procedure, this statement tells VBA to bypass any line in the
procedure that generates an error and to resume execution with the line that immediately follows the offending statement. No error message is displayed, so the user
remains blissfully unaware that anything untoward has occurred. There are three
things to note about implementing this statement:

- The trap applies to any executable statement that occurs *after* the `On Error
  Resume Next` statement.
- The trap also applies to any executable statement within each procedure that
  is called by the procedure containing the `On Error Resume Next` statement.
- The trap is disabled when the procedure ends.

Because the `On Error Resume Next` statement does nothing to resolve whatever caused
the error, and because skipping the offending statement might cause further errors,
this error trap is used only rarely.

To set a true error trap, use the `On Error GoTo` statement instead:

```
On Error GoTo line
```

Here, `line` is a line label, which is a statement that's used to mark a spot within a
procedure (line labels aren't executable). The idea is that, if an error occurs, the procedure containing the `On Error GoTo` statement will branch immediately to the first
statement after the line label. This statement should be the beginning of the *error
handler* code that processes the error in some way (see the next section). Here's the
general structure that sets up a procedure to trap and handle an error:

```
Sub Whatever()
    On Error GoTo ErrorHandler
    [regular procedure statements go here]
```

```
    ' If no error occurs, bypass the error handler
    '

    Exit Sub
    '

    ' If an error occurs, the code will branch here
    '

ErrorHandler:
    [error handler code goes here]
End Sub
```

Here are some notes about this structure:

- To ensure that all statements are protected, place the On Error GoTo statement at the top of the procedure.

- The last statement before the error handler line label should be Exit Sub (or Exit Function if you're working with a Function procedure). This ensures that the procedure bypasses the error handler if no error occurs.

- The line label is a string—without spaces or periods—followed by a colon (:) at the end to tell VBA that it's just a label and should not be executed.

Coding the Error Handler

The On Error GoTo statement serves as the mechanism by which errors are trapped, but the nitty-gritty of the trap is the error handler. The handler is a group of statements designed to process the error, either by displaying a message to the user or by resolving whatever problem raised the error.

The simplest error handler just displays a message that tells the user that a problem occurred. Listings 15.1 and 15.2 provide an example. Listing 15.1 uses a couple of InputBox functions to get two numbers from the user: a dividend and a divisor. With these values in hand, the procedure calls the Divide function, as shown in Listing 15.2.

note

This chapter's code can be found on my Web site in both Excel and Word versions:

http://www.mcfedries.com/ABGVBA/
Chapter15.xls

http://www.mcfedries.com/ABGVBA/
Chapter15.doc

LISTING 15.1 The `GetNumbers` Procedure Prompts the User for a Dividend and a Divisor

```
Sub GetNumbers()
    Dim done As Boolean
    Dim divisor As Variant
    Dim dividend As Variant
    '
    ' Prompt user for dividend and divisor.
    '
    done = False
    Do While Not done
        dividend = InputBox("Enter the dividend:", "Divider")
        divisor = InputBox("Enter the divisor:", "Divider")
        done = Divide(dividend, divisor)
    Loop
End Sub
```

The purpose of the `Divide` function, shown in Listing 15.2, is to divide the dividend argument by the divisor argument. To trap a "division by zero" error, an `On Error GoTo` statement tells VBA to branch to the `DivByZeroHandler` label. (Actually, this statement will trap *any* error, not just a division by zero error.) The division is performed, and, if all goes well, a `MsgBox` displays the result. However, if the divisor value is zero, an error will occur, and the code will branch to the `DivByZeroHandler` label. This error handler displays a message and asks the user if he wants to try again. The function's return value is set according to the user's choice.

LISTING 15.2 The `Divide` Function Divides the Dividend by the Divisor and Traps "Division by Zero" Errors

```
Function Divide(dividend, divisor) As Boolean
    Dim msg As String
    Dim result As Single
    '
    ' Set the trap
    '
    On Error GoTo DivByZeroHandler
    '
    ' Perform the division
    '
    result = dividend / divisor
    '
```

LISTING 15.2 (continued)

```
    ' If it went okay, display the result
    '
    msg = dividend & _
          " divided by " & _
          divisor & _
          " equals " & _
          result
    MsgBox msg
    '
    ' Set the return value and bypass the error handler
    '
    Divide = True
    Exit Function
    '
    ' Code branches here if an error occurs
    '
DivByZeroHandler:
    '
    ' Display the error message
    '
    result = MsgBox("You entered 0 as the divisor! Try again?", _
                    vbYesNo + vbQuestion, _
                    "Divider")
    '
    ' Return the user's choice
    '
    If result = vbYes Then
        Divide = False
    Else
        Divide = True
    End If
End Function
```

In this example, setting up the error handler was no problem because the potential error—division by zero—was a fairly obvious one. (Also note that in a production application you'd confirm a nonzero divisor as soon as the user entered the value rather than wait for the division to occur.) In practice, however, your error handlers will require a more sophisticated approach that tests for multiple error types. For this you need to know about error numbers. I'll discuss those later in this chapter, in the section "Err Object Properties."

Resuming Program Execution

In Listing 15.2, the error message displayed to the user asks if he or she wants to input the values again, and an If...Then tests the response and sets the function's return value accordingly. This example is a bit contrived because your errors won't necessarily occur inside a Function procedure or loop. However, you'll often still need to give the user a choice of continuing with the program or bailing out. To do this, you can add one or more Resume statements to your error handlers. VBA defines three varieties of Resume statements:

Resume	Tells VBA to resume program execution at the same statement that caused the error.
Resume Next	Tells VBA to resume program execution at the first executable statement after the statement that caused the error.
Resume *line*	Tells VBA to resume program execution at the label specified by *line*.

Listing 15.3 shows an example. The BackUpToFloppy procedure is designed to get a drive letter from the user and then save the active workbook to that drive. If a problem occurs (such as having no disk in the drive), the procedure displays an error message and gives the user the option of trying again or quitting.

LISTING 15.3   This Procedure Backs Up the Active Workbook to a Drive Specified by the User and Traps any Errors (Such As Having No Disk in the Drive)

```
Sub BackUpToFloppy()
    Dim backupDrive As String
    Dim backupName As String
    Dim msg As String
    Dim done As Boolean
    Dim result As Integer
    '
    ' Define the location of the error handler
    '
    On Error GoTo ErrorHandler
    '
    ' Initialize some variables and then loop
    '
    Application.DisplayAlerts = False
    done = False
    backupDrive = "A:"
    While Not done
```

LISTING 15.3   (continued)

```vba
        '
        ' Get the drive to use for the backup
        '
        backupDrive = InputBox( _
            Prompt:="Enter the drive letter for the backup:", _
            Title:="Backup", _
            Default:=backupDrive)
        '
        ' Check to see if OK was selected
        '
        If backupDrive <> "" Then
            '
            ' Make sure the backup drive contains a colon (:)
            '
            If InStr(backupDrive, ":") = 0 Then
                backupDrive = Left(backupDrive, 1) & ":"
            End If
            '
            ' First, save the file
            '
            ActiveWorkbook.Save
            '
            ' Assume the backup will be successful,
            ' so set done to True to exit the loop
            '
            done = True
            '
            ' Concatenate drive letter and workbook name
            '
            backupName = backupDrive & ActiveWorkbook.Name
            '
            ' Make a copy on the specified drive
            '
            ActiveWorkbook.SaveCopyAs FileName:=backupName
        Else
            Exit Sub
        End If
    Wend
    '
    ' Bypass the error handler
    '
```

LISTING 15.3   (continued)

```
    Exit Sub
    '
    ' Code branches here if an error occurs
    '
ErrorHandler:
    msg = "An error has occurred!" & vbCr & vbCr & _
        "Select Abort to bail out, Retry to re-enter the drive" & _
        vbCr & "letter, or Ignore to attempt the backup again."
    result = MsgBox(msg, vbExclamation + vbAbortRetryIgnore)
    Select Case result
        Case vbAbort
            done = True
        Case vbRetry
            done = False
            Resume Next
        Case vbIgnore
            Resume
    End Select
End Sub
```

The bulk of the procedure asks the user for a drive letter, saves the workbook, concatenates the drive letter and workbook name, and saves a copy of the workbook on the specified drive.

The error routine is set up with the following statement at the top of the procedure:

```
On Error GoTo ErrorHandler
```

If an error occurs, the procedure jumps to the `ErrorHandler` label. The error handler's `MsgBox` function gives the user three choices (see Figure 15.1), which get processed by the subsequent `Select Case` structure:

Abort	Selecting this option (`Case vbAbort`) bails out of the `While...Wend` loop by setting the done variable to True.
Retry	Selecting this option (`Case vbRetry`) means the user wants to re-enter the drive letter. The `done` variable is set to False, and then the `Resume Next` statement is run. If the error occurs during the `SaveCopyAs` method, the next statement is `Wend`, so the procedure just loops back (because we set done to False) and runs the `InputBox` function again.
Ignore	Selecting this option (`Case vbIgnore`) means the user wants to attempt the backup again. For example, if the user forgot to insert

a disk in the drive, or if the drive door wasn't closed, the user would fix the problem and then select this option. In this case, the error handler runs the Resume statement to retry the SaveCopyAs method (or whatever) .

FIGURE 15.1

If an error occurs, the error handler displays this dialog box.

Disabling the Trap

Under normal circumstances, an error trap set by the On Error GoTo statement is disabled automatically when the procedure containing the statement is finished executing. However, there might be times when you want to disable an error trap before the end of a procedure. For example, when you're testing a procedure, you might want to enable the trap for only part of the code and let VBA generate its normal runtime errors for the rest of the procedure.

To disable an error trap at any time during a procedure, even within an error handler, use the following statement:

On Error GoTo 0

Working with the Err Object

The problem with the error traps we've set so far is a lack of information. For example, the Divide function (in Listing 15.2) assumes that any error that occurs is a result of an attempted division by zero. However, there are two other runtime error possibilities:

■ **Overflow**—This error is raised if *both* the dividend and divisor are 0.

■ **Type mismatch**—This error is raised if either value is nonnumeric.

It's likely that you'll want your error handler to treat these errors differently. For example, a division by zero error requires only that the divisor be re-entered, but an overflow error requires that both the dividend and the divisor be re-entered.

To handle different errors, VBA provides the Err object, which holds information about any runtime errors that occur. You can use the properties of this object to get specific error numbers and descriptions.

Err Object Properties

The Err object has a number of properties, but the following three are the ones you'll use most often:

Err.Description—Returns the error description.

Err.Number—Returns the error number.

Err.Source—Returns the name of the project in which the error occurred.

For example, Listing 15.4 shows a procedure that attempts to divide two numbers. The Err object is used in two places within the error handler:

■ The error message displayed to the user contains both Err.Number and Err.Description.

■ A Select Case structure examines Err.Number to allow the handler to perform different actions depending on the error.

LISTING 15.4   This Procedure Divides Two Numbers and Traps Three Specific Errors: Division by Zero, Overflow, and Type Mismatch

```
Sub DivideNumbers()
    '
    ' Set the trap
    '
    On Error GoTo DivByZeroHandler
    '
    ' Declare variables
    '
    Dim divisor As Variant
    Dim dividend As Variant
    Dim result As Single
    Dim msg As String
    '
    ' Prompt user for the dividend
    '
GetDividendAndDivisor:
    dividend = InputBox("Enter the dividend:", "Divider")
    If dividend = "" Then Exit Sub
    '
    ' Prompt user for the divisor
    '
GetDivisorOnly:
    divisor = InputBox("Enter the divisor:", "Divider")
```

LISTING 15.4 (continued)

```vba
    If divisor = "" Then Exit Sub
    '
    ' Perform the division
    '
    result = dividend / divisor
    '
    ' If it went okay, display the result
    '
    msg = dividend & _
          " divided by " & _
          divisor & _
          " equals " & _
          result
    MsgBox msg
    '
    ' Bypass the error handler
    '
    Exit Sub
    '
    ' Code branches here if an error occurs
    '
DivByZeroHandler:
    '
    ' Display the error message
    '
    msg = "An error occurred!" & Chr(13) & Chr(13) & _
          "Error number:   " & Err.Number & Chr(13) & _
          "Error message: " & Err.Description
    MsgBox msg, vbOKOnly + vbCritical
    '
    ' Check the error number
    '
    Select Case Err.Number
        '
        ' Division by zero
        '
        Case 11
            Resume GetDivisorOnly
        '
        ' Overflow
        '
        Case 6
```

LISTING 15.4 (continued)

```
            Resume GetDividendAndDivisor
        '
        ' Type mismatch
        '
        Case 13
            If Not IsNumeric(dividend) Then
                Resume GetDividendAndDivisor
            Else
                Resume GetDivisorOnly
            End If
        '
        ' Anything else, just quit
        '
        Case Else
            Exit Sub
    End Select
End Sub
```

A Basic Strategy for Debugging

Debugging, like most computer skills, involves no great secrets. In fact, all debugging is usually a matter of taking a good, hard, dispassionate look at your code. Although there are no set-in-stone techniques for solving programming problems, you *can* formulate a basic strategy that will get you started.

When a problem occurs, the first thing you need to determine is what kind of error you're dealing with. There are four basic types: syntax errors, compile errors, runtime errors, and logic errors.

Syntax Errors

These errors arise from misspelled or missing keywords and incorrect punctuation. VBA catches most (but not all) of these errors when you enter your statements. Note, too, that the VBA Editor uses a red font to display any statements that contain syntax errors.

Syntax errors are flagged right away by VBA, which means that you just have to read the error message and then clean up the offending statement. Unfortunately, not all of VBA's error messages are helpful. For example, one common syntax error is to forget to include a closing quotation mark in a string. When this happens, VBA reports the following unhelpful message:

```
Expected: list separator or )
```

Compile Errors

When you try to run a procedure, VBA takes a quick look at the code to make sure things look right. If it sees a problem (such as an If...Then statement without a corresponding End If), it highlights the statement where the problem has occurred and displays an error message.

Fixing compile errors is also usually straightforward. Read the error message and see where VBA has highlighted the code. Doing so almost always gives you enough information to fix the problem.

Runtime Errors

These errors occur during the execution of a procedure. They generally mean that VBA has stumbled upon a statement that it can't figure out. It might be a formula attempting to divide by zero or using a property or method with the wrong object.

Runtime errors produce a dialog box such as the one shown in Figure 15.2. These error messages usually are a little more vague than the ones you see for syntax and compile errors. It often helps to see the statement where the offense has occurred. You can do this by clicking the Debug button. This activates the module and places the insertion point on the line where the error has occurred. If you still can't see the problem, you need to rerun the procedure and pause at or near the point in which the error occurs. This lets you examine the state of the program when it tries to execute the statement. These techniques are explained later in this chapter.

FIGURE 15.2
A typical run-time error message.

Logic Errors

If your code zigs instead of zags, the cause is usually a flaw in the logic of your procedure. It might be a loop that never ends or a Select Case that doesn't select anything.

Logic errors are the toughest to pin down because you don't get any error messages to give you clues about what went wrong and where. To help, VBA lets you trace through a procedure one statement at a time. This allows you to watch the flow of the procedure and see if the code does what you want it to do. You can also keep an eye on the values of individual variables and properties to make sure they're behaving as expected. Again, you'll learn how to trace a procedure later in this chapter (see "Stepping Through a Procedure").

Pausing a Procedure

Pausing a procedure in midstream lets you see certain elements such as the current values of variables and properties. It also lets you execute program code one statement at a time so you can monitor the flow of a procedure.

When you pause a procedure, VBA enters *break mode,* which means it displays the code window, highlights the current statement (the one that VBA will execute next) in yellow, and displays a yellow arrow in the Margin Indicator Bar that points to the current statement. See the done = False statement in Figure 15.3.

FIGURE 15.3
VBA displays the Debug window when you enter break mode.

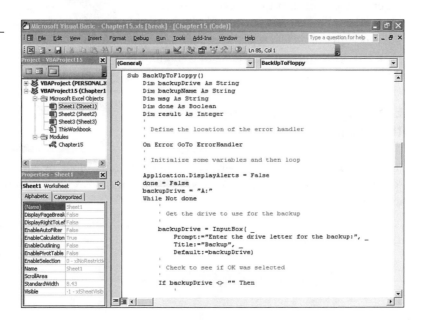

Entering Break Mode

VBA gives you no fewer than five ways to enter break mode:

- From a runtime error dialog box.
- By pressing F8 at the beginning of a procedure.
- By pressing Esc or Ctrl+Break while a procedure is running.

■ By setting breakpoints.

■ By using a Stop statement.

Entering Break Mode from an Error Dialog Box

When a runtime error occurs, the dialog box that appears only tells you the error number and the error description (see Figure 15.2, shown earlier). It doesn't tell you where the error occurred. Instead of scouring your code for possible bugs, you should click the Debug button to enter break mode. This will take you directly to the line that caused the error so that you can investigate the problem immediately.

Entering Break Mode at the Beginning of a Procedure

If you're not sure where to look for the cause of an error, you can start the procedure in break mode. Place the insertion point anywhere inside the procedure and then select Run, Step Into (or press F8). VBA enters break mode and highlights the Sub statement.

> ## tip
>
> Many of the menu commands that I discuss in this chapter have button equivalents on the Debug toolbar. If you don't see this toolbar onscreen, activate the View, Toolbars, Debug command.

Entering Break Mode by Pressing the Esc Key

If your procedure isn't producing an error but appears to be behaving strangely, you can enter break mode by pressing Esc (or by selecting Run, Break) while the procedure is running. VBA pauses on whatever statement it was about to execute.

Alternatively, you can press Ctrl+Break to display the dialog box shown in Figure 15.4. Click Debug to put VBA into break mode.

FIGURE 15.4

This dialog box appears if you press Ctrl+Break while a procedure is running.

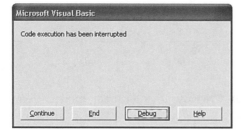

Microsoft Visual Basic

Code execution has been interrupted

Continue   End   Debug   Help

Setting a Breakpoint

If you know approximately where an error or logic flaw is occurring, you can enter break mode at a specific statement in the procedure. This is called a *breakpoint*.

To set up a breakpoint, follow these steps:

1. Activate the module containing the procedure you want to run.

2. Move the insertion point to the statement where you want to enter break mode. VBA will run every line of code up to, but not including, this statement.

3. Set the breakpoint by selecting Debug, Toggle Breakpoint (or by pressing F9; you can also click inside the Margin Indicator Bar, which is the vertical gray bar to the left of the code). As shown in Figure 15.5, VBA highlights the entire line in red and adds a breakpoint indicator in the Margin Indicator Bar.

Entering Break Mode Using a `Stop` Statement

When developing your projects, you'll often test the robustness of a procedure by sending it various test values or by trying it out under different conditions. In many cases, you'll want to enter break mode to make sure things look okay. You could set breakpoints at specific statements, but you lose them if you close the file. For something a little more permanent, you can include a `Stop` statement in a procedure. VBA automatically enters break mode whenever it encounters a Stop statement.

Figure 15.6 shows the `BackUpToFloppy` procedure with a `Stop` statement inserted just before the statement that runs the `SaveCopyAs` method.

> **note**
>
> The command that sets a breakpoint is a toggle, so you can remove a breakpoint by placing the insertion point on the same line and running the command again.
>
> To remove all the breakpoints in the module, select Debug, Clear All Breakpoints or press Ctrl+Shift+F9.

Exiting Break Mode

To exit break mode, you can use either of the following methods:

- Resume normal program execution by selecting Run, Continue (or by pressing F5).

- End the procedure by selecting Run, Reset.

FIGURE 15.5

When you set a breakpoint, VBA highlights the entire line in red.

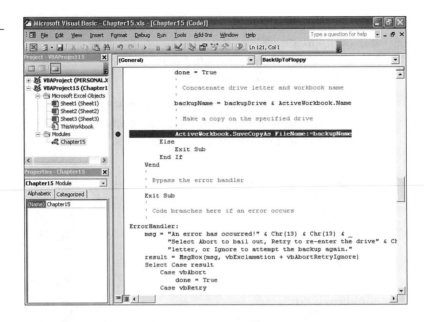

FIGURE 15.6

You can insert Stop statements to enter break mode at specific procedure locations.

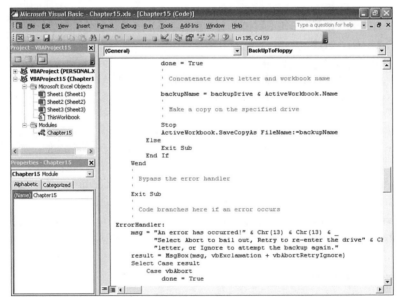

Stepping Through a Procedure

One of the most common (and most useful) debugging techniques is to step through the code one statement at a time. This lets you get a feel for the program flow to make sure that things such as loops and procedure calls are executing properly. You can use three techniques:

- Stepping into a procedure
- Stepping over a procedure
- Stepping to a cursor position

Stepping into a Procedure

Stepping into a procedure means you execute one line at a time (in break mode), starting at the beginning of the procedure. If you haven't started a procedure yet, you step into it using the technique described in the section "Entering Break Mode at the Beginning of a Procedure."

Alternatively, you might prefer to run your code until it's about to call a particular procedure, and then step into that procedure. To do this, set a breakpoint on the statement that calls the procedure. Once your code hits that breakpoint, step into the procedure by selecting the Debug, Step Into command (or by pressing F8).

Once you're inside the procedure, repeat the Step Into command to execute the procedure code one line at a time. Keep stepping through until the procedure ends or until you're ready to exit break mode and resume normal execution.

Stepping Over a Procedure

Some statements call other procedures. If you're not interested in stepping through a called procedure, you can step over it. This means that VBA executes the procedure normally and then resumes break mode at the next statement *after* the procedure call. To step over a procedure, first either step into the procedure until you come to the procedure call you want to step over, or set a breakpoint on the procedure call and run the project. Once you're in break mode, you can step over the procedure by selecting Debug, Step Over (or by pressing Shift+F8).

Stepping Out of a Procedure

It's very common (and very frustrating) to accidentally step into a procedure that you wanted to step over. If the procedure is short, you can just step through it until you're back in the original procedure. If it's long, however, you don't want to waste time going through every line. Instead, invoke the Step Out feature by selecting Debug, Step Out (or by pressing Ctrl+Shift+F8).

VBA executes the rest of the procedure and then re-enters break mode at the first line after the procedure call.

Stepping to the Cursor

Instead of stepping over an entire procedure, you might need to step over only a few statements. To do this, enter break mode, place the insertion point inside the line where you want to re-enter break mode, and then select Debug, Run To Cursor (or press Ctrl+F8).

Monitoring Procedure Values

Many runtime and logic errors are the result of (or, in some cases, can result in) variables or properties assuming unexpected values. If your procedure uses or changes these elements in several places, you'll need to enter break mode and monitor the values of these elements to see where things go awry. The Visual Basic Editor offers a number of methods for monitoring values, and I discuss them in the next few sections.

Using the Locals Window

Most of the values you'll want to monitor will be variables. Although watch expressions (discussed in the next section) are best if you want to keep an eye on only one or two variables, the Visual Basic Editor gives you an easy method to use if you want to monitor *all* the variables in any procedure. This method makes use of a special Visual Basic Editor window called the Locals window. You can display this window by activating the View, Locals Window command.

When your procedure enters break mode, the Locals window displays a line for each declared variable in the current procedure. As you can see in Figure 15.7, each line shows the variable name, its current value, and its type.

Adding a Watch Expression

Besides monitoring variable values, VBA also lets you monitor the results of any expression or the current value of an object property. To do this, you need to set up a *watch expression* that defines what you want to monitor. These watch expressions appear in the Watch window, which you can display by activating the View, Watch Window command.

To add a watch expression, follow these steps:

1. If the expression exists inside the procedure (for example, an object property), select the expression as follows:

   ■ For single-word expressions, place the insertion point anywhere inside the word.

   ■ For more complex expressions, highlight the entire expression.

FIGURE 15.7

Use the Locals
window to keep
track of the cur-
rent value of all
your variables.

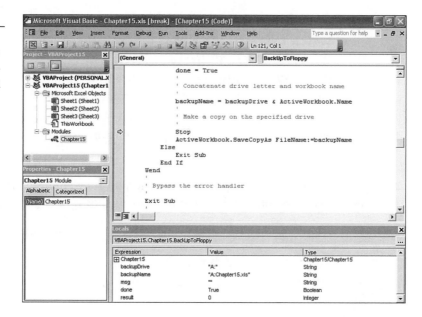

2. Select Debug, Add Watch to display the Add Watch dialog box, shown in
   Figure 15.8. (Note that in the vast majority of cases you can skip steps 3–5,
   below, and head right to step 6.)

FIGURE 15.8

Use the
Add Watch
dialog box to
add watch
expressions.

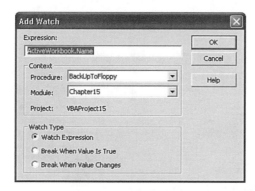

3. If the expression you want to monitor isn't already shown in the Expression
   text box, enter the expression. You can enter a variable name, a property, a
   user-defined function name, or any other valid VBA expression.

4. Use the Context group to specify the context of the variable (that is, where
   the variable is used). You enter the Procedure and the Module.

5. Use the Watch Type group to specify how VBA watches the expression:

- **Watch Expression**—Displays the expression in the Watch window when you enter break mode.
- **Break When Value Is True**—Tells VBA to automatically enter break mode when the expression value becomes True (or nonzero).
- **Break When Value Changes**—Automatically enters break mode whenever the value of the expression changes.

6. Click OK.

Once you've added a watch expression, you monitor it by entering break mode and examining the expression in the Watch window, as shown in Figure 15.9.

FIGURE 15.9

The Watch window with a few watch expressions.

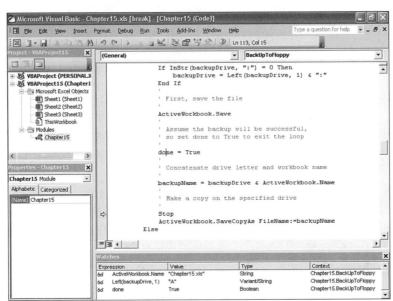

Editing a Watch Expression

You can make changes to a watch expression while in break mode. Follow these steps:

1. Select the Watch window by clicking it or by selecting View, Watch Window.

2. Click the watch expression you want to edit.

tip

The Debug, Add Watch command is available when you're in break mode, so you can add more watch expressions if necessary.

3. Select Debug, Edit Watch (or press Ctrl+W; you can also double-click the watch expression). VBA displays the Edit Watch dialog box.

4. Make your changes to the watch expression.

5. Click OK to return to the Debug window.

Deleting a Watch Expression

To delete a watch expression you no longer need to monitor, follow these steps:

1. Select the Watch window by clicking it or by selecting View, Watch Window.

2. Click the watch expression you want to edit.

3. Select Debug, Edit Watch to display the Edit Watch dialog box.

4. Click the Delete button (or highlight the expression in the Watch window and press the Delete key). VBA deletes the expression and returns you to the Debug window.

Displaying Data Values Quickly

Many variables, properties, and expressions are set once, and they don't change for the rest of the procedure. To avoid cluttering the Watch window with these expressions, VBA offers a couple of methods for quickly displaying an expression's current value: Data Tips and Quick Watch.

The Data Tips feature is one of the handiest of VBA's debugging tools. When you're in break mode, simply move the mouse pointer over the variable or property you want to know the value of. After a brief pause, VBA displays a banner showing the current value of the expression, as shown in Figure 15.10.

The Quick Watch feature displays a dialog box that shows the expression, its current context, and its current value. To try this, follow these steps:

1. Enter break mode.

2. Either place the insertion point inside the expression you want to display or highlight the expression.

3. Select Debug, Quick Watch (or press Shift+F9). The Visual Basic Editor displays a Quick Watch dialog box like the one shown in Figure 15.11.

If you want to add the expression to the Watch window, click the Add button. To return to break mode without adding the expression, click Cancel.

FIGURE 15.10

VBA displays
Data Tips when
you hover the
mouse pointer
over an expres-
sion in break
mode.

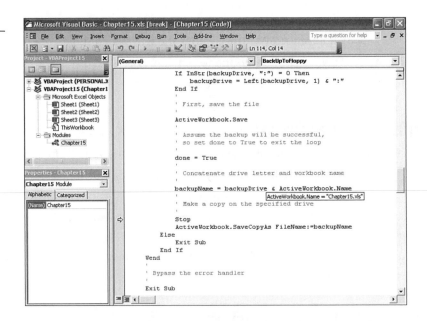

FIGURE 15.11

Use the Quick
Watch dialog
box to quickly
display the
value of an
expression.

Using the Immediate Window

The Watch window tells you the current value of an expression, but you'll often
need more information than this. You also might want to plug in different values for
an expression while in break mode. You can perform these tasks with VBA's
Immediate window, which you display by activating the View, Immediate Window
command.

Printing Data in the Immediate Window

You can use the Print method of the special Debug object to print text and expression
values in the Immediate window. There are two ways to do this:

- By running the Print method from the procedure
- By entering the Print method directly into the Immediate window

The Print method uses the following syntax:

Debug.Print *OutputList*

> *OutputList*   An expression or list of expressions to print in the Immediate window. If you omit *OutputList,* a blank line is printed.

Here are a few notes to keep in mind when using this method:

- Use Spc(*n*) in *OutputList* to print *n* space characters.
- Use Tab(*n*) in *OutputList* to print *n* tab characters.
- Separate multiple expressions with either a space or a semicolon.

Running the Print Method from a Procedure

If you know that a variable or expression changes at a certain place in your code, enter a Debug.Print statement at that spot. When you enter break mode, the *OutputList* expressions appear in the Immediate window. For example, Figure 15.12 shows a procedure in break mode. The information displayed in the Immediate window was generated by the following statement:

Debug.Print "The backup filename is "; backupName

FIGURE 15.12

Use Debug.Print in your code to display information in the Immediate window.

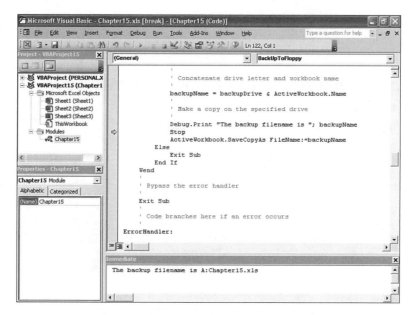

Running the Print Method in the Immediate Window

You can also use the Print method directly in the Immediate window to display information. Note that when you're in break mode, you don't need to specify the Debug object.

Figure 15.13 shows a couple of examples. In the first line, I typed **print backup-drive** and pressed Enter. VBA responded with A:. In the second example, I typed **?** **backupname** (? is the short form of the Print method), and VBA responded with A:Chaptr15.xls.

FIGURE 15.13

You can enter Print statements directly in the Immediate window. Note the use of the question mark (?) as a short form of the Print method.

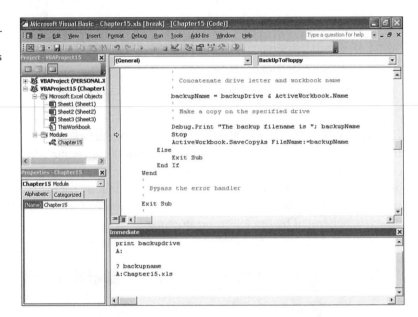

Executing Statements in the Immediate Window

Perhaps the most effective use of the Immediate window, however, is to execute statements. There are many uses for this feature:

- To try some experimental statements to see their effects on the procedure.

- To change the value of a variable or property. For example, if you see that a variable with a value of zero is about to be used as a divisor, you could change that variable to a nonzero value to avoid crashing the procedure.

- To run other procedures or user-defined functions to see if they operate properly under the current conditions.

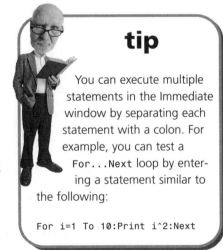

tip

You can execute multiple statements in the Immediate window by separating each statement with a colon. For example, you can test a `For...Next` loop by entering a statement similar to the following:

`For i=1 To 10:Print i^2:Next`

You enter statements in the Immediate window just as you do in the module itself. For example, entering the following statement in the Immediate window changes the value of the `backupName` variable:

```
backupName = "B:Chaptr15.xls"
```

Debugging Tips

Debugging your procedures can be a frustrating job, even during the best of times. Here are a few tips to keep in mind when tracking down programming problems.

Indent Your Code for Readability

VBA code is immeasurably more readable when you indent your control structures. Readable code is that much easier to trace and decipher, so your debugging efforts have one less hurdle to negotiate. Indenting code is a simple matter of pressing Tab an appropriate number of times at the beginning of a statement.

It helps if VBA's automatic indentation feature is enabled. To check this, select Tools, Options to display the Options dialog box and, in the Editor tab, activate the Auto Indent check box.

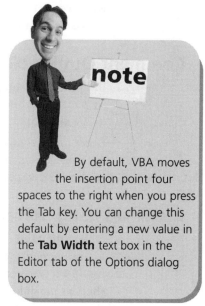

note

By default, VBA moves the insertion point four spaces to the right when you press the Tab key. You can change this default by entering a new value in the **Tab Width** text box in the Editor tab of the Options dialog box.

Turn on Syntax Checking

VBA's automatic syntax checking is a real time-saver. To make sure this option is turned on, activate the Auto Syntax Check check box in the Editor tab of the Options dialog box.

Require Variable Declarations

To avoid errorscaused by using variables improperly, you should always declare your procedure variables. To make VBA display an error if you don't declare a variable, add the following statement to the top of the module:

```
Option Explicit
```

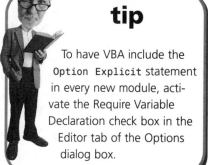

tip

To have VBA include the `Option Explicit` statement in every new module, activate the Require Variable Declaration check box in the Editor tab of the Options dialog box.

Break Down Complex Procedures

Don't try to solve all your problems at once. If you have a large procedure that isn't working right, test it in small chunks to try to narrow down the problem. To test a piece of a procedure, add an `Exit Sub` statement after the last line of the code you want to test.

Enter VBA Keywords in Lowercase

If you always enter keywords in lowercase letters, you can easily detect a problem when you see that VBA doesn't change the word to its normal case when you move the cursor off the line.

Comment Out Problem Statements

If a particular statement is giving you problems, you can temporarily deactivate it by placing an apostrophe at the beginning of the line. This tells VBA to treat the line as a comment.

Don't forget that VBA has a handy Comment Block feature that will comment out multiple statements at once. To use this feature, select the statements you want to work with and then click the Comment Block button on the Edit toolbar.

Break Up Long Statements

One of the most complicated aspects of procedure debugging is making sense out of long statements (especially formulas). The Immediate window can help (you can use it to print parts of the statement), but it's usually best to keep your statements as short as possible. Once you get things working properly, you can often recombine statements for more efficient code.

Use Excel's Range Names Whenever Possible

In Excel, procedures are much easier to read and debug if you use range names in place of cell references. Not only is a name such as Expenses!Summary more comprehensible than Expenses!A1:F10, it's safer, too. If you add rows or columns to the Summary range, the name's reference changes as well. With cell addresses, you have to adjust the references yourself.

Take Advantage of User-Defined Constants

If your procedure uses constant values in several different statements, you can give yourself one less debugging chore by creating a user-defined constant for the value (see Chapter 3, "Understanding Program Variables"). This gives you three important advantages:

- It ensures that you don't enter the wrong value in a statement.
- It's easier to change the value because you have to change only the constant declaration.
- Your procedures will be easier to understand.

THE ABSOLUTE MINIMUM

This chapter showed you how to use VBA's error trapping and debugging facilities to weed out errors in your code. You began by learning how to lay traps for those pesky errors that are inevitable in any reasonably-sized program. In particular, you learned the particulars of a four-pronged error-trapping strategy: set the trap with `On Error GoTo`; code the error handler; use one of the `Resume` statements to continue the program; and disable the trap (if necessary) with `On Error GoTo 0`. You also learned about the properties and methods of the `Err` object, including the useful `Number` and `Description` properties.

The rest of the chapter covered the art of debugging your procedures. You learned a basic debugging strategy, which involved determining what kind of error occurred—syntax, compile, runtime, or logic—and then either responding to the error message or using break mode to investigate the problem. You learned how to pause and step through a procedure, and how to use breakpoints, watch expressions, and the Immediate window. You closed the chapter with a few debugging tips.

Here are some places to go to find related information:

- The best way to stamp out bugs in your VBA code is to become familiar with the basic building blocks of VBA programming. These basics were covered in Part 1, "Getting Started with the VBA."

- An important part of trapping errors is letting the user know what's happening and, possibly, giving her some kind of clue how to fix the problem. Basic user interaction techniques are indispensable here, and I showed you quite a few in Chapter 12, "Interacting with the User."

- To help avoid errors caused by your users, you should set up your application's interface to minimize the possibility of improper data entry and to make it as easy as possible for users to work with the program. Creating a custom user interface is the subject of Chapter 13, "Creating Custom VBA Dialog Boxes," and Chapter 14, "Creating Custom Menus and Toolbars."

PART IV

APPENDIXES

A

VBA STATEMENTS

Throughout this book, I've introduced you to various VBA statements. (It's worth mentioning here that a *statement* is any VBA keyword or construct that isn't a function, object, property, or method.) These statements appeared on an "as-needed" basis whenever I wanted to explain a particular VBA topic (such as If...Then...Else and the other control structures you saw in Chapter 6, "Controlling Your VBA Code"). Although I covered many VBA statements in this book, I bypassed quite a few in the interests of brevity and simplicity.

In an effort to put some finishing touches on our VBA coverage, this appendix presents a brief, but complete, look at every VBA statement. I give you the name of the statement, the arguments it uses (if any; note, too, that required arguments are shown in **bold type**), and a short description. For those statements that I didn't cover in this book, you can get full explanations and examples from the Statements section of the VBA Help file.

TABLE A.1   VBA Statements

Statement	Description
AppActivate *title*, *wait*	Activates the running application with the title or task ID given by *title*.
Beep	Beeps the speaker.
Call *name*, *argumentlist*	Calls the *name* procedure. (Because you can call a procedure just by using its name, the Call statement is rarely used in VBA programming.)
ChDir *path*	Changes the current directory (folder) to *path*.
ChDrive *drive*	Changes the current drive to *drive*.
Close *filenumberlist*	Closes one or more I/O files opened with the Open statement.
Const *CONSTNAME*	Declares a constant variable named *CONSTNAME*.
Date = *date*	Changes the system date to *date*.
Declare *name*	Declares a procedure from a dynamic link library (DLL).
DefBool *letterrange*	A module-level statement that sets the default data type to Boolean for all variables that begin with the letters in *letterrange* (for example, DefBool A-F).
DefByte *letterrange*	Sets the default data type to Byte for all variables that begin with the letters in *letterrange*.
DefCur *letterrange*	Sets the default data type to Currency for all variables that begin with the letters in *letterrange*.
DefDate *letterrange*	Sets the default data type to Date for all variables that begin with the letters in *letterrange*.
DefDbl *letterrange*	Sets the default data type to Double for all variables that begin with the letters in *letterrange*.
DefInt *letterrange*	Sets the default data type to Integer for all variables that begin with the letters in *letterrange*.
DefLng *letterrange*	Sets the default data type to Long for all variables that begin with the letters in *letterrange*.
DefObj *letterrange*	Sets the default data type to Object for all variables that begin with the letters in *letterrange*.
DefSng *letterrange*	Sets the default data type to Single for all variables that begin with the letters in *letterrange*.
DefStr *letterrange*	Sets the default data type to String for all variables that begin with the letters in *letterrange*.
DefVar *letterrange*	Sets the default data type to Variant for all variables that begin with the letters in *letterrange*.

TABLE A.1 (continued)

Statement	Description
DeleteSetting *appname,section,key*	Deletes a *section* or *key* from the Registry.
Dim *varname*	Declares a variable named *varname*.
Do...Loop	Loops through one or more statements while a logical condition is True.
End *keyword*	Ends a procedure, function, or control structure.
Enum *name*	Module-level statement that declares an enumeration variable.
Erase *arraylist*	Frees the memory allocated to a dynamic array or reinitializes a fixed-size array.
Error *errornumber*	Simulates an error by setting Err to *errornumber*.
Event *procedurename(arglist)*	Class module-level statement that declares a user-defined event.
Exit *keyword*	Exits a procedure, function, or control structure.
FileCopy *source, destination*	Copies the *source* file to *destination*.
For Each...Next	Loops through each member of a collection.
For...Next	Loops through one or more statements until a counter hits a specified value.
Function	Declares a user-defined function procedure.
Get #*filenumber, varname*	Reads an I/O file opened by the Open statement into a variable.
GoSub...Return	Branches to and returns from a subroutine within a procedure. (However, creating separate procedures makes your code more readable.)
GoTo *line*	Sends the code to the line label given by *line*.
If...Then...Else	Runs one of two sections of code based on the result of a logical test.
Implements *InterfaceName, Class*	Specifies the name of an interface or a class to be implemented in a class module.
Input #*filenumber, varlist*	Reads data from an I/O file into variables.
Kill *pathname*	Deletes the file *pathname* from a disk.
Let *varname = expression*	Sets the variable *varname* equal to *expression*. Let is optional and is almost never used.
Line Input #*filenumber, var*	Reads a line from an I/O file and stores it in *var*.
Load	Loads a user form into memory without displaying it.
Lock #*filenumber, recordrange*	Controls access to an I/O file.
LSet *stringvar = string*	Left-aligns a string within a String variable.

TABLE A.1 (continued)

Statement	Description
LSet *var1* = *var2*	Copies a variable of one user-defined type into another variable of a different user-defined type.
Mid	Replaces characters in a String variable with characters from a different string.
MidB	Replaces byte data in a String variable with characters from a different string.
MkDir *path*	Creates the directory (folder) named *path*.
Name *oldpathname* As *newpathname*	Renames a file or directory (folder).
On Error	Sets up an error-handling routine.
On...GoSub, On...GoTo	Branches to a line based on the result of an expression.
Open *pathname*, etc.	Opens an input/output (I/O) file.
Option Base 0|1	Determines (at the module level) the default lower bound for arrays.
Option Compare Text|Binary	Determines (at the module level) the default mode for string comparisons.
Option Explicit	Forces you to declare all variables used in a module. Enter this statement at the module level.
Option Private	Indicates that the module is private and can't be accessed by other procedures outside the module. Enter this statement at the module level.
Print #*filenumber*	Writes data to an I/O file.
Private *varname*	Declares the *varname* variable to be a private variable that can be used only in the module in which it's declared. Enter this statement at the module level.
Property Get	Declares a property procedure.
Property Let	Assigns a value to a property in a property procedure.
Property Set	Sets a reference to an object in a property procedure.
Public *varname*	Makes the *varname* variable available to all procedures in a module.
Put #*filenumber*, *varname*	Writes data from the variable *varname* to an I/O file.
RaiseEvent *eventname*, arguments	Fires the event given by *eventname*.
Randomize *number*	Initializes the random-number generator. Omit *number* to get a different random number each time.
ReDim *varname*	Reallocates memory in a dynamic array.

TABLE A.1   (continued)

Statement	Description
`Rem comment`	Tells VBA that the following text is a comment. The apostrophe (') is more widely used.
`Reset`	Closes all I/O files that were opened with `Open`.
`Resume`	After an error, resumes program execution at the line that caused the error.
`RmDir path`	Deletes a directory (folder).
`RSet stringvar = string`	Right-aligns a string within a `String` variable.
`SaveSetting appname, etc.`	Creates or saves a setting in the Windows Registry.
`Seek #filenumber, position`	Sets the current position in an I/O file.
`Select Case`	Executes one of several groups of statements based on the value of an expression.
`SendKeys string, wait`	Sends the keystrokes given by *string* to the active application.
`Set objectvar = object`	Assigns an *object* to an `Object` variable named *objectvar*.
`SetAttr pathname, attr`	Assigns the attributes given by *attr* (for example, `vbReadOnly`) to the file given by *pathname*.
`Static varname`	Declares *varname* to be a variable that will retain its value as long as the code is running.
`Stop`	Places VBA in Pause mode.
`Sub`	Declares a procedure.
`Time = time`	Sets the system time to *time*.
`Type varname`	Declares a user-defined data type. (Used at the module level only.)
`Unload`	Removes a user form from memory.
`Unlock #filenumber, recordrange`	Removes access controls on an I/O file.
`While...Wend`	Loops through a block of code while a condition is True.
`Width #filenumber, width`	Assigns an output line width to an I/O file.
`With...End With`	Executes a block of statements on a specified object.
`Write #filenumber`	Writes data to an I/O file.

VBA FUNCTIONS

Although I discussed quite a few VBA functions in this book, my coverage was by no means exhaustive. VBA boasts more than 160 built-in functions that cover data conversion, dates and times, math, strings, and much more. This appendix presents a categorical list of each VBA function and the arguments it uses (required arguments are shown in **bold type**). You can get full explanations and examples for all the functions in the Functions section of the VBA Help file.

TABLE B.1   Conversion Functions

Function	What It Returns
CBool(*expression*)	An *expression* converted to a Boolean value.
CByte(*expression*)	An *expression* converted to a Byte value.
CCur(*expression*)	An *expression* converted to a Currency value.
CDate(*expression*)	An *expression* converted to a Date value.
CDbl(*expression*)	An *expression* converted to a Double value.
CDec(*expression*)	An *expression* converted to a Decimal value.
CInt(*expression*)	An *expression* converted to an Integer value.
CLng(*expression*)	An *expression* converted to a Long value.
CSng(*expression*)	An *expression* converted to a Single value.
CStr(*expression*)	An *expression* converted to a String value.
CVar(*expression*)	An *expression* converted to a Variant value.
CVDate(*expression*)	An *expression* converted to a Date value. (Provided for backward compatibility. Use CDate instead.)
CVErr(*errornumber*)	A Variant of subtype Error that contains *errornumber*.

TABLE B.2   Date and Time Functions

Function	What It Returns
Date	The current system date as a Variant.
Date$()	The current system date as a String.
DateAdd(*interval, number, date*)	A Date value derived by adding *number* time *intervals* (months, quarters, and so on) to *date*.
DateDiff(*interval, date1, date2,...*)	The number of time *intervals* between *date1* and *date2*.
DatePart(*interval, date,...*)	The *interval* given by *date*.
DateSerial(*year, month, day*)	A Date value for the specified *year*, *month*, and *day*.
DateValue(*date*)	A Date value for the *date* string.
Day(*date*)	The day of the month given by *date*.
Hour(*time*)	The hour component of *time*.
Minute(*time*)	The minute component of *time*.
Month(*date*)	The month component of *date*.
MonthName(*month,abbreviate*)	The name of the month associated with the specified *month* number.
Now	The current system date and time.
Second(*time*)	The second component of *time*.

TABLE B.2 (continued)

Function	What It Returns
Time	The current system time as a Variant.
Time$	The current system time as a String.
Timer	The number of seconds since midnight.
TimeSerial(*hour, minute, second*)	A Date value for the specified *hour*, *minute*, and *second*.
TimeValue(*time*)	A Date value for the *time* string.
Weekday(*date*)	The day of the week, as a number, given by *date*.
WeekdayName(*weekday*,*abbreviate*)	The name of the weekday associated with the specified *weekday* number.
Year(*date*)	The year component of *date*.

TABLE B.3 Error Functions

Function	What It Returns
Error(*errornumber*)	The error message, as a Variant, that corresponds to the *errornumber*.
Error$(*errornumber*)	The error message, as a String, that corresponds to the *errornumber*.

TABLE B.4 File and Directory Functions

Function	What It Returns
CurDir(*drive*)	The current directory as a Variant.
CurDir$(*drive*)	The current directory as a String.
Dir(*pathname*, attributes)	The name, as a Variant, of the file or directory (folder) specified by *pathname* and satisfying the optional attributes (for example, vbHidden). Returns Null if the file or directory doesn't exist.
Dir$(*pathname*, attributes)	The name, as a String, of the file or directory (folder) specified by *pathname* and satisfying the optional attributes (for example, vbHidden). Returns Null if the file or directory doesn't exist.
EOF(*filenumber*)	True if the end of file specified by *filenumber* has been reached; False otherwise.
FileAttr(*filenumber, returnType*)	The file mode (if *returnType* is 1) or the file handle (if *returnType* is 2) of the file given by *filenumber*.
FileDateTime(*pathname*)	The Date that the file given by *pathname* was created or last modified.
FileLen(*pathname*)	The length, in bytes, of the file given by *pathname*.

TABLE B.4   (continued)

Function	What It Returns
FreeFile(*rangenumber*)	The next available file number available to the Open statement.
GetAttr(**pathname**)	An integer representing the attributes of the file given by **pathname**.
Loc(**filenumber**)	The current read/write position in an open I/O file.
LOF(**filenumber**)	The size, in bytes, of an open I/O file.
Seek(**filenumber**)	The current read/write position, as a Variant, in an open I/O file.
Shell(**pathname**, *windowstyle*)	The task ID of the executed program given by **pathname**.

TABLE B.5   Financial Functions

Function	What It Returns
DDB(**cost, salvage, life, period**, *factor*)	The depreciation of an asset over a specified period using the double-declining balance method.
FV(**rate, nper, pmt**, *pv, type*)	The future value of an investment or loan.
IPmt(**rate, per, nper, pv**, *fv, type*)	The interest payment for a specified period of a loan.
IRR(**values**, *guess*)	The internal rate of return for a series of cash flows.
MIRR(**values, finance_rate, reinvest_rate**)	The modified internal rate of return for a series of periodic cash flows.
NPer(**rate, pmt, pv**, *fv, type*)	The number of periods for an investment or loan.
NPV(**rate, value1**, *value2...*)	The net present value of an investment based on a series of cash flows and a discount rate.
Pmt(**rate, nper, pv**, *fv, type*)	The periodic payment for a loan or investment.
PPmt(**rate, per, nper, pv**, *fv, type*)	The principal payment for a specified period of a loan.
PV(**rate, nper, pmt**, *fv, type*)	The present value of an investment.
Rate(**nper, pmt, pv**, *fv, type, guess*)	The periodic interest rate for a loan or investment.
SLN(**cost, salvage, life**)	The straight-line depreciation of an asset over one period.
SYD(**cost, salvage, life, period**)	The sum-of-years digits depreciation of an asset over a specified period.

TABLE B.6   Math Functions

Function	What It Returns
Abs(*number*)	The absolute value of *number*.
Atn(*number*)	The arctangent of *number*.
Cos(*number*)	The cosine of *number*.
Exp(*number*)	*e* (the base of the natural logarithm) raised to the power of *number*.
Fix(*number*)	The integer portion of *number*. If *number* is negative, Fix returns the first negative integer greater than or equal to *number*.
Hex(*number*)	The hexadecimal value, as a Variant, of *number*.
Hex$(*number*)	The hexadecimal value, as a String, of *number*.
Int(*number*)	The integer portion of *number*. If *number* is negative, Int returns the first negative integer less than or equal to *number*.
Log(*number*)	The natural logarithm of *number*.
Oct(*number*)	The octal value, as a Variant, of *number*.
Oct$(*number*)	The octal value, as a String, of *number*.
Rnd(*number*)	A random number.
Round(*expression*, *numberdecimalplaces*)	The numeric *expression* rounded to a specified number of decimal places.
Sgn(*number*)	The sign of *number*.
Sin(*number*)	The sine of *number*.
Sqr(*number*)	The square root of *number*.
Tan(*number*)	The tangent of *number*.

TABLE B.7   Miscellaneous Functions

Function	What It Returns
Array(*arglist*)	A Variant array containing the values in *arglist*.
CallByName(*object*,*procname*, etc.)	The value of the *procname* property of the specified *object*. Also can run the object's *procname* method.
Choose(*index*, *choice1*, etc.)	A value from a list of choices.
CreateObject(*class*)	An Automation object of type *class*.
DoEvents	Yields execution to the operating system so that it can process pending events from other applications (such as keystrokes and mouse clicks).

TABLE B.7 (continued)

Function	What It Returns
Environ(*envstring*|*number*)	A String value that represents the operating system environment variable given by *envstring* or *number*.
Format(**expression**, *format*)	The **expression,** as a Variant, according to the string *format*.
Format$(**expression**, *format*)	The **expression,** as a String, according to the string *format*.
FormatCurrency(**Expression**, *etc.*)	**Expression** formatted as a currency value.
FormatDateTime(**Date**, *NamedFormat*)	**Date** formatted as a date or time value.
FormatNumber(**Expression**, *etc.*)	**Expression** formatted as a numeric value.
FormatPercent(**Expression**, *etc.*)	**Expression** formatted as a percentage value.
GetAllSettings(**appname**, **section**)	All the settings in the specified **section** of the Registry.
GetObject(*pathname*, *class*)	The Automation object given by *pathname* and *class*.
GetSetting(**appname**, *etc.*)	A setting from the Registry.
IIf(**expr**, **truepart**, **falsepart**)	The **truepart** value if **expr** is True; returns **falsepart** otherwise.
Input(**number**, **#filenumber**)	**number** characters, as a Variant, from the I/O file given by **filenumber**.
Input$(**number**, **#filenumber**)	**number** characters, as a String, from the I/O file given by **filenumber**.
InputB(**number**, **#filenumber**)	**number** bytes, as a Variant, from the I/O file given by **filenumber**.
InputB$(**number**, **#filenumber**)	**number** bytes, as a String, from the I/O file given by **filenumber**.
InputBox(**prompt**, *etc.*)	Prompts the user for information.
IsArray(**varname**)	True if **varname** is an array.
IsDate(**expression**)	True if **expression** can be converted into a date.
IsEmpty(**expression**)	True if **expression** is empty.
IsError(**expression**)	True if **expression** is an error.
IsMissing(**argname**)	True if the argument specified by **argname** was not passed to the procedure.
IsNull(**expression**)	True if **expression** is the null string ("").
IsNumeric(**expression**)	True if **expression** is a number.
IsObject(**expression**)	True if **expression** is an object.
LBound(**arrayname**, *dimension*)	The lowest possible subscript for the array given by **arrayname.**
MsgBox(**prompt**, *etc.*)	The button a user selects from the MsgBox dialog box.

TABLE B.7 (continued)

Function	What It Returns
Partition(*number*, *start*, *stop*,...)	A String that indicates where *number* occurs within a series of ranges.
QBColor(*color*)	The RGB color code that corresponds to *color* (a number between 1 and 15).
RGB(*red*, *green*, *blue*)	The color that corresponds to the *red, green,* and *blue* components.
Switch(*expr1*, *value1*, *etc.*)	Evaluates the expressions (*expr1* and so on) and returns the associated value (*value1* and so on) for the first expression that evaluates to True.
Tab(*n*)	Positions output for the Print # statement or the Print method.
TypeName(*varname*)	A string that indicates the data type of the *varname* variable.
UBound(*arrayname*, *dimension*)	The highest possible subscript for the array given by *arrayname*.
VarType(*varname*)	A constant that indicates the data type of the *varname* variable.

TABLE B.8 String Functions

Function	What It Returns
Asc(*string*)	The ANSI character code of the first letter in *string*.
AscB(*string*)	The byte corresponding to the first letter in *string*.
AscW(*string*)	The Unicode character code of the first letter in *string*.
Chr(*charcode*)	The character, as a Variant, that corresponds to the ANSI code given by *charcode*.
Chr$(*charcode*)	The character, as a String, that corresponds to the ANSI code given by *charcode*.
ChrB(*charcode*)	The byte that corresponds to the ANSI code given by *charcode*.
ChrW(*charcode*)	The Unicode character that corresponds to the ANSI code given by *charcode*.
Filter(*sourcearray*,*match*, *etc.*)	Given an array of strings (*sourcearray*), returns a subset of strings (that is, another array) that match a criterion (*match*).

TABLE B.8 (continued)

Function	What It Returns
InStr(*start*, **string1**, **string2**)	The character position of the first occurrence of **string2** in **string1**, beginning at *start*.
InStrB(*start*, **string1**, **string2**)	The byte position of the first occurrence of **string2** in **string1**, starting at *start*.
InStrRev(**stringcheck**,**stringmatch**,*start*)	The character position (working from the end of the string) of the first occurrence of **stringmatch** in **stringcheck**, beginning at *start*.
Join(**sourcearray**, *delimiter*)	A string consisting of the concatenated values in a string array (**sourcearray**), separated by *delimiter*.
LCase(**string**)	**string** converted to lowercase as a Variant.
LCase$(**string**)	**string** converted to lowercase as a String.
Left(**string**, **length**)	The leftmost **length** characters from **string** as a Variant.
Left$(**string**, **length**)	The leftmost **length** characters from **string** as a String.
LeftB(**string**)	The leftmost **length** bytes from **string** as a Variant.
LeftB$(**string**)	The leftmost **length** bytes from **string** as a String.
Len(**string**)	The number of characters in **string**.
LenB(**string**)	The number of bytes in **string**.
LTrim(**string**)	A string, as a Variant, without the leading spaces in **string**.
LTrim$(**string**)	A string, as a String, without the leading spaces in **string**.
Mid(**string**, **start**, *length*)	*length* characters, as a Variant, from **string** beginning at **start**.
Mid$(**string**, **start**, *length*)	*length* characters, as a String, from **string** beginning at **start**.
MidB(**string**, **start**, *length*)	*length* bytes, as a Variant, from **string** beginning at **start**.
MidB$(**string**, **start**, *length*)	*length* bytes, as a String, from **string** beginning at **start**.
Replace(**expression**, **find**, **replace**)	A string in which one or more instances of a specified substring (**find**) in an **expression** have been replaced by another substring (**replace**).
Right(**string**, **length**)	The rightmost **length** characters from **string** as a Variant.

TABLE B.8 (continued)

Function	What It Returns
Right$(*string*, *length*)	The rightmost *length* characters from *string* as a String.
RightB(*string*, *length*)	The rightmost *length* bytes from *string* as a Variant.
RightB$(*string*, *length*)	The rightmost *length* bytes from *string* as a String.
RTrim(*string*)	A string, as a Variant, without the trailing spaces in *string*.
RTrim$(*string*)	A string, as a String, without the trailing spaces in *string*.
Space(*number*)	A string, as a Variant, with *number* spaces.
Space$(*number*)	A string, as a String, with *number* spaces.
Split(*expression*, *delimiter*)	An array consisting of substrings from a string *expression* in which each substring is separated by a *delimiter*.
Str(*number*)	The string representation, as a Variant, of *number*.
Str$(*number*)	The string representation, as a String, of *number*.
StrComp(*string1*, *string2*, *compare*)	A value indicating the result of comparing *string1* and *string2*.
StrReverse(*expression*)	A string consisting of the characters from a string *expression* in reverse order.
String(*number*, *character*)	*character,* as a Variant, repeated *number* times.
String$(*number*, *character*)	*character,* as a String, repeated *number* times.
Trim(*string*)	A string, as a Variant, without the leading and trailing spaces in *string*.
Trim$(*string*)	A string, as a String, without the leading and trailing spaces in *string*.
UCase(*string*)	*string* converted to uppercase as a Variant.
UCase$(*string*)	*string* converted to uppercase as a String.
Val(*string*)	The number contained in *string*.

Index